The JOkE

You All Woke Yet?

Donny Polidoro

The Joke
You All Woke Yet?
© 2022 by Donny Polidoro

All rights reserved solely by the author. The author guarantees all contents are original and do not infringe upon the legal rights of any other person or work. No part of this book may be reproduced in any form without the permission of the author. The views expressed in this book are not necessarily those of the publisher.

Printed in the United States of America.

ISBN-13: 978-0-578-38920-2- Paperback
ISBN-13: 978-0-578-39310-0-Hard cover
LCCN: 2022904325

Cover design: Lina Bean

Sermo Libre Publishing
Fort Myers, Florida

DEDICATION

This book is dedicated to every child in the Tri-State area that lost their life to cancer. Without their courageous fight, we would never have the courage to stand up and write, fight, and search for a better way of life. The greatest gift a parent can have, is a child's true love, every parent who loses a child deserves a first-class ticket to Heaven. To sit by their Angel when the time comes. God Bless America, and God Bless us All!

Table of Contents

Introduction 1

Chapter 1
The Resurrection Of The Democrats As America's Party 3

Chapter 2
Delaware, The Beginning 33

Chapter 3
The Glowing Green Thumb 49

Chapter 4
Foreign Policy 101 59

Chapter 5
Family & Faith 81

Chapter 6
46 Years In The Senate & Joe's Friends 97

Chapter 7
Their Playbook On How They Did It 119

Chapter 8
The Curse Of Joe Biden's America 235

INTRODUCTION

Before we go any further, let us be open-minded and understand that I hope you learn and react positively after reading this book. When you lived in the greatest country in the world one decade, then decades later you see it slip away from your family, you wonder is this a JOkE? It makes you so angry that you want to fight as our founding fathers did! The other side of war is where you can pick up a pen, tell the truth, and educate the future to secure a safe place for your family as our founding fathers did. This book shows how we keep fighting the same war generation after generation. How one boy from Pennsylvania, the birthplace of American Freedom, has so much hate in his heart against what freedom gave birth to. My fellow Americans, his political Party made him who he is. What has he done to America's future? All the reverse governing is to have one single thing over us…Power? He has sold out his country for power and wealth.

He has sold your children's future away for four more years of Domination!

When does the cycle of Kennedy's, Clinton's, Kerry's, Obama's, Biden's, Pelosi's, and identity politics end? Term limits are the only thing that can stop a career politician who sold his country down the river! Ask yourself that one question, for what and why is he allowing this to happen to America and Americans. He cannot help himself, he is in too deep! Joe Biden has more skeletons in his closet than the Grimm Reaper! I cannot type fast enough. Biden makes more anti-American moves than our enemies. As an American, am I to believe that this president has the power to resurrect a torn country? He has trouble controlling his dinner table! The Democrats used RCV voting an internet Drupal, a human, manipulated, if not manufactured virus, two impeachments, and mail-in ballots to take my country! A leader cannot be by the people if he is not for the people, and with his first one hundred days in office, he has shown he is not my president! The US is our home, our land, and our heartbeat. If we do not educate the younger Americans on the truth and the past, the future will be as disappointing as today.

Everyone during the Pandemic found a reason to see what is wrong with America and what is making us fail. America, its people, and how we managed the virus were spotlighted. One stupid act by one person became the world's foam finger to point us down. We just survived a medical attack on the planet, a racial riot civil war like the '60s, a revolutionary standoff between the people and the government, and now we face our enemy. We witnessed police getting attacked, and no one did anything. We saw a president be crushed day after day as another one stayed hidden in a basement. We had people ask why this is happening? In response, the Catholic boy from Pennsylvania makes poor decisions, making it worse. The virus attacked us; we hurt when we wiped our asses with newspaper; we were the ones watching people die and nothing being done. We were the ones who suffered, and this, time Americans are standing up. We will not allow our children to be hurt by the wrong person in the White House. If you take anything from this book, please vote with your heart, soul, and wallet because your heart, soul, and taxes make the world go around and keep it going around for future generations. Believe that!

Chapter 1

The Resurrection of the Democrats as America's Party

As I sit here on Easter morning, I think of Jesus the Son of God's resurrection from the tomb to the Right Hand of the Father. I cannot stop thinking of odd comparisons, how God plants things in our brains for us to figure out. Another prominent political son rises as the Son of God rises from the grave. As we fasted and held special mass services leading up to the resurrection, we too have had to fast and hold back as our freedoms were being mandated or taken away from us. The son of God brings together people of faith to rejoice in their beliefs. That Easter day will Spring us back from the dead and unify the Catholic/Christian Faith in God. As we see the resurrection of Jesus, it brings us together as a religion. In contrast, a revival of another son is pulling us apart. At a time of rebirth and reflection, Lenten sacrifices to heal and bring us closer to God; we have a Catholic President who does not see the power of a true leader that can reunite and confirm their faith in their country. We are, as Catholics, to believe during Easter that the Son of God will resurrect into Heaven.

The day Joe Biden came into office is the day the resurrection of immigration problems is back, the chaos in the Middle East has become an issue again, and now voting rights are back from the '60s. The resurrection of inflation, division among Americans, and the dropping of America down a peg has happened again. Jesus was betrayed in the garden of Eden by Judas for silver, wealth, and power; we Americans are betrayed by our politicians, who wish for us to be knocked down a peg. Not my words, those are the words of the

Obama and Biden administrations. When Obama and Biden were in office, they did everything in their power to pause American prosperity and superiority over the rest of the world. Obama said it best; you did not create this; it was done for you. Joe Biden earlier this year said it plainly, "that being American is nothing special."[1]. The goal of Joe and Barrack is to bring America and all its people down a peg and make the rest of the world on a level playing field. They will stop at nothing to win, to control and manipulate you. If we go down a peg, who rules the world? China or, possibly worse, the Taliban??

We must ask ourselves if the Democrat party should be allowed to go on after another failed presidential term, a failed Senate, and a lame-duck house of representatives that fight with the GOP but cannot stand up against their Party. If you are under 20 years old, you may have no idea of the real Democrat party. The Democrat party was once the heartbeat of the South. The confederates and proud defenders of freedom during the Revolutionary War. The Democrat party has set in motion to be the radical anti-American Party. Recent elections show Americans voting only on the color or race of a person and not their character and accomplishments. The people who benefited from years of progress and advancements by defeating the Party of the enslavers have become the Party of enslaved people. The slaves to the Government dollar, slaves to years of poorly run cities, schools, and lack of prosperity among neighborhoods.

Repeatedly the race card is played, and the effects set us back 20 years every time. Decisions made over anger and pent-up hate only hurt Americans and our future. We are not better off than four years ago as tax-paying Americans. Unfortunately, China has more international power and might after the pandemic. Russia plays pick up and takes over failing countries. The Taliban has an Air Force base and eighty billion worth of high-tech weapons. Illegals can break our laws, betray our trust, and get whatever they want. We are bowing down to the world. The game plan of Democrats to bring us down a peg has begun.

The Lenten season started around the same time Joe Biden became president. The time of Lenten season is to give up something you enjoy; this symbolizes Jesus's sacrifice in the desert for 40 days and 40 nights. Maybe Joe should have shown Lenten willpower with over 60 Executive Orders in his first one hundred days in office.[2] "In his first 100 days in office, Biden signed more than 60 executive actions, 24 of which are direct reversals of Trump's policies", said Kate Sullivan from CNN. Joe Biden is the biggest threat to America and American prosperity. To date, he is the first President in American History to lose more jobs than gain jobs in their first one hundred days in office. All because of the Executive order to cancel the Pipeline. Giving out free taxpayers' money is not creating anything. Canceling policies that kept our borders closed and safe has not helped one American at all. Closing mines, oil rigs, and pipelines do not only hurt people who have jobs in that field of work. Giving people free money to march illegally into our country only divides and starts more hate and anger. Do we have a president who is learning on the job after 50 years in politics? Or do we have a society woken to what Trump was saying all along? The swamp is full of monsters, and it needs to be drained. Congratulations America you have been Woke. Woke to a politician or a liar, you decide. He said one thing on the campaign trail to get elected and did something else after winning the election. I know some Constitutional Historian from the University of Pennsylvania can produce a better educational term to call him, but it is too simple. Real Catholic boy simple, he is one thing! One of the ten commandments is taught to every Catholic schoolchild. Do not lie! He said one thing and did another. That is lying. You lied about John Kerry's son and your son's business transactions. You lied about the Pipeline and stopping Fossil fuel jobs. You lied about being a president for all Americans. The media complains about transparency, but Joe Biden has been the most transparent politician in the last 13 years.

We have known Joe the JOkE for years, but nothing is new. Joe "the JOkE" Biden is a name that he has earned. Whenever Joe Biden is asked a serious question where he politically flip-flopped or lied and was caught in the act, he chuckles. The chuckle the JOkE that you think you figured out on me. He chuckles because he thinks you are the JOkE, and he tricked you, the JOkE American. That is where his awkward chuckle comes from, textbook liar. Watch old press interviews; it is right there. Kamala Harris does it too! The Democratic Party plays the angry White racist card against Republicans and nominates a 78-year-old White guy for president. When he knows he has been had or the gig is up, the chuckle comes out. The chuckle came out during the crisis at the border, the discussion on Hunter, and more recently, the disaster of what will become of Afghanistan. Where is Adam Schiff? Where is the outraged Democratic Party over Biden talking to the Taliban and making deals with the terrorist? Where is the outrage of the death of American soldiers fighting a surrender, not a battle? Why is it that Republicans and the people who voted for Trump are angry and taking action, as the other side makes excuses? Why is one side of America upset and cannot forget 9/11, and the other side is cool with what happened just 20 years ago and recently in Afghanistan. How does someone sit by and watch their country die? Simple, the Democrat party is not a party of Americans but American haters and anti-Americans. They attack America, and our soldiers pay the price every time while we allow them to lie and pass the blame. Well, guess what, Democrats? You own slavery, you own the 13 dead soldiers in Afghanistan, the death of millions of Americans because you opened the border during a mass Pandemic. Just say that again, during a mass pandemic where over nine hundred thousand Americans have died, one president closes airports and borders and works on a vaccine. Another president opens the border to millions of unvaccinated people, unhealthy people from over eighty countries. A Drug Cartel assists terrorists, rapists, and criminals in breaking America's laws, the same drug cartel that sells heroin. Hunter's heroin addiction and his heroin dealing friends are running the border. What are opioids made from? Opium poppy from Pakistan and Afghanistan? We have no gas and have gas shortages as gas prices rise, and what does Biden do? Ask Putin and Russia to start producing more fossil fuels for the world and become the leader of coal and oil. Another president makes us energy independent after decades of failed administrations. One president pushes for a Green Deal and puts the US in debt over non-proven clean energy solutions. Solutions like solar panels that we have to buy from China. Build Back Better by buying from China. Another president puts American and America first. If you still believe that Donald Trump ruined America in 4 years, but not the guy who has been in office for over 45 years, think again. Biden gave the Taliban an arsenal; he made gas prices go up; he lied about the vaccine first by downplaying its accuracy and dependability under Trump. For that, he now spends billions on asking Americans to get the vaccine. No America, the Democrats, and Joe Biden did that. You have done it now. Democrats go to your room. Adults are trying to run a country!

You cannot blame Joe; he is a product of what comes out of the Democrat party. Hate and division are the recipes to success, political smoke screens to blind your eyes from the truth. Then they let the people fight and divide why they reap the rewards. We must see that we are to blame; we know lifetime politicians and have seen this before. This is why the Democrat Party is for open borders, to find new voters to lie to. Use them and abuse them. Like a Pimp does to his stable, he treats his tricks like pieces of meat to make them richer. We are Joe Biden's whores, and the Democrat Party in control are the Pimps that use and abuse us. They hated the fact that Trump was a president for the people. They hated him because, after 47 years of kissing babies, taking photos, standing behind innocent women to take a good sniff of their hair! Joe Biden knew he would never be loved like Donald Trump was. After all of the pain which Joe has endured in the public eye. The loss of his wife and daughter, his precious Beau, and do not forget about the prodigal son Hunter and his drug addiction. He has spent years in public service slaving over a hot train ride every day to DC to help out Americans. He has given his life to making America and especially Delaware the most incredible place in the world, and still, no one loves him like they did Trump. After all of the free money, gifts, bridges, and roads he has built with his hands, sweat, and our tax money but still are not loved like Donald Trump was. Why did you ask? Trump did nothing but listen to the people, create jobs for Americans, make safer borders, safe streets, and a safe world. There was no free education for some, no free health care for some; instead, everyone prospers, or no one does. The Democrat Party and the Republican Party learned one lesson from Donald Trump. Listen to the people, and you will win. Unfortunately, Americans' love for Donald upset the career politicians who have now ruined generations of Americans for years. We are now paying the price for decades of American pride and love for one's country.

If you are a patriot today, then you salute a racist flag. If you are a freedom-loving American, you are a crazy White racist. Any way you show love for the USA and the flag, you are showing love for the racist history we endured, not the accomplishments we have made. The separation of political parties will put our country under tremendous stress and turmoil in the coming years. The career politicians who have used White voters for years to stay in office are now looking for new voters to manipulate directly because their time is up. They have used their whores up and now need a new batch to keep them Pimping; this is the old Jimmy Carter switch. A classic political strategic move. The top Democrats are career politicians, constantly training the left. They hold their lives over every vote, decision, campaign, and opinion. They have figured out the game, the political game. The goal is never to look as bad as they say their opponents are. You cannot sit down and put on a piece of paper in the last two years or even twenty years. What have the Democrats done positively for Americans moving forward? Barrack Obama and Joe Biden gave stimulus checks to big car companies. Now cars are the most expensive they have ever been. That helped who? Surely you know every bad, disgraceful and sneaky thing the opposite side has done. We learned how wrong Trump was as a politician before he even became a politician. They told us Donald Trump was horrible and how he could be an upstanding citizen like a career politician. The Brett Kavanaugh trial was a true example of how the facts, the truth, or even the results from a false narrative would affect a person's life and family. Every decision makes a reaction; every word falls on someone's ear. This comes back to maybe the oldest saying in the book. I can imagine my 3rd Grade nun pointing her finger at the class, "If you can't say anything nice, don't say anything at all"! That is not true in the politician game. If someone fact checks you and catches it, a lie is only a misspoken opportunity for an apology. Even then, you have to show it on Air even to get noticed. The 2020 election did not come down to the best interest of tax-paying Americans! They told us that Joe Biden was the best choice for our country's soul. They saved the soul of our nation from a racist president, is what we were told. How well does our soul look when the cartels rape women and bring death drugs across the southern border! How well does our soul look when the Taliban puts the women of the Middle East back 75 years and stops all progress of education and simple human rights. The soul of America looks good when a terrorist group kills 13 Americans; the group now controls an air force, an air force base, and billions in deadly weapons. May God save your soul Joe Biden!

I do not think people know or even really care about history. We were outraged in 2020 over the deaths from racism and racist acts of violence. We are angry at one racist police officer who was never proven guilty of racism but guilty of police brutality. It is so easy to blame and point fingers. If people knew their history, the country lost more American lives during the Civil war in our internal fight to end racism and slavery. We as a society have to realize that if we did not have the Democrat party, then we would have never had to fight to keep slavery or even the Civil War. The Democrat party has lied to a particular race of people for years. The Democrat party members were the owners of enslaved people. If Americans saw clearly and opened a history book and read a chapter, they would see who the slave owners were. The Democrat Party was the Party of the slave owners. So, when a whole group of young White Americans, young Black, and Brown Americans go out for an entire summer during a pandemic to protest racism and racist White political parties. Then goes and votes in a racist

White party and put in power who, the party of White racism? Are we sure we thought this one through? Are we sure we are fighting the proper fight? All this Woke, and now we are wearing yoke on our face. JOKE BIDEN PLAYED HIS BIGGEST TRICK AND JOKE ON YOU! He befriended Obama to stay in office. Welcome to politics, history, the truth, the way it has always been. Now you are genuinely Woke. The Democrat party never wanted slavery to end. They never wanted to let them be free, and they never wanted to fight. Lincoln pushed the Civil War, and the Democrats wanted to separate from the Union and be a set of free states. The Democrats would elect to split the new country in two before giving up Slave-ownership. Destroy our country before giving up their free labor. The Democrat Party is now the Party that points its finger at the Republican Party and calls them racist. It is the most significant Ponzi scheme of all time. Be the criminal but blame the police. This flip the script act is how we are in the mess we have today. The truth does not matter. The facts are of no concern. Who can lie and make people believe what you are selling is the goal?

When Joe Biden sat on the "The Breakfast Club Podcast with Charlamagne Tha God" Podcast and said, "You ain't Black" line.[3] It should have been that you are not voting Democrat if you are Black because we have done you wrong since day one. To think the Party of the Slave Owners is the same Party that called Trump a Racist. The same Party that made June 10th a national holiday. They praise themselves for the day slavery ended like they ended slavery. The Democrats ended slavery? You ain't got a brain if you think the Democrats stopped slavery. No, they started slavery, and you need to look at real history books! Just like how brothers and neighbors killed each other during the worse death count in America's history of war, the Civil War. We are at it again, fighting each other instead of the real enemy. How many setbacks as a country can we take? This is the narrative that brings a nation down a peg. Joe Biden said it himself in 2020 that being American ain't no big deal. While the whole campaign went on, Joe Biden painted the red-faced man as a racist, and Joe Biden was for all the people. It is about time we know Joe; after years of destructive politics in Delaware, it has had a toll on progress and the well-being of all who live in Delaware. If he cannot run a state as small as Delaware, then how can he run a country of 50 states. His track record speaks for itself.

In 2014, the **UCLA Civil Rights Act published its finding of Delaware and their public schools. Here is what the report says.** [4]

Black and Latino students in Wilmington, Delaware, attend schools with escalating segregation since the pioneering city-suburban desegregation plan ended, according to a new report by the UCLA Civil Rights Project. During the academic year 1989-90, when the metropolitan school desegregation plan was in effect, no students—of any race—attended intensely segregated schools (90- 100% minority). Today nearly 20% of Delaware's Black students and about 11% of Delaware's Latino students go to intensely segregated schools with overlapping concentrations of poverty. At the same time, Delaware's overall student enrollment grew more racially diverse.

- Intensely segregated (90-100% minority) and apartheid (99-100% minority) schools did not exist in metro Wilmington in 1989-90. By 2010-11, intensely segregated schools grew to a troubling 15% of schools in the metropolitan area, and apartheid schools accounted for almost 8% of Wilmington's public schools. Despite these serious setbacks, Delaware still reports less segregation than adjoining states that never had comprehensive metropolitan desegregation plans.

- In 2010-11, 47.3% of metro Wilmington students were low-income. However, the typical Latino student attended a school where 61.3% of students were low-income, and the typical Black student attended one where 56.2% were low-income. By contrast,

the average White student participated in a school where only 37.5% were low-income.

- In 2010-11, almost 90% of the students in Wilmington's apartheid schools were low-income, highlighting the extreme intersection between racial isolation and concentrations of poverty.

Numerous recommendations for addressing demographic change and resegregation are included in the report. For example, Delaware should develop state-level student assignment policies that reduce racial isolation and promote diverse schools. Policies should have ways for districts to foster various schools, recruit a diverse teaching staff, provide a framework for developing and supporting intra- and inter-district programs. And require that the state have diversity policies to assure fair access for all groups for both public and charter schools. Strong magnet schools and transfer programs within and across district boundaries should promote more racially integrated schools and minimize "White flight" to outlying districts. Within the Wilmington area, school attendance boundaries should be redrawn to mitigate the effects of the 2001 Neighborhood Schools Act, which reconnected residential segregation to school segregation. In addition, a controlled choice plan, which would alleviate the segregating impacts of school attendance boundaries, could be implemented. Collaboration between fair housing efforts and school desegregation policies should also be promoted.

This statement was published on December 18, 2014, about the UCLA Civil Rights Project findings of Delaware being a US state still operating their schools as America hated in the past.

Joe Biden once responded on the Senate floor about the Civil Rights movement. Joe stood in front of the Senate floor, Americans watching from home and the world, and President Joe Biden said," he didn't want his kids to grow up in a racial jungle." [5]. He made clear by his record and the Civil Rights article he never changed the schools after his hate speech in 1977. He has never altered just learned how to lie and smirk. Joe Biden's record and the statistics speak for themselves. The findings by Civil Rights groups pointed out his state and their failures towards the advancement of people of color. He has never changed. He just figured out a way to change the past. The new media, new millennials, the new Americans that take our freedom for granted and paint racism like Pretty Little Trees are being fooled. Again, you are Joe Biden's whores, and he tricked you into another slut move. How does our soul feel now? He sold his soul years ago down the river of illegal dumping for political kickbacks. As he ruined communities, fellow Americans, and future voters, he just opened the state up and let foreign people become his new whores. He is not only destroying our future, but with the help of the Socialist Democrats, he is also destroying our history.

The Democrat lies that Americans and America stole their country from others and had been tormenting the world for centuries. Then China, Russia, Germany, Japan, Cuba, England, France, and even Spain must feel like the Devil's God Father at lucifers baptism. If we are the country with a tainted soul, then other countries must have a free pass. The Democrats want you to believe that America started in 1999 when Monica Lewinsky raped Clinton, Lebron James was baby Jesus in the manger, and Trump and White America were sailing the Nina, The Pinta, and the USS Ronald Regan into New York harbor to kill all the foreigners. Oh yeah, we also had Covid-19 in our muskets, and voting is not allowed by women, people of color, or homosexuals. Don't you remember 2019 when Trump ordered death to all who will not kneel! Please wake up and see that you and your negative thinking are killing America. We are allowing negative media, lies about history, and unfaithful truth to spread like cancer as Betsy Ross sews as fast as she can. For what now we kneel before the flag, Democrats started that. Now we burn the flag with our enemies; Democrats gave them that. Now we see the effects of lies, hiding in your basement, and what political and national division does. The Civil War is upon us once again. Yes, the Democrats did them both.

Joe Biden was never going to vote to allow schools to open up to any American who wanted to attend it. Imagine all that hate in Public Schools as his wife was a teacher of education in the public school system. Hell, his kids went to the most expensive, elite private school in Delaware. What was he worried about? He knew his kid's school was safe from segregation. The Pimp out pimped the game. If I cannot segregate them, I will join them in the White House. What did Joe Biden do to better Obama's terms as president? Did Black America benefit from him and Barrack in office? UCLA report seems to differ! The facts show something different than what he tells us. The past can never be changed, but lies and misinformation cannot make the future. The Democrats are who they are. The people who vote for Democrats are to blame for voting these people in office. Take responsibility and be proud of your actions and words. Speak up about how happy you are about your decisions in life and the 2020 election. Put signs in your yard and wear the proud shirts "Ridin' with Biden." Be proud of what you put into office. Be proud of how you will save our souls and America's soul. You have chosen a President and a party that does not care about the future of Americans. They clearly showed that by their past and plans for the future!

Joe Biden has been a thorn in Lady Liberty's sandals for a long time. A true Roman Caesar tragedy. We will fall from the inside, not from outsiders. Your country will turn on you, and you will not solve a problem but create another. In the end, the Democrats do no good and are not held accountable. When we sit and look at what is going on, it is hard to understand that this guy has been in politics for a very long time. He should be so seasoned and aware of how things work, but it seems like he is learning on the job. All those years and still learning on the job. That is like being an assistant waiter for the rest of your life, never taking a table's order, by learning the menu. Never be responsible for your tables and customers. Always just learning and in training as an assistant waiter. It is unheard of when you look at the years and knowledge that Jill and Joe Biden should have. Or was it all a trick pony show, you know, smoke and mirrors? Dr. Jill Biden and President Joe Biden have over 95 years in public service, and still, we hear and see the worst decisions made in American history for our children and the school systems in America. Jill Biden is like a janitor throwing sawdust still on throw up in the hallway. Look back at what was learned from years of division and fighting after the Civil war. What did we learn by making all people equal and fighting each other to end slavery?

The Democrats and Republicans have learned nothing. Hate is worse now than ever. The playbook the politicians are using is still working. They argue on the hill while we fight in the streets. We have all played into their hands, and now we are whores in the stable. Step out of line, and you are canceled. Step out of line, and you are cut off and called a racist. Are we up against the wall as Americans? Have we voted in our last free election as of 2016? Is America the country now a myth like Atlantis once was. Are we the new Mayan culture? Once a great society but now a tourist trap on a Carnival cruise excursion? What will America become with Democrats in power? Real simple, one-party rule "Autocracy." Joe was a genius! The true politician pulled one more rabbit out of his blue hen cap. The whole world went from hating themselves to having a person to blame for everything. The one person to blame was us! The one person who represented us was just an easy target. They could care less who the GOP or America votes for; it is their way or the cancel way. We have finally learned from the cancel cry wolf syndrome, and they are now about to cancel us. We have screamed at mountain tops and cried wolf one too many times. We are on the verge of being worse off than our parents or grandparents. That would be the first time in American history that will happen. Never before have we had less than what our parents had. After two world wars, disease, pandemics, countless terrorist attacks, and the thing that is killing us is ourselves.

Please do not vote Republican, Democrat, Independent, or whatever Party you used to be in the next election. The next election and every election after, vote American. If it is not suitable for all Americans, then it is not good for us. Every person should grab their remote and talk into the search microphone. Search 9/11 and watch what happens to America and us because we read books, educate our female population and choose to love a mouse. They hate us for it! We have freedoms that others in the world die for and beg to come to this country. Our security as Americans is at a higher level in August 2020 than before the attacks on NYC on 9/11. One President, George Bush Jr., told the terrorist to run and hide because here we come with American might and power. Joe Biden, our new president, tells the terrorist that we are leaving, please, as he leaves behind and hands over America's military might and ammo to attack our way of LIFE. No-one stopped Hunter from sleeping with his dead brother's wife [6]; that was his way of life. We never stopped his freedoms. No one ever stopped Joe Biden's brother from never paying back a civil lawsuit in the millions after a fatal car crash; he also left the country and hid.[7] Must be a Biden trait they learned in Scranton, PA, how to hide. No one went after your brother and stopped his life and his freedoms. Still, you tell us how to live; you tell us who to let in our country and schools. You have started the second most dangerous time in America's history in the last 50 years. You have made the terrorist relevant again. The Democrat voter has put America, its allies, and its freedoms back 20 years. Mickey Mouse, concerts, football games, and proms mean nothing if we are not safe to go outside anymore! Even worse now, the Taliban has weapons of mass destruction. For real this time, Joe Biden reloaded the terrorist. Is this even on the news? Is this what the left feed media is talking about? No, they still have The Trump is wrong and GOP racist script going strong. The Party of slave owners, segregation, and bigotry is calling the kettle Black. Do you know why the Democrats, a party full of old White people, tell you about old White racism that has poisoned the soul of America? Because they ran out of old White people to vote for them, they now needed to load the country with foreign people to be reelected. The Civil Rights new voting law must be passed.

The first batch of old racism during the civil war was the Democrat party.[8] Then, they turned their backs on voters during the Civil Rights reform to retain old White voters from the South after the Civil War. That is also called the "bandwagon-jumping party," wherever the votes are, that is where a Democrat politician will be. Then again when they voted Woodrow Wilson for President from 1912 to 1916. Wilson supported the KKK; he also gave the KKK money and downplayed their violence in the media to vote for him. **(9)** They are the Party of what people? The game of talking out both sides of their mouths and screwing over the people who believe in them! It is shameful to blame America's problems on one Party and not the real culprits. The Democrat Party is the oldest political party in America.[10] The Republican Party was formed from the old Whig party that fought the Democrats against slavery and the Civil war era.

The Republican Party was a minor political party destined to fail because the Democrat party put a seniority committee process in order. So, the most powerful seat of every committee chairmanship was awarded automatically based on seniority, not on skill or will for the people, which gave power, especially to long-serving Southerners. This is the same plan they have for the new Voting Act. To control the vote over long-standing politicians, you know, like Joe Biden. Which set Black Americans back even more. They blame others, but the Democrat party holds the trophy of shame of racism in history. The reason to control the elections was to keep the slave owners in power. If the vote went by seniority rule, they could stay as long as possible and appoint whoever they wanted.

The Republican Party was started to stop the ridiculous power control the Democrats made by changing voting blocks and realignment of party ideology in the 1800s. In the 1930s, the Democrat party emerged as America's Party. Since then, they have elected more presidents than any other party. They come into power and tell lies and shame the opposition and you into voting for crazy liberties paid for by the taxpayers of America. After every failed attempt to make the greatest country in the world that ever-existed utopia for all, on a taxpayer. They still try and will always fail. Unicorns are not real, and taxpayers' dollars pay for everything. The Democrats from Douglas to Wilson to Kennedy to Clinton to Obama to Biden have lied to Americans, blaming the conservative parties trying to put Americans back in chains. Yes, when the Democrats were in power, people were in chains. Now the chains fit only tax-paying Americans. When some smart ass says the founding fathers enslaved people, they are partially correct.

The founding fathers were called the Democratic-Republican party until the Party split during the Civil War. The Republican side helped free slaves and died for America's soul to be saved. The Democrats have no direction, and they have no purpose but to divide the country once again. Reagan and Trump were the last two who saved America from failed unqualified politicians. Every decade they reinvent themselves not for America but to find a new group to latch onto. After every failed election run, the Democrats use crowd control, and the party heads rush to figure out their failures. So, when you go to the job interview, and the hiring person says you need a bachelor's degree to work here, and you only have an associate degree, what should you do to get hired? Perhaps those next two years should be spent bettering yourself to get that job and prove that you can do it. Instead, do the Democrat thing, blame the guy hiring for being a racist, and cancel his business.

Crowd control, Walter Mondale started the Democrat New Deal that made all Democratic factions vote together for party rule and power control.[11] Pelosi and her games with Schumer are a pure example. The politicians go back to their states, tell their voters one thing, and come to DC and vote on party lines. No opposition, one for all, or we all fail together mentality. America does crowd control after every Democratic presidency also. That is why they need new factions, new foreign voters, new party voter lines, longer election cycles, and now no voter ID required. They lose an election, call foul with Russian collusion, then fight to pass a Voting bill that allows foreign citizens to vote, illegal people to vote, and no identification when voting. So, did they want more Russian collusion? Well, they are not the first ones to cry Russian wolf or Russian-bear interference in our elections? If we pass their voting bill, anyone anywhere in the world can vote in America's elections. They have a say in what my government does with my taxes. After an election where Joe Biden had the most votes in American history, voting is still flawed. After telling me that Trump undermined American Democracy, Joe Bien and the Democrats now tell me elections are biased, racist, and not fair. America WTF is going on.

The Democrat party is made up of distinct groups that have different interests all over the place but still come together to control the voting process. The various parties represent other races, religious views, identity, gender politics, and money and spending. These factions make up the Democrat party because they cannot stand on one message alone. Pro-America! Pro-America would not go with a Black coalition that tells us we are systemically racist. Pro-America would not go with the Socialist Democrat faction is against capitalism and freedom of work. The founding goals on which America was founded. Pro-America does not go with the Democrat party because the Party would have only one clear message and purpose then, America. All these diverse groups under one umbrella can vote out any challengers. There is the Moderate Democrat group made up of Delaware's Chris Coon and Amy Klobuchar; they are the ones that play both sides of the fence. They believe in moderate values and less spending like a Conservative Republican but realize the population in their state has changed, so they go where the votes are, foreign and uneducated. This more conservative section is the smallest group in the Democrat party because they are the closest to the center with common sense with Republicans. They know and understand that nothing is for free, and everything has a cost in the future, but they are still not courageous enough to take a stand.

The next faction of the Democrat party is the Conservative Wing. This group is made up of mostly Southern Democrats. West Virginias Joe Manchin and Arizona Senator Kyrsten Sinema are members of this faction. They believe in the same things Republicans do but have to run as Democrats because of years of lies to the people in that region who no longer trust the Republican party. They believe in being fiscally responsible and in conservative spending. That has not been the case under Biden because their states' voting base is changing. People will not be voting for these two in 2022. They had enough of the old rich guy from West Virginia and the teacher from Arizona. The next Party of the Democrat party or the flavor of the month vote club is the Libertarian wing. This coalition consists of Chuck Schumer, Al Frankenstein Franken, Pelosi, Obama, and Biden. John F. Kennedy was a big believer in this Democratic caucus. So, most people associate Democrats with just being liberal and Republicans being conservative. The people who started the Liberal Democrat movement did so in the 20th century. So, how does this caucus relate to the Democrat party of today? How did they associate themselves as liberals when the Democrat party started way before the 20th century? I do not think people know who they are as a voter. I hope this helps.

The starters of the Liberal Democratic movement took hold when the Civil Rights of humans were being extended to all Americans at the time. Why not help and support all Americans? These principles were started by Democrats like Woodrow Wilson, who helped reenergize the KKK. Guys like Truman, Ted Kennedy, and Lyndon B. Johnson. A group of men who had nothing in common except power and control. The Liberal wing of the Democratic Party makes up about 47% of all Democrats.[12] Most of them see themselves as very liberal instead of the other half of the same Democrat party, who say they are more conservative and moderate. So, half of Democrats believe in Civil Rights for all, and they will help pay for it through their taxes. Instead of a new hospital, let us give civil liberties like voting and public schools. What? The other half the conservative Democrats like Civil Rights for all; they just are not paying anymore. They paid enough. So, a real struggle inside their Party, 47% of Democrats vote as a Liberal Democrat and 50% of the Democrat party vote as conservative or moderate. But wait, there are still more factions or Democrat groups of politicians, so about ten in total.

So, ten factions or groups of voters who register as a Democrat are either Liberal or conservative? What? So, Democrat politicians represent ten separate political groups of Americans or voters who vote Democrat at every election. So why have so many factions? Keep reading. It gets good.

The next faction of the Democrat party is the Progressive part of the Democrat party. Is this you? Then you are like George McGovern, a Democratic Senator, and the tremendous Democratic screamer Howard Dean. Who got a bad rap for being happy? You may also recognize Tammy Baldwin and Ted Kennedy. Bernie Sanders, the one independent Senator votes with the Democratic caucus of the Progressive wing. Their beliefs are the New Left deal of the '70s and '80s that believed in rights for all. Social progressive agenda for Americans of all color, sex, and religious freedom. Well, not the spiritual part; they fight those groups a lot. They fight on arguments that they created. Problems created by them or their Party in the past. They relight the flames of division and anger among Americans. They are always screaming and pushing for human rights. Who is against Civil Rights and liberties for all Americans? Only the natural enemies of America. The people who hate us and blew up two buildings in New York on 9/11 hate our way of life. This is how they steal voters from other parties, mask their views, and use their color, race, and sexual preference as a weakness against voters' minds. Propaganda, if everyone hates you, then everyone is out to get you.

The next faction of the Democrat party that helps all Democrats but mainly those who respond to my caucus, not others, is the Democrat Socialist Wing. So, the Socialist Party in America is the Democrat's politicians in America. Do you know other Socialist governments and parties in history? Let us name a few and learn from others' mistakes before shooting ourselves in the face with a stapler. The Republic of China, Cuba, Afghanistan, Korea before the split, Nicaragua, Vietnam, Yemen, and not to be least and last but the Soviet Union factions before the fall of the USSR in the '80s.[13] Reagan stopped that cold war, and he was a Republican, in case you forgot. So why would the Democrat party have a Socialist party wing when the names of countries I listed are the names of every country we have fought in the last century. Why would the Democrat party, the party for Civil Rights, be aligned with a fellow party of Socialists? Does the Socialist government ideology come from countries where the Civil Rights of citizens are not granted?

So, one group of Democrats believe in Social and Civil Rights, while another group of Democrats believes in curbing Civil Rights as a Socialist government. But if you vote Democrat, you are voting for both people; they both represent you. Why would the Democrat Socialist Party be made up of people of Cuban descent, African Descent, North Korean descent, and from the country with the least Civil Rights for women in the world, Afghanistan?[14] The leader of the Socialist Party of the Democrat wing is AOC, Rashida Talib, Cori Bush, Ilhan Omar, and somehow Bernie Sanders is in this group too. These women left Socialism to come to America! Both sides of the fence Bernie Sanders took his free honeymoon to Russia during the Cold War[15] and badly talked Regan to the Russians as he voted for Civil Rights with the Progressive wing. He also voted for Socialist Government control on the other Democrat wing. What the hell is going on here?

The Democrats are the Yankees of the nineties. Anybody good became a Yankee to win, win, win. Socialism, the Party of Bernie Sanders votes for governmental control of your finances, entertainment, and your children's future. Through any means necessary, the people will follow the Socialist Government. They will be lied to and manipulated to believe this is the best way of life. They are trying to sell you on a fake narrative, like the most fabulous honeymoon spot destination in the world, the Kremlin. When the Cold

War was at its worst, the people of Russia, East, and West Berlin were breaking down brick walls to escape. Bernie Sanders was being flown in on a private jet for an all-expense-paid honeymoon to Russia. Way to go, radical new Democrats who hate Trump so much, Bernie Sanders takes gifts from the country who worked with Trump to steal the election.

Then why did only Trump have an impeachment trial and an investigation into Russia gate, and they found nothing. Bernie Sanders honeymooned with the country that worked with Trump to steal the election. On the other side, the hypocrites say nothing about Bernie's vacation. The same lousy country who helped Trump get elected also filled Bernie's hot tub with bubbles during his honeymoon! So, who and what Party is colluding with Russia, again and again? The Socialist Party of the Democrats makes up the smallest group of the 50% of Democrats who associate themselves with being Liberal. Wow, that is a lot to take in. So, if you sneeze and you feel that you might need medical attention but have no insurance but are happy that the tissue was free from the food bank down the street, then you are a Socialist Democrat. This Party is how Bernie gets more votes than he deserves!

The Socialist Democrat is the part of the Democrats who were the Wall Street occupiers. The people who lie about other rich people and the poor people hate more. The Socialist Democrat, the Party of what You make, is Mine. This is the Party that pushes pain and inequality through years of oppression. Like Cuba and China, ask AOC's parents about Socialism. So, one more time, in case I am not getting this through, some of the Socialist countries today are China, Afghanistan, Cuba, and Venezuela. Do these countries value Civil Rights, abortion laws, voting laws, education, and standard healthcare? They do not match up with America's values. But for some reason, the Democratic Socialist Party is made up of people from these non-human right's friendly countries. Ironic or a plan to bring us down from within. Vote in the enemy, and the enemy will vote us out. The party faction was started by Bayard Rustin[16] in 1974 to help with gay rights, nonviolence against gay people, and Socialism. Did I just type that in one sentence? To support Democracy and the rights of all humans by just one economic rule. Sheep for the slaughter, just like China, Cuba, and the Taliban ruled Afghanistan. No, Thank You, check, please. Bernie Sanders uses hate as a campaign tool. His supporters feel the same way. One of Bernie Sanders's supporters shot a Republican Congressman while playing softball. He shot and tried to kill him over the election, overlies and propaganda from Bernie Sanders.[17] So much anger from listening to a politician's words. The riots and violence that a politician on January 6th fueled happened before, on June 14, 2017, when a Bernie Sanders supporter did it first!

Why would one Party, the first party of America, need so many different legs to stand on? Because they amputate a specific group of party voters every voting cycle. Identity Politics! They all vote together, but their majority kills a part of their minority. They hurt themselves and then need to scramble or damage control and bring in millions of voters from other countries to fill the vote box. A simple plan of replacing Americans with whoever they want, and all done by Bernie Sanders, the oldest Socialist I know. Why does the Democrat party, enslavers, now push for more Black voters, Brown voters, and Asian voters? The voters of slavery have never stopped keeping people in chains. Instead of their arms and legs shackled now, their minds and hearts are in chains. The Democrat party is currently under significant damage control from themselves and their actual past. Next time you go to an old salve plantation on a class school trip, look for yourself. Do not read my book and blog, cancel, or hate me. I am you, an American who was lied to. I will not be Trump brainwashed; I do not need him to teach me. I lived it; I am an American.

The Republicans are another party gaining too much power, so abolish them. When not reading from the teleprompter, Joe Biden talked about autocracy right early back in his term. That is the plan, one-party rule, the Democrat party. No campaigning, no town halls, no elections, challengers, just one-party government. There have been more Democratic presidents than any other party in America's history. The first registered Republican President was Abraham Lincoln. There have been nineteen presidents that have been Republican party candidates. The Democrats have had twenty-one registered presidents, and most recently, since the 1900s, the Democrats have been in power for sixty of the last 120 years. The Republicans have been in power for sixty of the last 120 years. So how do we compare even tenures at the helm?

Some say the Democrats who were in control during the most painful times in history did the worst. Others hate capitalism and the military might; the Republicans always build up both with every budget. The problem is the battle of which Party is better or more suitable for Americans. When in reality, both parties should be Pro-America all the time. The party lines are the problems for Americans! Every day, our leaders tell us how bad we are as Americans. The two American political powers separate themselves like the plague. We, the people, come together for the country's good, and the politicians cannot stop fighting. This has created the hate and division that we face today. A party must explain why and how, and another party blames everyone else. They start the problem, and then we must fix it. They burn every bridge they cross, and we rebuild it! The Party of the division of America since the Civil war is still the same Party of division today, The Democrats.

So, when The Democrat party was tearing down statue after statue of America's past citizens that made this country what it is today, they must ask themselves who did we tear down, whose racist past was up there. The Democrat past was the statues up there, and the misinformed Democrat youth was now canceling the old leaders of the Democrats. The tearing down of old Democrat statues is how they deal with their past. You are too stupid to learn, and they are too smart to let you find out. Look up every statue ever commissioned in America's history.[18] Since 1901, all records have been kept on file. The history of the Confederacy is always in Democrat politics. Even Bill Clinton pushed for the White vote to win his first election. You will be amazed at the campaign swag that Bill Clinton and Al Gore had for re-election in Arkansas. A matchbook with a confederate flag on it. Get the White vote, then go on Arsenio and be hip with other voters. In 1992 Al Gore and Bill Clinton used the Confederate Flag on Buttons to help with campaigning in the South for the White House.[19]

They play on both sides of the fence. Kennedy used his mom on the campaign trail for votes, using his Catholic upbringing as a tool to manipulate voters. He had an affair the whole time in the White House with Marilyn Monroe.[20] Joe Biden's mentor and ideal President Jimmy Carter took pictures with confederate flags during his campaign for votes. Whose vote? The White racist Democrat vote. What is the faction for the White racist voter of the Democrat party? The Democrats seem to lose badly after specific terms and all to ex-war heroes of America. Ulysses S Grant, Rutherford B. Hayes, Teddy Roosevelt, and James Garfield. All were union soldiers who fought for our country and then went to fight in Congress for the people. The same wave of ex-military is running again in 2022 to defend America and its sanity. The one fear that China, Russia, and the Democrats saw firsthand on January 6th. Was freedom!

You can silence us, segregate us, lie to us, and steal from us. A whole new race of American Patriots was born that day. Somehow the ride of Paul Revere suddenly appeared again in 2021; the ride down this time took place on Monroe St. in DC and not down Lexington in MA. The cry was not to warn about the British but to warn us about the Democrats. The January 6th event showed that America would not go down without a fight. The Democrats do more to tear us apart. They scare us so bad that it drives us together; Antifa, Proud Boys, The Third Way, and Pro-Trump protestors were all there on January 6th.! Both sides of the political fence were climbing the walls together! The Democrats seem to find the uncanny act of making America greater by using our most incredible talent. Freedom against us! When a politician in office threatens the Republic throughout America's history, it only fuels Americans to move! They have no problem showing the darkest side of America's past as if they were not a part of it.

The Republicans were the enslavers, and they fought themselves during the Civil War. Like a guy on the Jerry Springer show, pretending not to be the father. The Democrats gave birth to racism in America by fathering their love for slavery and power over other humans. The new Democrats enslave us by using control of our wealth, your education, your health, and your vote. They can swear an oath and hold their hands on a Bible, but if they do not believe in the words of the Bible or the Bible itself, what oath was sworn? Trump was a pure example of Obama's unwavering hate for thy country. What do you think Biden is doing, making Americans come together or falling apart? He is the next Democrat president who fails the people that trusted him for decades! He has failed the military and the police officers, and now he insults Ukraine again. Biden and the Democrats have to open the border and bring in refugees; no true American will ever vote left.

The Democrat party has been the Party of killing grandfathers and fathers of other countries in wars. They were then bringing their children and grandchildren into America as refugees to live free in America. Thinking the refugees forgot the past because we will give them free taxpayer's money. We are the only country that goes to war and kills generations of people, then brings the youth of that country here to live! We killed your father, but now you're an American refugee! Then years later, when the left needs a political low-blow or a way to trick young, uneducated voters, they scream anti-sympathy. They use the war and the refugees for votes. Peace man, Joe Biden already lost his son. Does Joe see what happens when you live an angry life? He said the lie so much he is starting to believe it. So scary! He is doing it again; this time, everyone is a refugee from a pandemic war! America fought WW2 less than 65 years ago and dropped two bombs destroying generations. How many people ate sushi this week? We fought Mexico for two centuries. Look outside at who is mowing your house.

We fought the dirtiest fighting war in history, the Vietnam War, The Afghanistan war, and the cold war. Is there anybody from those countries in America today? The answer is YES to all those questions.

We are the only country with enemies but let their people come in and out of our country. We send soldiers to fight and shoot and kill the enemy, and then when they come home with stress and anger, they run into those same nationalities at Disney World on vacation. We allow the enemy to live in America. Damage control, we bomb your family members because we all voted to fight the war because we are a republic of Democracy. Then the Democrats sell the world that Republicans are the bloodthirsty warmongers and push anti-war propaganda. When a war has to be confirmed in Congress by both parties. The Democrats are okay with allowing our enemy to roam free in America. After a battle, no other country in the world does that, no one. No other country in the world does this during a pandemic. No one.

We need to wake up! We have let over two million people in America since Joe Biden took office, less than a year. More people than the population of some American states. For whom are the Democrats fighting? Why would this be the primary concern in the middle of the worse pandemic in one hundred years? Why are Democrats so angry at unmasked Americans in grocery stores, schools, football stadiums, churches, and restaurants. So mad that we fight with each other! Though the border is wide open, letting millions of covid carry people into America, now starting global strains mutating and killing at a higher percentage. Why?

The person following the science would allow contamination of a controlled subject. When scientists do tests in a lab, do they mix test samples with the open-air contamination and see what happens? Is that science to open the border and let unvaccinated people work, walk in our grocery stores, and attend our children's schools to see what happens? Is that why the Teacher Unions will not go back to in-person, because they pronounce the names on the student roll call. Do they know what or who is in the classroom they teach? Why would a president and a first lady who is a doctor and a schoolteacher allow unvaccinated children to attend school? Or attend with unvaccinated teachers? When does the doctorate make sense, she is a science follower, plus a doctor, plus a schoolteacher, and this is still happening to our children's education? The first lady has been a school teacher her whole life, and America's children have just suffered unimaginable education loss!

Why are so many people ready to call Trump a racist because he shut down travel? Why does Joe Biden let the unvaccinated immigrants travel free through our country, on who's money? The Taxpayers pay for it all! There is no science behind that. Next, will it be global warming now caused by Covid? You act like the Republicans are dumb and intellectually challenged; you praise science and mock the unvaccinated. You do what Democrats do best damage control. Do we know who is not getting vaccinated, has someone taken a poll. Maybe that would be a fantastic way to hold an election year; only vaccinated people can vote? Politically correct, the war is on the unvaccinated; they will get people sick! So, they cannot vote at polls to keep everyone safe; it seems fair! If you are not allowed on a cruise unvaccinated, why are you allowed to vote? Then we will know who and what Party believes in science. Only vaccinated people can vote; if 60% of the vote is Democrat and only 13% are Republican, we have a clear answer. If the count goes the other way, we will know a different answer. Then after we see, we can point a finger. Until then, we are only feeding into the media hate game.

Who are the haters of America now? Say it with me, America was founded in 1999 when Monica Lewinsky raped bill Clinton and Kamala, and Hillary saved the world, freed the enslaved people, and her friends started the internet. Al Gore and Barrack Obama began Twitter, the NBA was started by Lebron James, and Joe Biden was at a funeral his whole life crying over his family members. Then giant evil monster Trump came from NY and climbed the buildings like King Kong, swiping at planes in his hair. To fuel his orange hairspray rage, he ruined Narnia and Utopia for the children. Got It, History 101, now go and vote!

The Democrat party has mastered the 24hour news cycle and the way to spin the truth to uneducated voters. When you control four-fifths of the leading media channels, you can spin any news any way you want. Kamala Harris compared Pearl Harbor to January 6th.? That was to compare the people on January 6th to a Kamikaze airplane pilot bombing Americans with their planes. No, I see the comparison; one guy flies an aircraft into people like 9/11 to kill them. At the same time, other people walked through the Capitol building stealing a Senator's laptop. So, bombing an aircraft carrier filled with American soldiers, or Nancy Pelosi's computer, right! Pearl Harbor was an attack; January 6th comes around every year. Those statements by Kamala Harris fuel hate and division.

The door to the Capitol building is like a bank vault and can only be open from the inside.[21] Those lies and horrible comparisons make you look at your neighbors like a terrorist who flies planes into buildings or our navy. It shows in how they vote too! After the 2012 and 2020 elections, people do not vote with their hearts or what is good for our country. The people who vote over anger never make the right choice for their country. For example, we wanted to crush Donald Trump over an alleged affair with a porn star. The media, never knowing if what was true or not, pushed the narrative that he did the crime.

What type of crime is having sex? Trump must be a criminal; he had to of done it. He is fat, bronzed tan with a comb-over. Who would ever be attracted to a loser like him? Also amusing because a porno star might have had sex for money with someone famous. As this goes on, the Governor of New York has been in office for three terms, a true career politician just like his father. He has now come out and has been charged with harassing numerous accounts of inappropriate touching and a nasty toxic workplace environment. The flip the switch hypocrisy is beyond comparison. A civilian millionaire had sex with a porno star years before taking public office, and he must pay for past unethical, not criminal, moves he conducted at that time. It never was proven, and he still should be held responsible. We look the other way for years, and the Governor of New York rides off into the sunset undamaged and with no trial. His brother is still full of smiles on TV, making lies about a past president as his brother does worse things to women.

The prosecution of Jefferey Epstein shows that Bill Clinton visited that island on Epstein's plane. What does Hillary Clinton do? She announces she might run for office in 2024 because Trump is a monogenous pig. Americans are now being split into two sections. One believes the lies, and one does not. Almost like a Civil War all over again, a war for what this time.

It is up to you to decide the team you are playing for! The right team is supporting the constitution of the United States of America. The other team votes with hate, racial blinders, past wars, past presidents, past lies, and distortion. We are now looking at another 9/11 because the Biden team fails to value any American's life as much as they love theirs. They sold America on racism and how the Republican Party has been the leader, not the fighters of racism in America. The Republicans cannot live without it; they voted Trump a White man to bring racism and White power. Then what did the Democrats vote for? They voted an old White man into office just like we did. Now the world and China use that fake racism tag on us and our American freedom.

The Barrack Obama un-American tour all over again. Go around the world to countries that were here long before us and point out America's faults and disagreements to the world. Like a desperate husband who complains about his wife to try and get laid at a bar. The spinning game has begun like a cheap roller coaster at a local church parking lot. As it goes faster and faster, the spin confuses you, and you cannot focus on what is happening. You try to yell and make a noise, but your cheeks press towards your ears, all of a sudden, it happens! The kid down the end who has been living high on the hog lets go and throws up on the whole coaster ride. He cannot handle his soda, four cotton candies, and the stress. We just elected the asshole who throws up on the roller coaster. The kid afraid of blood and passes out is about to do your surgery. The guy with the worst lawn and overgrown hedges is about to be your landscaper. The chef who does not wash his hands after a cigarette wants to make your salad. We just gave the keys to the Porsche to a person with no license.

We elected someone who hates America and the people who love it. Please get him off the ride before the carnival closes down. Please stop the cycle of every Democrat politician finding a way to blame someone else than creating chaos or a problem that we all as a nation must fix. The Party of peace, the Party of stopping the hate, the Party of respect and equality for all, the Democratic Party, made sure the world and you knew who to hate on. Remember Sunday school, Joe, hate is a strong word. Your hate for us speaks louder than words, and now America sees the outcome of voting in a true politician. Your 46th President, a Life-Long Democrat Joseph Biden, has shown the Democrats true colors, and they are bright. Bright as the blinding sun. Good morning: I am glad I could wake you up!

Chapter 2

Delaware, the Beginning

I am from the East Coast area, so some people might be in disbelief when I explain what kind of Delaware Joe Biden has created. The long-standing history that made a small state so relevant in American history is now being diluted and stripped of any class and dignity. The lifelong politician has been sucking the state dry, so dry you can see the bottom. This state is full of incredible history, unbelievable fishing, and of course, it has no sales tax for visitors. With that said, this state should be the shining beacon of a career politician and his willingness to stay in office. As a career politician, Joe Biden's history in Delaware is now a playbook for other up and coming politicians.

He learned from one of the Master of Politics. A Kennedy, the top-tier political family of America. Not the well-known John or Bobby Kennedy, but Ted Kennedy, the golden boy who never could be polished up as his brothers could. His dad never excepted him to be like his two brothers. Ted was in political office for 47 years as a Senator for Massachusetts. Wait 47 years; that sounds familiar. After disgracing the family, Ted Kennedy got a tramp stamp of USSR & China on his back and vowed to ruin America. The people of America could never trust him after the Chappaquiddick Island cover-up.[22] He could never win nationally as his brother did. Joe Biden used his political charm to stay in office for over 40 years as Delaware changed. For the worse, some say, only history is the accurate measure of one's success. I can only give you the facts about the state, and then you decide, or better yet, Americans should take vacations to places where politicians are running for office.

If a person cannot run their state correctly, they will never run 50+ states correctly. The voting laws the politicians push for should be for the voter. A person running for office should be known publicly at least two years before the election. The people should know and have stats on politicians, just like the stats for the Super Bowl. The results of an election are far more critical than a sporting event. I do not believe a state of hard-working Americans voted and kept him in office for over 40 years. I do not believe it! What a life the Bidens have lived because of the people of Delaware.

The Biden sons went to great schools and had a top-notch life.[23] Joe Biden served the people of Delaware from 1973-2009 as a US Senator. The state of Delaware has had a vital part in America's history and how we live today. The founding fathers knew their biggest challenge was responsibility through years of trial and error. That meant being able to fix problems and take responsibility for their actions. Some are worse than others but still never looking back on what could have been or not going backward away from the progress, and freedom America deserves. Delaware is the first state to start it all, the ratifiers of the constitution.

Delaware was the first state of the Union, a once-proud symbol of American Pride and strength. A state that brought together all thirteen states to ratify the US Constitution and start the American journey. How ironic the children of Delaware brought together this nation, and now a son of Delaware tears apart the same country. The Swedes settled upon Delaware in 1627. Today Delaware ranks 49th in capacity among the United States. Delaware's nickname once was the "Diamond State," Thomas Jefferson gave it due to its strategic location on the east coast. The state flag of Delaware has a Militiaman on it that symbolizes the crucial role of the citizen-soldier to maintain American liberties. Another part of the flag is the water representing the importance of ports to commerce and growth.

Delaware is the second smallest state in size and is ranked 11th in per capita per square mile. For every square mile, there are 508 people. To better understand the size of the state and the population per capita. Delaware is the second smallest state behind Rhode Island; the population is ranked sixth highest in America. More people live in Delaware than Wyoming, and Wyoming is the second-biggest state in the United States. Delaware is sixth in density by population rank behind Guam, US Virgin Islands, Puerto Rico, American Samoa Islands, and Rhode Island, to name a few.

According to US NEWS, Delaware's population grew 2.57% and is ranked 46th in best places to live in America. Compared to the United States, the state of Delaware's average cost of living is 2.7%higher than the national average stated by bestplaces.net home review for new buyers.[24] They show that Delaware is higher in the cost of living, with groceries being 5.9% higher than the national average. The previous study was done before the inflation hike of 2021. Health care is 11.6 % higher, utility housing costs are higher than the national average. The only thing lower and by only 4% lower than the national average was Amtrak Joe's public transit, a selling point for moving to Delaware as a new homeowner. In 2021 the population grew despite a world pandemic, refugees by the thousands. There are many remarkable facts about Delaware's history besides the Biden's.

The size of Delaware will never change the state is the first state in the country to be built out. No government-owned public land is available for development. Before starting construction, every project, highway, or infrastructure deal must be resourced from a private owner. On the other hand, the state's population has seemed to increase dramatically over the past two decades. With most newcomers not coming from this country at all, he is passing on a Joe Biden Refugee Location program to all of Delaware, if they like it or not.

Suppose you cannot find the American votes to win; move in people who will vote for me. I would bet you if you took a poll of 1000 people walking in and out of BJ's Wholesale Club right now off Rt.1 before the Delaware bridge entrance to go back to New Jersey. If you asked them where they were born, what would they say? If you asked those one thousand people who the owner of enslaved people was during the civil war of America, who would they pick? Republicans or Democrats? Do they even know the answer?

Delaware's demographics are the same demographics coming over the Southern border today. A blueprint for changing the USA for good. Delaware, a once-proud blue-collar working state, is now a politically correct time bomb. Joe Biden himself on the tape said in the '80s; you cannot go into a Dunkin Donuts or a 7/11 and speak English anymore.[25] Please fact-check me. I would love for you to see it and read it for yourself. After years as a career politician, he has to find new voters to stay in office. A once-familiar face to Americans on a train going to work just like them is now a vision of free American taxpayer money to foreign people he lets enter our country illegally every day!

It is with our money, not his. Joe has no bank, and he is not the wealthiest person in America; it is being paid with on our taxes, our kid's future taxes, and their kid's future taxes. Like most America today, Delaware is not the same place; Joe has used up generations of hopes and dreams into one big White Lie. A lie was so big that you could not hide the problems facing the people of Delaware, crime, pollution, and health issues. The days of career politics have crushed the future of politics in Delaware. The career politician has devastated the places that gave them a career. Every debate, every news segment is about how to fix years and years of Damage and Hate. Democrat Damage Control is all we do anymore. After four years of progress, a peg or two was taken down because it was viewed as American Exceptionalism. Like a four-letter word, we are scorned for being proud Americans in America.

Democrat Damage Control has been going on for years in Delaware, and thanks to Biden, there is no end in sight for the first state of the Union. So, I know I am ragging on Delaware and its people, you must be saying by now. We get the point it is a tough place to live. No, not at all; I am showing you what bad leadership does to a great state, a country, and the world. Leaders are what made people run into battle during 1776, and leaders are what people who lived in Delaware their whole life need right now.

Also known as the First state, Delaware lies along the Delaware River and the Atlantic Ocean. Pennsylvania borders it to the north and Maryland to the south. Across the Delaware River lies the state of New Jersey. The Delaware River was a significant body of water in the growth of the Americas. The river helped George Washington cross so that his army could recapture Trenton on Christmas night in 1776.[26] The night of the birth of our Savior Jesus Christ was the perfect time to start the birth of our great nation by crossing the Delaware river and taking back what was ours. Now that is an actual leadership move.

The Delaware River and the state played a massive part for and against America during the revolutionary war. Delaware was divided, and the lower counties had less enthusiasm in fighting their friends Great Britain. They had a good relationship with the government and were allowed more independence and freedom than other parts of Delaware. The "Blue Hens" nickname for the University of Delaware is an odd mascot choice. The army of Delaware was known as the Delaware "Blues" due to the color of the state flag, Colonial Blue. This name was changed during the battle of Brandywine when Delaware troops laid down their arms so the British army could march into and take over our country's capital at the time, Philadelphia. The State President at the time, John McKinley, was taken prisoner, and the British controlled not only Philadelphia but most of the transport lifeline known as the Delaware River. This act changed Delaware "Blues" to the Delaware "Blue Chickens" among Continental soldiers. That being said, it is a lousy mascot to be known as deserters and chickens of war. Go, Delaware!

The history of our country is fantastic, and we should always reread and relearn the actions of the past so they do not repeat themselves. Delaware has and always will be a significant focus point in American history and how we grow as a country. Dover Air Force Base is a substantial airport for our military. In the state of Delaware, our United States Government has the most important Air Force Base to protect the East Coast. It supplies all cargo for US troops in Europe and the Middle East. So, when he gives up the Air Base in Afghanistan, a significant lifeline for stability in the region, people are confused. You question how a person does not understand the importance of giving over a fully-loaded Air Force base in hostile foreign territory. Delaware relies on the Dover Air Force base for more than just protection from overseas. The Air Force base is the lifeline of that area and everything surrounding it.

The Dover Air Force Base is located southeast of Dover, the capital of Delaware. The total value of resources equals $5.7 billion, including aircraft, capital assets such as land and buildings, equipment, retail sales, base operations, and maintenance. Some figures show how much military Joe Biden left behind in Afghanistan. You now have something to compare it to. They estimate around eighty billion dollars- worth of military weapons is now in the hands of the Taliban from the takeover of the Air Force Base.[27] So, Joe Biden gave the Taliban around 14 Dover Air Force bases worth of equipment. Also, he has new 2022 budget cuts for US military funding. He is having a garage sale from his basement. God, please help us. Joe Biden and Barrack Obama were shrinking our military when countries like Russia and China moved in where they liked.[28] Scary! Funny when Trump was in office, China and Russia did not blink without asking permission. Trump was the first president in years to not start a war or a conflict! Now with Biden, just as when Barrack and Clinton were in office, it feels like 1939 all over again.[29] The story gets better.

The United States realized the importance of a strategic airbase on the West Coast due to the attack after Pearl Harbor. So, ten days after the worse attack on the US government, the US activated the base in

Dover, Delaware. So, after the first worse attack on US soil behind 9/11. It only took two days for America to come together and fight back as a nation. Joe Biden turns his back on the importance of an airfield during combat and hands over military might to the world's biggest enemy, Terrorism. Dover airbase is now the most crucial air command to offer air supplies to military conflicts, humanitarian efforts, and across the US as well. This base houses over 10,000 soldiers at any one time. Dover is home to the Department of Defense's largest and most advanced airport in the United States.

The Dover Air Force base is seen in every US mission. The importance of air support during battle is crucial to minimal life loss and any counter-attack unseen. The United States has total air superiority during any war, from drones to fighter jets. The eyes in the skies. Not only is Dover Air Force Base important due to military combats and missions, but it also feeds the economy. Dover Air Force base generates around $331 million each year for its area. That does not include jobs created from vets that stay in the area and work in air and space-related fields. Like most things during Biden's watch, the Dover base has seen better days. The economy around the base has shown what happens when you take something for granted and do not respect and take care of it. The base has been forgotten in some people's eyes in the military. Instead of renovating certain areas, they close down old ones and rebuild right next to them. Government waste that the taxpayer funds. As the Delaware River, when you do not take care of something, the damage is hard to stop and reverse.

The town of Dover has an unemployment rate of 10.3%, which is higher than the US average (6.0%). Dover has a higher income tax than the US average also. This lack of support for the base leads to lower-income or non-educated jobs taking over. A lower cost of living comes from making less income. The average income in America is just below $29 thousand a year. In Dover, it is below $23 thousand. The base was once a significant force in the economy is now diminished year by year.

The lifeline of Delaware's economy in 1776 is the same as it is today. The position of a state surrounded by three larger states is key to the success of Delaware. The river that once was a lifeline to economic freedom, allowing such a small state to compete globally, has been mistreated. Like most waterways that see so much traffic, the river has pollution, but the Delaware River is more polluted for some reason.[30] Like the fifth most polluted river in the country. Is bad leadership to blame? Why or who would sell out their state's lifeline, and for what? In 1956 a survey of the Delaware River was done by the US Army of Engineers; it shows that with the annual flooding of local waterways and maintenance to the basin, the river will remain pollution stable.

There has been pollution since the river was called the Lenape river. In 1609 the water quality of the river went from drinkable to polluted. In the coming decades, the river just got worse. The Clean Water Act in the late '70s and '80s helped save the river, wildlife, and the businesses that need the economic income that it brings. Even during the 2020 election year, the river was the main selling point for Joe Biden and his expertise in Green Technology. The question came up numerous times about Delaware's commitment to the environment, while facts showed that pollution in Delaware is among the worst in the country. Air quality and life expectancy around the river are damaged too. It is not called the Biden River; it has been cleaned before because the Johnson administration tied up loose ends after Kennedy was assassinated. Kennedy refused to sign the bill, and it sat on his desk until Johnson took over.

In 1966 before Biden was ever in political office, Senator Edmund Muskie, a Democrat, and his bi-partisan subcommittee member Senator J. Caleb Boggs, a Republican from Delaware, secured the bill's votes. Their bi-partisan partnership led to the vast support of the bill that mainly added air quality. Though a small but significant step in Delaware's future and the states surrounding the river. So, when 1973 rolls around, you think a young Senator would learn a thing or two. You would think that the heir of DuPont and a College graduate would understand these things before running the state of Delaware for decades.

A boy from Scranton, Pennsylvania, another state that uses the river just as much for its success, would be all for river protection and air quality for the people living near it. The US government spent nine hundred million dollars in 1968 alone just on the Delaware River to restore the quality of life on and around its waterways. The pollution in the Delaware River improved from 1967 to 1973 until the industrial boom of Delaware. Delaware could only compete with neighbors who had more to offer by letting things slide when big money came to town. Tax cuts, Tax breaks, Environmental overlooks, and items of that nature. When DuPont opened its enormous plant in the '70s, a small New Jersey town over the bridge had 1000's homes built up for employees and their families.[31] No one ever blamed Joe Biden. He has had a pass for some reason. It is like being a lifeguard at a pool for 47 years, and there have been numerous drownings, and the water is green. Who is to blame? Never will he admit to failure or not being up to the task.

We all know the story of DuPont and its Asian partners that put harmful chemical plants in our country and pollute our waterways. No, you never heard of the DuPont's; OMG, look it up; that is ten books or five movies in itself.[32] Look it up; it is a great read. When you are done reading, you will start attacking the grocery store teenage bagger when he asks for paper or plastic. Paper, please. In Wilmington, Delaware, where DuPont is headquartered, the water has a higher "Forever Chemicals" concentration than any surrounding state.[33] Over 1.3 million Americans in New Jersey, Philadelphia, and Delaware alone have been affected. Over 320,000 residents have been harmed by the Delaware River and its runoff in Delaware.

This summer, my wife lost her niece to cancer, a 13-year-old girl who never had a chance to live a whole life because of a politician's greed. She grew up in that area and lived near Dover, DE, most of her life. The book was dedicated to her and every child who lost their fight against cancer. Cancer was the cause of 29% of all deaths in Delaware last year. That is one-third of Delaware's population being impacted by a lack of local and state government agencies failing to act. Yes, now after soldiers at Dover Air Force Base are becoming ill. Finally, Biden and Delaware are going to clean it up. The problem they face is that it cannot be cleaned. They are called "Forever Chemicals." They named it, not me. The buck stops with you, Joe!

I bet it did stop with you, right at your back pocket! Still during the election, I laughed as I saw Joe Biden and the New Green Deal, and the environmentalist with the progressive left spends trillions to make energy. The manipulation does not end after he is even in the office and won. He still must keep the narrative and lie about how Green he is and how he can change America for the better. Forever Change us with Forever Chemicals. Imagine if the Governor of Alaska let an oil company dump illegally, and we never had King or Sockeye again. Build Back Better?

In July 2020, the University of Pennsylvania published an article stating that the Delaware River is considered safe only for "secondary contact," NOT SWIMMING in BOLD LETTERS. What, stop the nonsense? Less than a month later, after Joe Biden found out about the article, a national advocacy group named American Rivers proudly published the Delaware River the "River of the Year" because of its improvements in water quality. The group **E360.Yale.edu** did the article and posted the American River society awards findings. The group American Rivers is based out of, you guessed it, Washington DC and has thousands of volunteers who want to tear down over two hundred Americas dams on rivers nationwide. They say that we must restore fish and wildlife habitats by tearing them down. Watch out, Nevada; you are next!

So, who is correct, the state of Pennsylvania and its College or an environmental group from DC? How did the river get so bad that we cannot directly answer the outcome? Is it safe or not? Who is playing cover-up or telling the truth? Not something the river has much say in anyhow; pitiful thing gets used and abused still to this day. What factors led to a problem so bad? Which companies are to blame for polluting the river? What politician was on watch as all of this went on!

Biden has made deals his whole career in Delaware, deals that have affected all of us. Have you ever had a credit card? Guess where and when they became the mega giants today? Delaware with help from our good friend and trusted blue-collar chum Joe Biden. He has made deals with everyone for whose benefit? For himself and his friends. Joe once said in an interview that he does not trust anyone. A man at 70 years old said he does not trust anyone. Do you know why? Because we cannot trust him. In the 1970s, Joe Biden would do anything to stay in power and be loved. He might have been the Senator of Delaware, but he worked for DuPont for 47 years. Just like how Hunter works for foreign money and Joe has shown him the way. In the '80s, the credit card boom was here but only for the rich.

No working-class man could get a card with money on it. So, what did blue-collar Joe do? He and Governor DuPont at the time let bank lobbyists write a wish list to the leaders of the state? If they allowed this, they would move all their cooperate offices to Delaware. Then the big companies with their Unions will make their employees vote for DuPont and Biden. A credit card company could move to Delaware and do what they wanted for people and their credit. While other states had laws to protect blue-collar Americans, Joe told banks they could charge whatever they wanted in annual interest and late fees.

The new rules would allow the banks to foreclose on debtors' homes if they fell behind on payments. Since the Governor also owned the most significant business in the state, they also cut corporate taxes that year. These events were the birth of a monster that was not wealthy, inventive, or even a man of the people. He let his big-money donors and self-governing state officials have the ability to cheat people out of their futures.

We all have credit cards, and we all know what can happen if we do not pay the debt back. The stories, the movies, and the politicians who fight for a free school and free rent during a pandemic ignore this truth. The Senator for decades never battled for credit card debt. So, when he sat there on the Charlamagne and said, you ain't Black if you vote for the Trump. He said you ain't Black unless you got credit debt from the JOE. Trump does not have credit card companies as friends; Joe does. The banks on Wall Street know Joe! JP Morgan and others profited from this political power move, and it was a rich corporate business dream come true. Even when the Federal Government would try to stop Delaware, Biden was in the Senate telling all his friends how much they could make. By the 1990s, almost all the biggest credit card companies were raking it in. So, he said that Trump and his rich White friends are getting richer while he is in office. OMG, what a good observation Joe.

I might add, Joe's net worth is over one hundred million dollars. After 47 years in office, I did not know you make 2 million a year as a Senator. In the late '90s, every state adopted this as law, and that started the Corporate America hate game as the Democrats every year play to the poor blue-collar workers of America. Antifa, the riots are all against big money America and their rich greed. Remember the Wall Street camp out? Democrats fought corporate greed and Wall Street billionaires for the little helpless Americans. Joe Biden and Democrats in office helped create a financial crutch that has crushed Americans' futures for decades.

Everyone, and I mean everyone, knows someone in credit card debt. There is no difference between the loan shark and a credit card company. They will both take something from you if you do not pay up. The All-American Blue-Collar hero is a bullshitting liar. He allowed the banks to set such high-interest rates that there was an escalator effect on paying it down once you got in debt. They created terms like monthly minimum, 1% cashback, and free drinks as you waited for your plane. The interest rates to pay back $100 were 18-20%. So, for those borrowing one hundred dollars, you have to pay back $120. Suppose you do not pay it back all at once. If you do payments and the monthly minimum, you will pay back repeatedly. This game is how they keep you in debt. The more you spend, the more you get back. So, they charge you a 21% interest rate and give you 1% back if you spend it on what they tell you to. This is a destructive cycle for any borrower and not what a politician should be doing while in office.

In 2010 the EPA came out with data showing that the DUPONT company dumped over ten million pounds of waste into the river.[34] The EPA investigated and found the quality of life in and around the river changed dramatically for the worse due to the unchecked dumping of "Forever Chemicals," as they are called. These consist of hydrogen chloride, titanium, iron, and titanium ore, mainly from their plant north of Wilmington. Over decades they violated permit limits that lawmakers set. They released more than they were supposed to release. That year DuPont earned $3 billion in profits and paid a fine to the state of Delaware for $500,000.00 for violating pollution levels for the past six years. Only $500K for ruining millions of lives forever with "Forever Chemicals."

The New York Times in 2016 had an article saying that DuPont dumped chemicals into the river for years, and politicians did nothing but look the other way. Years of demanding work and millions of taxpayer's dollars were spent in the '60s and '70s, and for what. DuPont can pay off politicians, and they would look the other way. The only problem is that you still smell the sewage in the air when you look the other way. It was not until 2016 that the politicians of Delaware, minus Joe Biden took action and recently, in 2021, landed a massive lawsuit for $50 million and, most important, responsibility for damages done.

The Delaware River, in the last five years, has had a significant comeback in wildlife returning to the areas damaged. Still, to this day, you cannot swim, drink, wash clothes, or brush teeth with water from the Delaware River or its runoffs. The only thing is to flow down a rapid in a tube just like a tourist. Every year thousands travel to the Delaware River to ride down in lines.[35] Do you think they know how polluted the Delaware River is?

The waterways around the river are also seeing a considerable eco-change. In 2010 the Delaware legislators took responsibility for decades and centuries of neglect from local and state politicians. For a long time in Delaware, you could do any kind of business you wanted by greasing some palms. The big corporation started somewhere; money, greed, and power have led it to Delaware. The people still must live here, work here, and play here. The history of dumping illegally in the Delaware River has gone on for centuries. At the turn of the century, primarily all the slaughterhouses lined Delaware and Pennsylvania along the river. They lined both sides to have drain runoff straight into the Delaware River. During WW2, the pollution was worse, and the sailors were told to ignore the stench.

Delaware's new legislators made it priority number one the year after Joe Biden went to the White House. The leaders held people accountable and made them pay for real this time. When Joe Biden was a Delaware Senator, DuPont paid a fine of $500 thousand. It seems low after having profits for DuPont were three billion that year. In 2021 over a dozen public utility companies were forced to settle on damage to natural resources during the '80s. After years of putting off, a settlement ordered by a judge that ruled damage to the river was first discovered back in 1983. For 40 years, they waited till everyone died off before blaming the proper people. It could not have happened when he was still in the Senate. He blocked all resolutions, court orders, and public knowledge of the damage to Delaware and its people due to Forever Chemicals. He could not face the music while there, so he hid again and sneaked out the back door.

After he was left office in 2008, an actual Delaware bi-partisan legislation passed almost unanimously on pressing the people responsible. The PPR's as they are known, got a pass from their friend Joe.[36] He looked out for the people all right, the people that would line his wallet, support his family, and fund his lavish lifestyle. A true politician, Joe Biden used and abused his power to get what he wanted. Take a good sniff Delaware and try not to cough on the Joe fumes.

He has not lost his touch, though. The Delaware basin project will receive billions in funding from the new bill passed in 2021. After years of harm and sickness due to allowing big corporations to make billions on the health of Delaware residents. Now he puts a couple of billion into fixing years of damage, and who pays for it, we all do. The American taxpayer will pay for what Delaware politicians did to Delaware. Just like we all pay for higher prices at the gas station, but canceling the pipeline hurt only Trump, right? The Delaware basin foundation will receive funding to fix what? The same stuff that the lawsuit that just passed in March of 2021 is supposed to be paying for. So, wait, we are paying for something to be fixed twice; who is receiving that money? Is that his retirement money so he can have another mansion in the Hamptons with Barrack?

Senator Tom Carper, a Democrat, pushed hard for the funding already on its way. So, after the lawsuit settlement in March 2021, the environmental leaders of Delaware got together to talk about how to spend more money than the new Infrastructure bill will offer them. The Delaware environmental leaders met at the DuPont Nature Center along the Wilmington riverfront in April 2021. This book writes itself. So, after years of destroying the environment and the people's way of life, the polluters meet with politicians to fix their created problem. See the pattern? I will make a mess, and we all must pitch in to fix your mess. The Republicans are racist and unkind because they do not want to repair the lot that the Democrats created by not listening to the Republicans in the first place.

The irony that DuPont is involved with politicians to fix the environment is laughable. Like a murderer sitting on his own jury, the jury that convicts him. They should have no part in removing Forever Chemicals from areas that will never recover. They should have never been allowed to keep doing damage year after year. Who was on watch when this damage was done? Who was around to see the towns up and down the Delaware River decline? If only the people of Delaware had someone during those 40 years of significant pollution to watch over the state, and it is their most fantastic resource.

Joe Biden has made it a point in his career to screw over Americans, because why? Money, power, greed, and never being responsible. Every low-income town along the river is now affected by the damage done over years of neglect. The Dover Air Force Base has Forever Chemicals dumped all over it.[37] Years of political bargaining to get richer and the poor pay the price. Anyone can see the whole state is on a downward spiral after years of JOkE Biden; even the average income in Delaware is below the US average. Delaware's citizens have been working their whole life to make someone else rich and keep the politicians in power. His infrastructure bill is a mockery of how politicians can run our cities and towns into the ground due to horrible views on how America should be run. He is helping failures waste more taxpayer money and get nothing done but hurt our children's future with debt.

If you want to make a real difference in Americans' lives, please resign and never come back, or better yet, just Hide! Take your whole team with you. JOkEs of the Biden circus must go. Just like you and your son were easily corrupted by foreign money, your cabinet, the Teacher's Unions, the DOJ, the Military Elite, and all involved are only worried about money and staying in power. The Lie to hurt Trump is killing us. Spend, spend, and spend when you have no money left to spend. Please do not take our children's future and then their children's future and flush it down the polluted Delaware River.

How about Delaware sells all of Joe's properties, Jill's dresses, and jewelry and tells Hunter to give over the China check he got and pay back the families who lost someone forever. The Biden's never paid any price for the damages to Delaware that are now Forever Chemicals that are forever killing people of Delaware. Forever Chemicals kill people, forever!

Chapter 3

The Glowing Green Thumb

When Hurricane IDA hit the coast of New Orleans in 2021 as a category four hurricane, the worst since the 1850s, and the first thing Joe does is blame climate control. Yes, I understand that we are depleting the Earth of natural resources. We reheat the waste from years past into our atmosphere using fossil fuels. So, when I get yelled at by a guy who has polluted the tri-state area with bad political and personal policies, I have had enough. I must speak out. Young Americans want to know why the climate is so bad and how the Earth is changing at a dangerous pace. Now suddenly, wealthy billionaires wish to go to space and colonize?

The leading cause of climate change comes from career politicians who spent a lifetime looking the other way on people's health. He was in Wilmington, right down the street from the industrial boom. He has changed the state's landscape from once farmlands and fields to pollution-spewing Nuclear, Chemical wastelands filled with Municipal County mega billion-dollar plants. We have been doomed, folks. He is not worried about global warming because he helped contribute to it. He says he traveled the world; Joe Biden says he has talked to every politician and looked him in the eyes for the last 50 years! When did America see a natural decline in the health of its earth? We noticed a change in how we breathe, live, and grow food, especially the rapid deterioration of America's health. About 50 years ago!

The world is not hurting from mother nature. Mother nature is breaking because our leaders made environmental moves without considering our health or the planet's health. Global warming has been through years of bad policies made by allowing big money to run your politicians; it is a lobbyist vs. activist standoff.

Again, another problem that is crushing us as a country was made by a politician. First, financially, medically, and now our safety. A governor who lets companies put chemicals in the ground forever has no right to tell anyone to Build Back Better. You built it first, and now we are fixing your failures. Is Joe Biden ever going to be held responsible for anything? Damage to his state and the people, now mother nature pays for the damages done from humans. Today even mother nature says, wake up! Every action has an equal or more powerful reaction, including when you fail to do your job as a politician. When you stopped worrying about The People and started worrying about who you are. Our leaders have failed; they stopped protecting us and only protected their wallets. Global warming is real, but mother nature is not to blame.

Joe Biden blasted coal and cut the pipeline when entering the White House. For the first time in a long time in America's history that we were Energy Independent, the whole reason we could leave the Middle East for good. We do not need their oil anymore; what does he do? He closes a pipeline, and now gas prices are up—a career politician who was in the game of talking out both sides of his mouth. In one swipe of a pen, he took away our freedom, and now we again rely on someone else's fuel, the way they refine it, and whatever they want to charge. Plus, now the new conflict in the Middle East makes sense. So, we canceled the pipeline on day one, lost American jobs, sent the production, employment, and profits overseas. Plus, we now must transport from across the ocean. Has anyone ever heard of an oil tanker leaking anyone? Then drive on highways, so spend gas to transport gas, double pollution burger, anyone. Then still must use a pipeline locally to pump it into gas stations.

Does that make sense, and the gas prices are now over a buck more per gallon? Just like his hero, Jimmy Carter, did. We had the pipeline secured and finished. If a leak occurs, we have a 24-hour monitoring system on the pipe. Damage is minimal, and it is a quick fix and clean-up. Over the oceans have shown us with one oil tanker leak can due. The damage we are talking about and the loss of coral and sea life in the billions. That is if we catch it in time. The pipeline was the safest way to transport that fuel without damaging a helpless fish. The ocean has had enough damage! The United States cannot trust Russia with our elections but buying massive amounts of energy is perfectly ok with everyone. Foolish me, are we looking at this all wrong?

Ask yourself three questions, and the outcome is clear. Stop step back and think about who would benefit by stopping the pipeline. Who will be affected at the pump? Who will be crushed by it being canceled? The second question is straightforward, and we are the ones paying for it at the pump. Gas has risen 50% since Joe Biden took office. To answer the first question, who benefits from the pipeline closing, Russia, you know Trump's friends who helped him get elected? Who eventually will be crushed by Russia in the end, Hunter's so-called oil coworkers, friends, and paycheck, Ukraine? So, when the Democrats had you fooled again with two wasted impeachment trials, the truth did come out.

Ukraine was lied to by Hunter Biden, and the Ukrainian president had every right to worry and ask for help from the US government. Russia did interfere with the elections, Russia is about to invade, Russia hacks our Oil companies to help Joe Biden become the leader of the free world from his basement. Yes, one more thing, gas prices rise, and some gas stations are closing due to lack of fuel. Hackers from Russia! Joe Biden hacked the pipeline and blamed it on Russia. Putin made a couple of billion, and Joe ruined another significant part of America.

Joe Biden has been a big reason Delaware is the first state built out. From 1950 to 2010, privately owned farmland has shrunk in Delaware by half.

What does that mean, no fresh produce and fruit and livestock? Shipping in from other states means other farmers are working, not ours. Smaller farms in an area mean less fresh breathing air. Farms help produce a healthier environment because the ecosystem in a farm is self-contained. Unlike dumping chemicals in a river, the farm compost system makes farms eco-friendly. Plus, you offer people in the area fresh produce that is healthier than any fast food.

Delaware was once a thriving farming area; the flag of Delaware has a revolutionary soldier on one side and a farmer on the other. In 1930, Delaware produced more peaches than any other place in the world. In the early 1920s, the whole state was farmland from cow farms to chickens, and fresh fruit trees covered the peninsula. A once-free open state covered with open lands of hard-working Americans to a state with no ground for sale. The liar who says he has had a green thumb his whole life changed the landscape of Delaware. A once sprawling American farmland filled with migrants from both World Wars built up a better America. The land that has now been sitting for years, covered in layers of pollution, covered over so it cannot be seen. Forever Chemicals can be hidden but never fixed, and they are forever. Like most things done during Biden's helm as a state Senator for over 40 years, brushed over and hidden from plain sight. Corruption in Delaware has been done with a pen, a gun, and even a shovel.

Two things can be said about Delaware's problems from pollution. Someone committed the corruption crime, and the people responsible for our safety and wellbeing failed to do anything or looked the other way. Knowing the career politician, Joe Biden was thriving for, I can bet that his pockets are enormous and that people got sick and died. Jump ahead to the end of his political career, and it was true, Joe Biden has tarnished the health and environment of the State of Delaware. Let us take a look at a guy who wants to "Build Back Better" a whole country in just four years with billions of taxes payers' money. While in the last 46 years and trillions of dollars, he destroyed one tiny state. If this chapter does not touch heartstrings and make you realize how taking a handout or looking the other way can hurt even a tiny child, I do not know what will.

For some reason, Joe Biden has an ego problem that does not work well. He could have been the best Senator from the farm State of Delaware by producing food, agriculture, and being a good ole American. Instead, he competed with North Jersey, the "mini–New York," Philadelphia, and Camden. I am a better politician than you just watch. I can make the big business come here; you will see. We have seen the fish, birds, and wildlife move away.

A once central farming area in the United States is now Delaware. Like Wayne's World made fun of in their movie in the 1990s, hello millennials, you are not the first ones. Great, we are in Delaware, wow Delaware. He has ruined a good thing for who? The people of the state, their lives have not gotten better from growing plastic instead in apples.[38] Their health did not improve from breathing in toxic fumes; the wildlife did not get stronger from swimming and drinking in a river filled with ten million pounds of toxic waste. Not just DuPont alone, 100's of other companies had a free pass to use Delaware and its people's land as their toilets. They used Delaware as a wastebasket, and nobody said anything because Joe Biden was on the watch.

When Joe Biden talks about how he lost his son to a form of cancer, does he realize the pollution that his son had to grow up in by living in Delaware? He grew up in Wilmington near all the pollution. Is that why Joe Biden hates America so much? Did he not think of the long-term consequences of nonstop pollution to an area? Land, water, and sea. Joe Biden's environmental approach is like a three-part movie. First, we kill the water, which leads to air pollution. Water and the air make rain clouds, leading to the death of animals and people living under them. If nothing can breathe, eat, or grow, then the land dies away as things move on before they die off. The Earth is covered by over 70% of water. How long until Joe ruins other oceans or all of them with his financial friends through the globe.

Joe has been looking the other way to allow big business foreign money, and his greed led to the deaths of thousands of people who live in Delaware and the United States.[39] The disaster that the Delaware River became in the '70s, '80s, and '90s should be a clear example of how Joe Biden has no green thumb at all. He sat back and took handouts from every illegal dumper in the state and other states. He let that go on under his watch, and while the people of Delaware got sick and died, he got rich and smirked. While he sat in Wilmington, the pollution ran down rivers and streams, affecting everyone in the state one way or the other.

So, when Joe Biden or any politician opens their mouth on the national stage about how they can fix the environment or Build Back Better, please take a good look at Delaware. At how he put Forever Chemicals in the area he calls home. Delaware has taken too many steroids and never entered the gym! Delaware is a pure example of Joe Biden and his infrastructure bill. They spent the money but did none of the work to see results. Highway 1 heading towards New Jersey through the Delaware Bridge has been under construction for 20 years, no lie. Just a constant day-to-day grind. Building back better is the responsibility of the States to maintain and fix roads in their state. We pay taxes, people; that money is there. His infrastructure bill will waste more of taxpayers' money and does not do what he says it will do. Joe has a green thumb, all right. It just glows from pollution and counting so many Benjamins.

A recent article **from the EPA Superfund Sites in Delaware on August 9, 2021**[40] states that the pollution was terrible after 40 plus years of damage during Joe's terms. After 20 years of recovery, billions are wasted, people are dead. The land is now safe to be on, but do not touch anything. But it is safe! Wow, how convenient; now the land is under the containment level, and soon people and wildlife might be back. So, let us get this straight first; he ruins it by taking a back seat to be a caring, responsible elected official. He polluted the land for 40 years and looked the other way; all the while, he hides away in DC and plays homemaker with OBAMA (I want to know who the wife was and who was the husband) as people have to clean up his mess. He hides away so others can clean up his mess and make the taxpayers fix his pollution to America. Then when he needs every millennial to be dumb and vote disastrous, he has the government-funded DC lobbyist EPA draft a report on how Delaware and its decades of corruption and pollution just vanished.

Joe Biden could not build a peanut butter jelly sandwich without messing it up. Please, America, take it from a person who dedicated a book to a 13-year-old girl who battled rare cancer her whole life and why because she grew up and her family lived in Delaware. That shit is not right. Republican, Democrat, whatever you are, she had no choice to decide what political party to join; she never lived long enough.

Countless family members of mine, who lived and their families worked at plants in Delaware, died from pollution and work conditions. Then they brought the disease home to their wives doing their laundry. Their kids hug daddy and breathe in the pollution he just carried home. For what, a Tupperware craze of the '80s? We went from glass bottles to plastic bottles to save thirty cents a bottle. How many lives were lost for thirty cents a bottle? Today, how many children die of cancer in Delaware because of years of neglect decades before? Forever Chemicals, Joe Biden let companies spill, dump, and pollute Delaware with Forever Chemicals.

The name Forever Chemicals comes from where and who? The EPA, the same people who flipped their story in 2021, are under the budget thumb of Joe Biden. The same people that told the world of Forever Chemicals are the same people who gave Joe Biden the green thumb approval. What a JOkE; politicians control the budget committee that oversees funding for these agencies set up to protect Americans. This is what politicians learn from years in office! Follow and become their hero, fellow career politicians. An honest day's work is all the American people ask for. Car oil and cow farts are ruining the planet we live on. Not politicians who allow Forever Chemicals to be illegally dumped on their watch.

When a politician says he will do anything, look up their history on that subject. All of Joe's friends and family members are not qualified to mow my lawn, let alone be in the power of the greatest country of all time. We have allowed the lie to take over the lie and cover up the truth. Now we have set our lives the lives of our children back 20 years because of Joe's hate and lack of work ethic. Nothing he could have done in Delaware could ever overlook the damage he caused. DuPont can open up a thousand Children Cancer Centers; they helped cause it.

Biden could erase sales tax and pay people to stay home and be lazy. They will eventually die from drinking the water and breathing in the air. Joe Biden could have done anything he wanted, a young and new politician at the most crucial time in America's Civil Rights history. The stage was set for a blue-collar boy from Scranton to save the state and be the voice for the people. Instead, he sold their vote for the term after term of big money Donors and Union Voting frauds. If you cannot see the writing on the walls, then taste the Forever Chemicals in the soil. Take your time. They will be there forever.

The same EPA article published in 2021 tells of countless areas in Delaware ruined by municipal and industrial waste. The companies have no names in the article. They are labeled as PRP. Potentially Responsible Parties is how the EPA marks the polluters. So, if they are "potentially" liable, why are they fixing, cleaning up, and lining the pockets of who is in charge? You, the EPA, and the US government! So, the companies responsible for polluting Delaware range from city municipalities, private companies, industrial giants, and even the US government. The pollution to the groundwater came from burying drums one hundred feet in the ground. That leaked into streams, creeks, and drinking wells. Also, an explosion fire at one facility caused ground leaks that spilled into the waterways and the groundwater. After years of non-regulations and government cover-ups, the groundwater in some areas will be an ongoing treatment and testing to ensure the pollution levels stay manageable. When I was a kid and swam in the Delaware River because we were told it was safe, you could feel the Teflon and oils on your bathing suits. A sore throat and ear infection were common after swimming in Joe Biden's pollution.

For years Joe Biden allowed DuPont and numerous PRP municipal utility companies to ruin the ground in Delaware. Joe Biden let these companies live ABOVE THE LAW, the same line he used on Trump. When Trump built his casinos, could he ruin the Atlantic Ocean they sit on? Donald Trump was bashed during the 2016 election for being a rich White guy in power. Like every friend and coworker of Joe Biden. Do you think even for one moment that Joe Biden could ever think about the consequences? A career politician never worries about the outcome; they simply blame someone else after being in power for decades. Never taking responsibility is an excellent trait in a Democratic politician's playbook. There will be no green deal; there will be no Build Back Better. There will be wasted taxpayers' dollars; we all can remember Obama's shovel-ready jobs.[41]

They were ready all right, ready to build Obamas Hawaii mansion, his Martha's Vineyard Plantation, and his 33-million-dollar Library in Chicago commissioned in August 2021. Do you think Joe Biden lied, saying he was in Delaware during the Afghanistan evacuation, or was he in Massachusetts at his friend's birthday party laughing it up? You wonder how a guy could ruin so many lives and healthy futures for handouts, and he stayed in power for too long. Maybe this was not the first election stolen. How does a stumbling double talker win term after term? Is Governor Cuomo the only Democrat that lied about how many people died during the pandemic? We might have found another. How does someone who never fought for the rights of the people of his state remain in office? Joe Biden has changed the landscape of Delaware forever. By adding Forever Chemicals to the soil. In the early 1900's Delaware was all farmlands, and it fed the East coast. The air was clean, the rivers and streams were clean and safe for everyone to enjoy. The landscape today is far from and agricultural giant it once was. So, when he yells at the TV screen during a press conference, is it the Forever Chemicals making him stumble while he speaks! He squints and taunts you over climate change and not caring like him, not loving the Earth, and being anti-environmental like Trump was. Does he add the part where he said Forever Chemicals were added to the state's soil while he was Senator for 47 years? Maybe I am dreaming, and perhaps the world just crawled under a rock, but people die of cancer, and one day it will come back and bite him in the ass. Karma is a Bitch, Joe!

Chapter 4

Foreign Policy 101

I cannot write this book fast enough. When I started my research for this book, I looked up all the failed choices and votes this president has made. JOkE Biden releases our troops on the eve of 9/11, 20 years after the attack on American soil. Of all times, why, so he can look in the TV screen, shed a tear for Beau, and say I got them all home. So, you can feel sad, and he can play on your heartstrings. Joe excuses and double talk on why we are leaving Afghanistan never made sense then and still today.[42] So, when a soldier signs up for war and combat to go and defend our freedom and country, you tell him, please do not get hurt. They know what they sign up for; that is why we call them heroes, Joe. A police officer, a firefighter, and soldiers sign up to fight death as a daily job hazard.

That is why countries have soldiers and not the whole place takes up arms and dies. We have soldiers to fight wars and battles on foreign soil, not here in America. Why Am I telling you this? Your son was a hero that signed up to fight terrorists; now, he fought and died for nothing. That was his plan to show his pain inside over the death of his son, so America, you can understand. It worked on the people of Delaware for over 40 years, and indeed it can work on you one more time. I did it for Beau! I gave the terrorist weapons for Beau! I helped

13 American soldiers die because of Beau! All to be a hero in the eyes of himself.

His son tragically died of a brain tumor long after serving in the Army. A soldier knows why they sign up for service, duty, and honor. Be a commander, not a coward. If you would ask his son about the decision, what would Joe's son Beau say? What would a military vet say after Joe Biden removed a significant force from a terrorist-producing country in the Middle East after years of securing stability for not only Americans but the people and women who live there in fear? Americans are the wrong people who let women have rights, like learning and reading? Where is the Me-Too Movement now? Get on a plane, travel to DC, and demand action! When I started writing this chapter, the sun never shined anymore. I was so mad, angry, confused, and then I got it like a light bulb on the top of my head. Like everything a politician does, especially the Democrats, you need to step back and look at the big picture.

This hurts when you cut through the deceit and lay out what JOkE Biden just did again. We just gave terrorists who hijacked four planes and flew them into American landmarks in the hope of killing thousands of people another shot.[43] We just gave them a whole airbase full of planes on the eve of 9/11. JOkE Biden, I cannot believe that not one person in your cabinet or even your family would not say, hey, Joe, you are making the wrong move. You think your dead son, an Army vet, would appreciate how you left like a coward. You and Barrack Obama have made a point while you had the power to bring us down a peg, decimate our military and give the enemy billions and billions of dollars and weapons. Iran nuclear deal and 150 billion dollars of cash under Barrack Obama. Joe Biden gives even more to the same people who hate America. Who is voting for you and Barrack? Do they both need to be held legally accountable every time a terrorist attack occurs in the future? Did you aid and support them? You gave them weapons! You have made every country in the world less safe. Now with weapons that we designed. Taxpayers just supplied the Taliban Army. The chapter should end now; that's it; what else do I need to say to get you Woke.

The worst attack in American History on nonmilitary civilians since Pearl Harbor, and you think we need to leave for good. We controlled the country for over 18 months with 2500 soldiers; now, we need 10,000 to hold an airbase. Please resign just over that; you are the biggest threat to America, plain and simple. Impeachment 2022 needs to start immediately. Like Lenny in Mice and Men, just a dumb, straightforward, and simple move, again by another Democrat politician. Is he trying to make more pain and hurt, so we have to go back in 20 years and do it all over again?

When I step back and try to wrap my head around a moron and his simple brain to let terrorists out and not only free but more powerfully armed than they had ever been in their history, JOkE Biden gave them an airbase, and they are fighting us and our allies. I have to tip my hat; Joe may be so dumb he does not even realize what he just did. When we were attacked on 9/11, we were stable as a country, with no race riots, no pandemic, and enjoying life. Some Americans tried to blame Bush Jr. because he was a Republican, but we all came together to fight the bad guys. Joe has awakened and woke up America's youth to how great we are and can be when attacked as a nation. He has raised the hatred in America towards extremist terrorism from across the sea. They can try to push the January 6th people as terrorists, but American's will never forget real terrorists from 9/11 and what happened to us that day.

Joe and his Democrats can try to change history and repaint the uniforms' colors during the Civil war, but it does not matter. His lies and his division games are ending. They can push any lie to try and overshadow a day like 9/11. The division, the racism, covid vaccine mandates, and especially hate towards law enforcement will stop. When your building gets blown up, and every race, creed, color, religion, nationality, and political party is in there and dies together. All our pity fighting means nothing; Joe Biden has awakened America's true enemy. Any person who tries to take our freedom. It does not matter your color or political party. Everyone loves and uses freedom in our country.

God Bless America! Joe Biden gave the Taliban billions of dollars of weapons to hate, even more, the true enemy of all non-Muslim religions worldwide. He is a Catholic, and he just gave the Catholic haters weapons to kill Catholics. Plus, they hate Jews, Christians, Lutherans, and Baptists! They even hate the one day a week fake Christians reserve as Holy. Those who voted with hate against Trump voted with anger misinformation and supported a terrorist enabler.

This is not the first foreign policy blunder that Joe has gotten into. He has been keeping the fight in the Middle East going for decades. He helped start it, too, with a moral choice. A vote! Let us see Joe's history of voting on foreign policies and how they have affected America. He has been in office since 1973; the US has been in countless wars, conflicts, missions, and now the second retreat in American history. What has America's boy done to stop the wars and destruction going on in the world we live in? How has he impacted terrorism worldwide after being in office for over 40 years? What has he done to secure your freedom? Joe is still learning after 40 years that the first thing to a robust foreign policy is never bowing down and running away. Still, after all these years, learning is starting to take its toll on our freedom. When he plays both sides of the fence as he does throughout his career to stay in power, you see the true politician.

Since 2019 the tearing down of America's past began. They taunted Americans from the Republican side, as every statue was a Democrat enslaver. The pain was not mutual because we did not put them up; Blue Dog Democrats and career politicians did. So, when Joe Biden lets these American military symbols and the fight those Americans endured be demolished and tarnished. That was a Democrat moment in time, not the moment to be proud of, but it happened, and we as Americans have learned from our troubled past. Those statues were mainly of Democrat enslavers. Those statues might have hurt the feelings of a teenager who does not understand a sacrifice more significant than yourself, like signing up for a war in the 1800s. To enter a war for your country was once seen as admirable! Almost certain death to a young soldier on the front lines of a musket battle during the Civil War.[44]

The soldiers in Afghanistan were fighting a terrible racist anti-freedom group called the Taliban. We defended the freedom of every woman and child in that country. Our soldiers put their lives on the line for us, them, and the rest of the world. A monument should come up for the fallen thirteen soldiers who died at the airbase. When we look back on the final days of Joe Bidens, the last "custard" stand, like a boy at the custard stand, "I'll take Rocky Road," you idiot! After years go by and the refugees we defended and died for decide to change their minds, then what. Will they have the right to tear down those monuments? Is that fair, are we so brainwashed as a society that we accept self-failure?

When Obama and Biden told the world that Americans are not worthy of exceptionalism.[45] Who was listening? Do we believe that we are the racist haters of the world and the worst people of all time? The worse people because we live in a country with enslavers. Then if we remove every statue with a negative view on slavery, the word Democrat should be torn down just like a statue. The word alone brings back views of hate, slavery, plantations, confederate flags waving in the wind, and of course, the Civil War.[46]

As millions die to come to our lands and live in our part of the world. Why, why live where the devil sleeps. Why live in America, the land of hate and anger towards non-Whites? Why vote Democrat when they were the enslavers? Because they know it is a lie, they are taught better than we are about American history. Will we let a group of cancelers erase those thirteen heroes' sacrifices? Just as the Democrat party pretends to erase the Confederate Army from history! Joe Biden already tore down the monument of those thirteen soldiers and every statue of every soldier that served for those twenty-some years to keep us safe when he turned tail and ran away. He created another Korean War and another forgotten victory. He started another Vietnam War where we blamed each other instead of the true enemy.

The battle for freedom from terroristic radical Muslims in the Middle East is brought home to America. We see it at a Jewish synagogue, a UPS shipping center, and another military base. The people left behind will be forgotten, tortured, starved, and beaten. Our soldier's honor will be tarnished just as they did in the '70s under Kennedy, Johnson, and Nixon. We created another failure, an unwinnable war, when we walked away.

Joe Biden watched, lived through, and dodged the Vietnam war. He should have known better. [47] He had bone spurs, yes bone spurs! He was there and saw what we did wrong; we blamed each other and took our eye off the goal. The path America is on now after Joe Biden ended our watchful eye on terror is scary. He put our soldiers in a dangerous position. Then he humiliated every vet that served. Then he made more angry young men and women enemies of America by our involvement in their country after a weak show of retreat. Making more radicals hate America, and now Joe gave them weapons to train their new army.

Only a traitor working for the other guys would do such a thing. In WW2, America, China and Russia fought off the German and Japanese attacks. They fought the Axis of Evil, the horrible Hitler allies that wanted to take over the world. Today America, China, and Russia are the new Axis of Evil. Joe Biden is working with the enemy as he tells us that Trump and Putin were stealing the election. The US president and his party are now helping with the Taliban, killing innocent people who do not believe in their ideology. Death to all infidels. The Germans and the Nazis at the time of WW2 caused mass genocide on a particular religious group. The Nazis raped, beat, and murdered the Jewish people. The Taliban does the same thing to their people, plus they fly our planes into our buildings and harm

Americans. So, during WW2, do you think the president worked with the Japanese Navy before Pearl Harbor?

A good comparison to Afghanistan is WW2! Do you think we wanted to trust Hitler that he would allow Americans and Christians to come across the enemy line to safety? You know, at German checkpoints, but now at Taliban checkpoints, show your Biden Card! There is no difference between the Taliban of today and the Nazi German machine of the past. The hate for a particular group or group is a mutual trait between both groups. The only difference between 1941 and 2021 is that our leaders in command are working together instead of pretending to hate each other. When you play battleship, do you show your board? Would you park a new car somewhere unsafe and leave it unlocked with valuables inside? No, no, no. The only difference is our commander-in-chief is not up to the task of making America great.

From the Democrat enslavers, Hitler, Nazis, and Taliban today, the enemy of freedom and human rights has always been there. Pure evil will never stop showing its ugly face. Hidden in a Communist country somewhere, someone hates us for overeating, drinking beer, and watching football on Sundays. Cowards will never stop blaming others for their problems. It is our leaders who cannot waiver and show fear. They buckle under the dollar and the power of greed. Our leaders keep up the constant fighting, and the media does not let peace prosper. Joe Biden is the enemy of America again, and his party of Democrats is still the same Jim Crow lawmakers of the past. The President is working with the enemy now instead of being a leader of the free world.

Joe Biden and his Axis of Evil leaders released Covid-19, controlled the world's economy, rattled the 2020 election so America's progress would be at a standstill. Joe Biden sat in his basement and sold the fool voter on the racist White Republican future to come instead of being honest about the years of hate on his team. Nobody bothered to look up the truth, and we have damaged our future forever. They are hurting the next generation forever. Forever Chemicals in Delaware and now forever consequences in America. When does forever end?

Joe Biden has been in political office for almost 50 years. He started as a local politician in Delaware and then was a Senator of Delaware for over four decades. He has made a career out of bad foreign policy votes and moves. In 2021 when he left Afghanistan and the world open for another 20 years of terror attacks, he knew better. He has been around for some of the worst and best US military conflicts. He knows how to use military might and how to downplay us, too, like when he was the vice president. After being elected Senator, Joe Biden had to decide, on party lines, of course. He was put to the test in his first year in public office. At that time, America went through the Yom Kippur War. This event set up the destabilization and the wars in the Middle East for the last 50 years.[48]

Joe Biden was Senator working with his mentor Senator Ted Kennedy. Nixon was president at the time; he needed votes to tempt India and Egypt to step out of peace talks with the whole Middle East. He hoped he could gain new allies for America. Instead, we created enemies for life! The seasoned Democrat Congress plucked young Democrat Senators to push Nixon and pass this horrible US foreign policy that would start conflicts that we still face today. Quite frankly, he does not even remember voting on it![49] Joe Biden followed along party lines with his first vote in office. He has never changed; he was never a bipartisan politician; he just played one on TV. So, he was always the grey fox in the hen house. He was once a sheep too, Baaad Joe!

The next conflict he was involved in voting for was the Lebanon multinational intervention conflict that up-started the creation and needs for the UN to be more involved in America's military future. Why? Because voting on conflicts was significant, as long as the conflict is not in our backyard. The next war or played down attack that we call a conflict, or a skirmish, was in 1983 the Invasion of

Grenada, then the Invasion of Panama was at the end of the eighties. All fights leftover from the Cold War have been going on since WW2, when Russia saved America and the world.

During WW2, Japan, Germany, and Italy were the Axis of Evil. The bad guys of WW2! Germany warned Japan to leave the sleeping giant out of the war, America. Instead, they insisted Japan attack China and Germany attack Russia from the west and meet Japan in the middle. China was nothing then and would have fallen as fast as Kabul in 2021. The Axis of Evil would have controlled all of Asia, Europe, Africa, and Australia and left Canada and the US for WW3. But Japan did not listen and attacked Pearl Harbor forcing the Americans to enter WW2. This led to the US being victorious after Japan surrendered. Russia was the saving grace; because of that act by Japan, Russia was able to fight off the German westward attack losing over twenty million citizens and soldiers during WW2.[50] That sacrifice by their whole country defeated the Germans and saved the Europeans, Americans, and others to fight smaller armies like Italy and Japan.

When the war was over, Russia was never given the same respect as the US, and they never were given the same empathy either. Russia lost more people in WW2 than any other country involved in WW2. They wanted parts of Germany; they wanted security and wealth from losing so much. This fight was between Stalin and then-president Franklin D. Roosevelt, a Democrat. He also wanted security and payback for losses of life after the war ended. After Roosevelt's death, Truman took over the last five months of the war and found out about the Manhattan Project. That was the bomb Roosevelt was making to end the war of all wars. Truman, a Democrat, decided to drop the bomb. He also dropped the bomb without telling any of our allied troops about the plan. They never knew of the project.[51]

So, Joe Biden was not the first Democrat president that left their allies in the dark just like he did during the withdrawal from Afghanistan in 2021—left in the middle of the night! Joe, they call that a walk of shame or a tramp trot home in the dark.

Well, back to history, after dropping the bombs, America was declared victor of WW2 and all the spoils that came with it. Russia was left to fend for itself as we kept and still have a US base in Germany. Russia does not. Russia was mad, and the Cold War was started and never stopped. It began with a Democrat in office that needed a victory lap and a victory speech. America entered the war in a coalition as the Allies against the Axis of Evil. We joined as a coalition of Allies to defend freedom in the world. This was never settled, and we still had Cold War conflicts well into the late 1980s from that failed policy with our Allies.

Another conflict Joe Biden could have learned from was the most significant victory and show of force by any country in the world's history. President George Bush Sr. sent American might and restored order as they ran out the Iraqi Army from Kuwait. They were restoring peace in a few hours. We came, we saw, and we kicked ass. Restored power and left. The No-Fly Zone enforcement over Iraq called Operation Desert Storm. It was such a massive event for America that Topps baseball cards did a set about the victory; it is impressive. We controlled the air by depleting the Iraq air force and stopping hijackings with help from our UN allies.

This war was left-over from failed US foreign policy from the Carter administration. Yes, they are bringing it back full circle! Yes, Jimmy Carter and the Democrat party voted to involve the US in the Yom Kippur War. Jimmy Carter was one of Joe's mentors, a hero, and he visited him after winning the election in 2020. Joe and Jill Biden visited ex-president Jimmy Carter. CNN had a special about the great American president Jimmy Carter during the 2020 elections; you know, propaganda.[52] Damage Control because they knew about Kabul from day one, and time was running out. Destabilization of all the countries in the Middle East to say there is a problem. A problem you created by withdrawing troops.

Joe Biden could have taken a playbook from Bush Sr. about wartime conflict negotiations and tactics. Instead, Joe Biden chooses

Jimmy Carter's playbook, all results equal failure. Why would today be different if it did not work during Carter's presidency? China and Russia are still the same players, and England has a less global impact now. We are not better-off; Joe was alive in the 70's he should know this. And when all else fails, open the borders, get new voters, and forget about the last ones I just screwed. Damage control! From the damage they created. When Joe and the media say he ended America's longest war by freeing the Taliban and giving them weapons? First, that sounds stupid and makes no sense. As dumb as letting all murders out of jail and giving them guns, let's see what happens. Does the crime wave of 2022 ring a bell?

Another failed Foreign Policy by Anthony Blinken and President Joe Biden. Russia and the Cold War is America's longest war, and it still goes on today. The truth is that Joe and the Democrats created this and other problems. They build them, feed them, keep them going, and create more hate. They are playing cowboys and Indians like a TV show from the '60s. Joe Biden and Putin play bad cop, good cop. While they frustrate the people who put them in power. Autocracy, one power rule, China, Russia, North Korea, and now the Democrat-led America. When he said he stopped the longest war in United States History, the cold war with Russia has been going on since the end of WW2, and it continues today. I blame you, and you blame me, and we get rich as the people grow angry against someone else. With the fake proxy war in Ukraine, Russia and the US are fighting over Ukraine now! The playbook of Democrats is written in history; you have to wake up and read it.

Right after Joe Biden was elected to the Senate in 1972, there was a conflict in the Middle East. After Joe Biden was elected vice president, there was a conflict in the Middle East. Right after Joe Biden was elected president, there was a conflict in the Middle East. Who would have guessed? Let us go back, so Richard Nixon, a Republican Senator from California, started the EPA and stopped the war in Vietnam. Yes, Republicans came from California and liked the environment at one point!

Nixon won by a landslide against the Democrat nominee that year. Nixon, a California Republican, beat a Southern Democrat that year. After such a comprehensive victory, the Democrats started damage control and eventually crushed Nixon with the Watergate Scandal, and he resigned before being impeached. They did the same playbook to Reagan. After multiple failed impeachment attempts, they even tried an assassination![53] So, the two impeachments for Trump were just the Democrat damage control playbook at use after a horrible election cycle. They have done it before! Did I just read you the Trump Presidency or the Regan Years? Ronald Regan was almost crucified for giving the Taliban guns in the '80s to defend themselves and fight Russia at the end of the cold war. Every time the Democrats lose an election, they lose bad, to Nixon, Regan, and Trump. They start damage controls and do whatever they can to stop progress and hurt America. All so they can blame the sitting president.

So, after Nixon won the election, damage control took center stage for the Democrats. They did whatever it took to make Americans, especially the younger generation, hate the Republican party, the party of their parents.[54] They told us that Nixon hated hippies, but he was from California, home of the hippies. They did the same to Trump and Regan. Regan was against drugs, and Trump did criminal reform for real with Kim Kardashian and Kanye West, but they were both racist White guys, remember!

Nixon did do some good things that Democrats have adopted or kidnapped as their philosophy, but we see otherwise after years of actual science. Nixon started the EPA, and he ended the hated Vietnam War[55] that had no direction anymore; he was president during the first US moon landing. Still, Nixon has never been seen for anything else but a crook and a fool giving the peace sign.

He was the starter of the EPA to protect the environment against big companies and illegal dumping. To stop guys like Joe Biden and corrupt Democrat Governors that ruin states and families with Forever Chemicals. Illegal dumping was a major problem back then. If he started the EPA today and helped curb Climate change, people everywhere would have baby Nixon's as their children's names. Recycling would be called "Nixon," put the paper in the "Nixon Bin." He would have been a superman to Forever Chemicals so people would not get sick in Delaware. Nixon was an actual president of the people; he was the total opposite of Biden. Nixon started the war on cancer, and Joe Biden added thirty new types of cancer to Delaware. Nixon created the EPA, and Joe Biden let companies ruin Delaware and put chemicals in the ground and water forever. Nixon was anti-Communist, and Biden was friends with China and Russia. Nixon is seen as a clown. But before you read this paragraph, I bet most of you did not know anything about the EPA part.

Nixon also started the anti-missile system to protect us from terror attacks, and Joe Biden gave billions to Terrorists that attacked America. Nixon and Regan came from California as Senators and crushed the elections. Trump came from every part of America and crushed the election.

That scared the Democrats. A Republican candidate can come from California and sweep an election. Educate yourself. No one likes to be taken as a fool. Nixon also faced dishonest and damaging political low blows during many conflicts, leading to his resignation. Nixon and Trump will be remembered for their impeachments, not their work ethic. They were not being politicians but being taken by politicians. They never feared the work ethics that make America so great. It does not matter your color or race; if you put in a good day of hard work done right. The keyword is done right. Then you will be respected and rewarded. If the job is done right, there is no need to Build Back Better. Build Back Better from what failed policies of a generational politician.

Joe Biden and the Democrats did the same thing to Trump and America as they did in the late '70s. The Democrats and Damage Control Czar number #1 Jimmy Carter. Jimmy Carter was elected to run the Chair of the Democratic Governor's Campaign Committee in 1972. This group ensured all Democrats agreed on TV and kept party politics indoors. So, after Nixon was in office and was doing a decent job pointing America in the right direction, the Yom Kippur war of October 1973 took place. (56) The Senate, after the 1972 election, was primarily bi-partisan. The country hoped that the two sides finely would agree and be very bipartisan for the country's sake! This never happened after Nixon's election.

Unfortunately, it turned into Nancy Pelosi school girl politics once more. The Democrats damage-controlled politics in the 1972 primaries painting Nixon as an old White man who hated everyone, who was not like him.[57] Sound familiar 2020? They painted him literally as a tyrant. That Nixon was anti-hippie, pro-China, pro-Soviet, and against anti-war demonstrators. First, he stopped the war! They lied and lied and pushed a racist narrative during the 1972 primaries. Biden and young Democrats still use that same anti-age slandering against their opponents. Carter did the same thing against Nixon. Joe Biden did it first against Coggs from Delaware in 1972.[58] Then again in 2020 against Trump. They pushed the narrative that an anti-age ultra-right wing conservative square that runs for office cannot relate with younger Americans, Black voters, and not with the hippies. This anti-age slander was against WW2 vets, and in 1972 the voting age was changed from 21 to 18 years of age. So, the anti-age damage control worked. That year the Democrats widened their lead in the Senate and the House. That made the Yom Kippur War vote more instrumental in Nixon being untrusted, unliked, and cheated out of office.

The irony is that a 77-year-old man today used dirty politics to beat an older man while younger. So, once they controlled the Senate, they controlled Nixon's power and held up much-needed military support to Israel. In October of 1973, the Arab-Israel conflict #IV took place. Israel was supported militarily by the USA against Egypt, Syria, Saudi Arabia, Algeria, Jordan, Iraq, Libya, Kuwait, Tunisia, Morocco, Cuba, Sudan. That group was militarily supported by the Soviet Union, East Germany, North Korea, and Pakistan.[59] I am not making this up. It is 2020 all over again. Let us see what happens.

The war or conflict between Israel and the Arab states over recognized statehood and land occupation has been going on before Christ. Making it worse are bad politicians. The lack of respect for life almost led to a nuclear war between Russia and the US over supplying arms to each side. The Democrats in the house and Senate held up the confirmation for Nixon to send aid to Israel, and that help would have negotiated a ceasefire. The Democrats used political football or filibustering, and this act made support for Nixon go down in the polls and hurt America's dominance in the worldwide arena. Yes, the filibuster was used to hurt Nixon Republicans and cause more death in the Middle East.[60]

Please do not lecture me on the filibuster, Joe! We looked weak and almost had another war on our hands due to bad politics. The Democrats' action in Congress held up military, medical and humanitarian aid to Israel; and made more advancements possible by Soviet Union aid to Syria and Egypt. The Cold War started, and this was one of the most dangerous times in America; the Soviet Union had puppet characters to use as weapon launchers. They would give the nukes to Cuba during the Bay of Pigs and the Cuban Missile Crisis. They would have given the Syrian Army weapons and given them the power to start WW3 as they sit back and watch twenty-seven million other people die this time.

When the Yom Kippur War took place, it was during the holiest of days in the Jewish community. A time for peace and prayer. The Arab coalition ran by the Syrian and Egyptian Army were fed arms by more prominent countries like the Soviet Union and North Korea. America helped with aid to Israel, but the mega power in the Israel corner made other countries cautious for an all-out war with the US. Plain and simple, American involvement would deter countries from attacking the Jewish nation of Israel. So, the Congress which leaned Democratic found an opportunity to use this against the landslide winner Nixon. Party politics to play with another countries fate. To use American exceptionalism and might against its own country. Barrack Obama did that, Joe Biden did that, and Jimmy Carter and the

Democrats of 1973 had no problem either. Divide our country politically to win an election.

Make anti-humanitarian efforts and let people die to push a narrative of division. The Democrats did this in 1973. It sounds like 2009, 2014, and 2021 all over again. The first year in office is when Joe Biden creates a conflict in the Middle East. The Obama and Biden playbook creates unrest and political tension by undermining American exceptionalism. Damage control so we can have leverage in the next election. They held up aid by filibustering and dragging their feet in 1973. What did this do?

It made our trusted allies Israel question our loyalty, and it made their superior Air Force demolish the enemy. When a dog is against a wall, he will attack. They knew this made Nixon, American Loyalty, and American power look weak. How could we help you when America is in turmoil? We are divided, and we are still fighting over the Vietnam War? That Nixon stopped and ended. A house divided cannot stand, or in his case, be a trusted ally! That act of holding up aid to our partners caused so many more lives and put the Arab states back 50 years. While assistance was being held up, the Israel Air Force had no choice; they pounded both sides. The politicians in America also were playing both sides.

After the third Arab-Israel War, Egypt realized that they could not keep being defeated and turned the page at the same time into the 20th century. Before the Yom Kippur War in 1973, the Egyptian president traveled to America to talk with the United States on peace talks in the Middle East. Egypt cut ties with the Soviet Union and was leaning towards peace, or so we thought. In October 1973, during a holy time for the Israeli people, they were attacked from both sides by Syrian and Egyptian armies, surprising and stunning America. Nixon met with the Egyptian president and the Saudi prince in June of 1972.

After talks were completed, Egypt cut ties with the Soviet Union and resumed peace talks with Israel, but something changed. In July of 1972, Egypt went to Moscow, and the conversations were negative, and the outcome was worse. Syria was able to get more Arab states to join the attack, which led Egypt to either be in or out. Congress was dragging its feet before the November elections in two months, putting Nixon at a standstill until the Democrats could control more seats, meaning more power and influence. The attacks against Israel started in October of 1973. Nixon's response and aid were held up through politics, making it seem sympathetic to Egypt.

Israel never stopped bombing Syria-who was led by the Soviet Union. Egypt got kicked out of the Soviet Union, Syria accepted them, and was able to talk Egypt into an Arab-Israel war number four. Nixon looked weak and ineffective because of the political game by the Democrats, who called this a victory for American Democracy. More worried about a strong stance against the Soviets, while thousands more Arab and Israel people died.

The Soviet Union nor the US lost anything. Israel gained more land and essential spots like the Gaza Strip, which is still fought over today. The Suez Canal reopened for safe international travel again. Egypt eventually decided to sign a treaty deal with Israel in 1974; they had little choice after the Israeli Air Force was so dominant with airstrikes.

The US would help talks between Israel and Egypt, creating peace in the Middle East. Syria and the other Arab states kicked Egypt out of the Arab alliance, making the Soviet Union even more potent. With influences in the Middle East that still exist today. When the US embassy closed in Afghanistan in 2021, China and Russia kept theirs open. Politics made tensions grow; America and Russia still play puppet politics with smaller nations today. Ukraine 2022 is a pure example! Nixon was trying to end the war in Vietnam and conflicts in the Middle East because he was a soldier during WW2. Nixon was a veteran of political service, but politics are not fought fair like on a battlefield.

The estimated deaths of the Arab-Israel Fourth War were troubling. Egypt's unexpected ceasefire meant that Syria now took the brunt of the Israeli military. Creating more casualties of war, more anger in the Middle East, and it never stopped the fight, just made a new one. The battle and betrayal started numerous conflicts and terrorist attacks like 9/11! The Yom Kippur War began in 1973, but it never ended; extremist Arab Islamic states have only grown more hate. How does this make America look? They hated us so much they flew planes into buildings. The politicians in Congress caused more lives to perish in 1973 and 2001. The hate war against the Western world started with the hate against freedom and peace.

The war that Joe Biden said he ended in 2021 is the same war he helped vote for and start in 1973. A career politician is his own worst enemy. The Democrats' deals in Congress took more lives by holding up aid. The politicians' games to have a pissing contest only caused more people to die and eventually terrorist attacks on the Western world ever since. They look as if we stepped into their religious world and got involved, and we did. It had to start somewhere, and this is the piece of the puzzle that stuns me.

After allowing generations to fight in the Middle East from 1960 to today, we allowed them to enter our great nation. As we held up aid one decade ago as thousands got slaughtered. Decades later, we open the door to crowds of mourners. We will never learn that when we cause harm, anger, and rage through war, only harm anger and rage exist towards us. Games in politics played by career politicians only take lives. The goal of a government is to worry about their people, safety, and future. How does playing games with military aid and taking sides with Egypt behind our allies' back help that?

We pushed Israel against the wall as they faced the Arab alliance attacking them on a holy day with significant military support from Russia; they had no choice but to fight back. America, their only ally aid at the time, was being held up by party politics; they had no choice but to attack and unleash hell on their enemies. This anger and battle are now a generational war. The games played by politicians in the '70s are still being cleaned up today. Attacks on freedom and attacks by suicide bombers flying into buildings still occur. All those attackers came from countries against the US and Israel in the Yom Kippur war of 1973. Way to go, Joe!

He still causes pain for that region; it is his go-to spot for pain and division. Kill many people from the Middle East, and the world pays attention. He knew what would come from leaving Afghanistan; he helped vote for the war to continue in the '70s. Before evacuating, he never offered peace talks; they would not listen to him. The Middle East terrorist groups know JOkE Biden! They were not going to trust him again! This action created so many problems for the Middle East that they still fight today's Yom Kippur war.

Only now do they have a clear view of their enemy thanks to Joe and his Democrat friends trying to harm Nixon; it ended up hurting us all. From that ceasefire to the war on the Western lifestyle, it has begun again. The Democrats in Congress to make Nixon weak made us all soft and the world less safe. Party Politics, Carter, Kennedy, Biden, and Obama are all to blame. The party politics that we play here affect worldwide events. The anger came from the politics the US played with real lives in the Middle East.

What do you not remember? Of course not. But guess who does, every generation that lives in that war-torn area. Their families' grandkids all remember the US involvement in the Yom Kippur war. The Soviet Union does not exist anymore; East Germany does not exist anymore. Guess who does; the US is their number one enemy and target.

This chapter on America's wars and foreign policy goes way back in history. History is what keeps us from making the same mistakes repeatedly. Biden loves science, but he failed history in his Ivy League education. At an expensive Catholic Prep school for boys, all those years never taught you humanity, dignity, and the importance of human life. The Israeli and Arab relationship is still an ongoing fight today in 2022. The children of that area still suffer from politicians' choices. Unfortunately, the same warriors and countries in the Arab-

Israel Fourth War are still the same today. Later generations are just fighting the same fight from year to year. What policy is that? What kind of career politician would go back into another war with the Middle East?

The Democrats held back aid to the Israel army, and Joe helped them vote on party lines. Now today, Joe gave mega military assistance to the Taliban in 2021. Where is the Democratic Congress on this vote? Where is the outrage against an American president giving aid to our allies, let alone our biggest terroristic threat in 20 years? The world's biggest terrorist got assistance right away from Joe Biden when he entered office. In 1973 he voted against aid to Israel while they fought the same countries, enough said. JOkE Biden used you again, America. Never Forget because the Middle East will never forget the actions of 1973. We will never forget 1973 either; we are reminded every September 11th.

The problem with the Democrats is telling the truth; they have learned to lie about America as the rest of the world does. The problem with the drug cartels is that they are too powerful because; why? Because Americans consume too many drugs, and we are all addicts? The problem with telling the truth is that they have nothing to run on if they do not play the hate card first. The truth about drug cartels, human smugglers, the actual crime rate in Philadelphia, racist voting laws, and anything else they want hidden will always be covered up. Because the policies and left thinking only destroy and never build back, they definitely cannot Build Back Better. So, when people leave South America because of drugs and cartels, the blame goes to whom? Who do you think runs the cartels? So, the Mexican cartels are now retired old Italian mafia? No, they are South Americans. Their people make, sell, and give drugs to children.

The same South Americans coming over the Southern border are also killing their own people. The Taliban and ISIS are a group of Catholic redheads from Ireland? No, it is Muslims and people from that region. The people fleeing the Middle East are running away from people in the Middle East. They do not like what their people have created. They can blame the Western world and our open views, but they all throw their kids over a fence to get here. It is the same in the US! Who commits the most crime on Brown and Black people in America? I bet you it is not cops! They blame the police officer's routine got old fast, and it does not work anymore.

The cartels are native South Americans. The Middle East terrorist is typically a Muslim. The criminals are the people you see in your town due to open borders during a world pandemic. Tell the truth; now we have people from ninety countries entering ours for a better life. A better life than what their people and their government could give them. We open our doors, our wallets, and our country. Tell the truth that Mexican cartels are killing Mexicans, that the Chinese government holds Muslims in camps to change their thinking. We allow people to come here and be free, and what do the Democrats do? Divide them as soon as they enter. They ran away from their home because it was a horrible place, only to join America's fighting divisive government. We face another Civil War created again by the Democrats where people will hate, separate, and harm each other.

The hate in America was built on lies, disinformation, and media propaganda. The war has begun, and the only good thing is that seventy-five million people voted for Trump. The fake voters, fake news stories, fake hate crimes, fake evacuation stories, fake Covid response, the fake Russian hack, inflation, high gas prices, the fake war on drug crimes, and the defund the police movement are all who? The Democrats. The same people letting the cartels make money and ruin Mexican lives are the Democrats. The murder rate is up because Joe Biden is in the office! The same people that are letting the Taliban regain power and ground are the Democrats. The same people defunding the police allowing crime to crush cities, are the Democrats. The people who want to shrink the military and kick out all unvaccinated soldiers are the Democrats. The people who locked down cities and towns, causing more harm than good, are the Democrats. The people allowing the cartels to bring in drugs, killing millions of Americans, are the Democrats. Look in your local town and see what is being ruined around your town.

The hate shown by the Communist Socialist Democrat party of America should be abolished once and for all. The party should be broken down, so each group must run under a separate party name. The liberal and Socialist left cannot be under the same political umbrella: nice try, Obama, grouping all colors and races to compete against the Republican vote. The first Black president started with this division, and his idiot lapdog keeps it going. When asked about segregating Delaware's public schools, Joe Biden said he did not want his sons in a "racial jungle"[61]. His sons went to a private school on private transportation, not racial jungle buses.

This man is now the party of the Black voter, the Brown voter, and any other minority they can find. The Circus is in town, and JOkE Biden and Barrack Obama are looking for the first clowns to jump out of a burning building into a bucket of water. Any takers?

Chapter 5

Family & Faith

Joe Biden was baptized Catholic in Scranton, Pennsylvania. He went through tough financial times through his childhood and struggled. Stop the bullshit. Enough with the misleading sympathy stories on life. Joe Biden and all his sons went to the most prestigious and private Catholic school in the State of Delaware at the time. The tuition now is $28,000 a year just for high school, not including transportation, books, and other supplies. The school has been that way since its founding in 1932 by John Raskob, a Democrat campaign manager who held the Democratic National Committee meetings in his house. When Joe Biden went there, for a struggling out-of-work-family, tuition was not affordable. He and his two brothers all attended that school. His two sons graduated from there as well. Did you know while he was Senator, and your schools were changing for the worse in Delaware, that your taxes were paying forty-three thousand dollars a year to put the Biden boys through Catholic Prep school?

So, in 1984 a US Senator's average salary was 72,600 dollars. That means he paid over two-thirds of his salary before taxes, food, housing, and savings to his two son's educations. No wonder he took the free train every day. No wonder he is horrible at financials, and inflation is awful. No wonder he passes bills that our grandchildren will pay for. Who is in control of what the Senate makes? In 1986 an average salary of a US Senator was $75,100.00 that year. Five years later, the average salary was $125,100.00 a year. [62] In just five years, they received a $50,000 a year raise. Today a US Senator's average salary is $174,000.00 a year. In the five years, it went up by $50,00.00, but in just the last 31 years, it only went up by $50,000.00. That is quite a raise. Before we even talk about faith and family, he already lied.

Joe has learned one thing from being Catholic the art of guilt and becoming a martyr. Jesus died for our sins! God the Father gave his only son. Things you learn as a faithful Catholic during childhood and into adulthood. You can take it as a sacrifice for the greater good of humankind or as a tool to victimize a particular group. The art of using something as a crutch that you bear works the best as guilting others for being non-bearing of such a task or tragedy. Trust me, I know I have been an alter server half my life. So, this is the pot calling the kettle Black, and I am calling you out Joe Biden on your faith. Because when it is all said and done, and we pass on from this earth, we must face the actual test—acceptance into Heaven or damnation into Hell. As told in our religion, the proper judgment of life after death is not by our words but by our actions on earth. That is the key to Heaven, to be a good Catholic while on earth. Lying is not an effective way to start. Just saying, the ten commandments and all might have mentioned lying.

If Joe Biden can get others to feed into his lies and exaggerations, then the act or the sin of lying is justified. Because you believed in someone, not knowing they were a liar does not make you an accomplice to his lies, you were tricked. Does Moses ring a bell yet, Joe? What other commandments did you break? What other tricks did you try to pass onto America?

His hate and anger stemming from the loss of his son have changed his presidency and the way he thinks. He had lost control of his soul when he started cheating on America. Watching this story of Joe Biden's political career is like watching a movie where Jesus is the director and Karma is the editor. From the beginning to the end, it is like every negative anti-Catholic after-school special from the '80s. When a just and morally wrong decision comes back to bite him in the ass, he just does it again. He has polluted rivers, lied to grieving families, supported the Cartels, gave weapons to the Taliban, and even stole someone else's words to run for president. [63]

When will he learn and feel the taps on the shoulder from God? God has been taping him on the shoulder for years, but Joe is so sold to the devil that he cannot even think about stopping and smelling something else than a women's neck. God works in mysterious ways. Karma is real, and Joe Biden and his career are pure examples. If you cannot see it, then maybe you can read it. Joe Biden ran for president before 2020 and 2012. He ran in 1987 but dropped out three months into the campaign due to lying and plagiarism of a speech he took from another politician's years before him.

So, when you are in college and struggle late at night to finish before the deadline, do as Your President did. Instead of putting in the work, the guy you voted for lied and stole speeches to trick voters. [64] He stole someone else's words and tried to lie and play the people as a fool. It did not work. He was caught, and what did he do? He resigned and ran back to Delaware and hid. We have all seen this movie before. Lie, run, and hide. In the Delaware escape room, Joe, Jill, and the family dog hide from the reality of the life they created.

The irony is that Joe Biden is a clown when he talks off prompter and the English language baffles him off the cuff. He has a problem with words, and he cannot get a statement out, a proper name, or even answer a simple question. The problem is not his early childhood stutter, another guilt trip to voters. It cannot be his age and dementia knocking, and some think no one is home upstairs. He does not care enough to do the work and be involved. It is sad, but it is a trait of many people; they just do not care. He has to squint, lower his voice, and talk low as he tries to get the point across. We see it as a shame and an older man, but he thinks he tells me something I do not already know. So, what is the irony? The irony is that God has punished him for eternity with a blabbermouth. God has made his lies spew out of his mouth. He is the new Jim Carrey in the Liar-liar movie. God has damned him to blabber and disclose information. He has not made a complete statement since 1987!

When he stood in front of America and resigned from running for president in 1987 because the truth came out, he lied to get people to vote for him. After nothing is done and he gets his old job back. What does that show young American's and fellow politicians? That it was OK to LIE! In the Catholic religion, we believe in God; you know, the one God the Taliban hates, just to clarify. Joe Biden gave the anti-Catholics weapons to kill us all. He keeps on fighting God's will and keeps on losing because God cannot be lied to.

He has had a fight on his soul, and he knows he lost the acceptance to Heaven, so take everyone with him to Hell! His mentality is that we are all sinners just like him; admit it, you are all bad, not just his family. In his brain, heart, and soul, he sees only the worst traits in American's and America. His life has been a slap in God's face as he used people's heartstrings to get re-elected year after year. Being sworn into the Senate in a hospital room where his son can be pictured in a cast after the accident is just the beginning. God has nominated him, not you, not me, and not the helpless! God has done this punishment to him! If you think I am being too tough on a political figure, just ask a parent who lost their child to cancer while living in Delaware during his terms in office if they care?

It should be easy to find a phone number to call and complain about a lousy politician. You should not have to wait until others take action or until people start dying to be a good politician. The statistics are one thing that does not lie. Every year in Delaware, 18% of all deaths are of a child with some type of cancer. Black people and Whites are the highest two races that are affected. That is concerning because Black people only make up 23% of the population but die at the highest rate of any race in Delaware. He is killing his voters and lying right to them. That brings us to the first time Joe lied and tested God's will.

Now, remember I am calling it as I see it, Joe Biden, the straight shooter from Scranton. Joe, the American dream will save our country's soul and us from destruction and the tan man. Joe Biden was sold in 2020 as a savior to the world again. He tested God's will. Jesus is our savior, not Joe Biden; he is a basement rat. He was the man going to stop the hate, crime, rape of our country and save its people's future. He was going to bring our country back into God's good graces. You absolute fools.

Joe Biden has more skeletons in his closet than the Grim Reaper. He has lied and has paid the price from the big man. Joe Biden's first wife was a well-educated, intelligent daughter of two hard-working parents. She and Joe went to private schools and met on Spring break in the Bahamas. Remember is poor upbringing as a child. Tough childhood growing up, they were vacationing during spring break in the Bahamas. A real son of hard-working parents like Joe lies about would be at work during spring break and not traveling to a foreign country.[65] Another example of Joe that God has witnessed! They went to Syracuse together and eventually moved back to Delaware. When Joe was running for the Senate, he would travel long hours back and forth to DC, not by private car paid for by the US government as every other politician did.[66] He would take Amtrak, a train system that makes stops every so often and never on time. A train is almost always running late.[67] This was how Joe Biden said he was a member of society and one of us. Or was it a way to be free, not in control of time or your travel? A car ride took only 20 minutes more than a train ride. A train is never on time; it is not only a saying but true.[68] Amtrak is not the fastest way home! The front door of the Wilmington train station is where Joe Biden lived in 1972? No, he still would have to drive home from the train station.

The train ride is how a husband could come home late and have something to blame it on! He could say he missed the train or the smell of perfume on his clothes came from being next to someone on the train. He could grab a drink on the way home on the train. Why would a man who worked long hours and was in a power position take a long train ride to and from work if he did not have to? This was his way of getting out of being there for his wife, who was home alone struggling with three children during the holidays, and the most significant campaign run of all time.

As the world fell in love with a young Democrat, his wife was home alone, waiting for her husband. Do you not think a mother of three has a suspicion of cheating or an unloving spouse? Jill Biden's first husband sensed she was cheating. He talks about his ex-wife Jill and her turning him down to do what?[69] Jill Biden's first husband bought her tickets to see Bruce Springsteen in concert, and she declined because she had to work for her boss, Joe Biden, during his campaign run. When he won his first Senate seat, Jill was at the hotel with him, "working on his campaign."

Joe has been working late, and the train ride was his excuse for being so distant. One claim says they met after Joe Biden bugged his brother for a blind date. Jill Biden talks about meeting his wife, and she says, "it was an irony" no, Jill, it was a wife's intuition.[70]. She admits to going to the hotel that night to celebrate, celebrate what? The stories do not match up, but nothing Joe says ever does.

If he drove home every night like a good husband, he could have gotten a Christmas tree on the way home, and he could have been home for the holidays with his family like a good father does. Does every politician work during Christmas break in DC? I do not think so. It is just not adding up. His wife was driving with three children to get a Christmas tree when she perished in that fatal accident. Then to make things worse, he blamed the truck driver for being drunk and reckless.[71] Later, this was found to be false, and it might have been the other way around from what police reports say.[72] Instead of just leaving dead dogs lying, he added to the pain and pulled more heartstrings.

Jill Biden's first husband suspected cheating, and reports say the timeline fits with her volunteering during his campaign. Joe Biden made a conspiracy about his wife's death; he made people question the event after lying about drunk driving. He brought it from a tragedy to a scheme. Was he dating other women when his wife and daughter died? Was Jill Biden lying to her husband and having an affair? What does God think about cheating and infidelity? Just another reason why when he says he is saving our country's soul, you should be saying, please worry about your soul. Joe Biden pushed the narrative that Trump is the lying White man I am just a grieving widow. The blame game that God hates. What does this mean if it is true? It says a lot about his family's actions and events.

Events like when his son Beau died, and Hunter got his dead brother's wife addicted to heroin and cheated on his wife as well. What did Joe have to say about this? "We are all lucky that Hunter and Hallie found each other as they were putting their lives together again after such sadness. They have mine and Jill's complete support, and we are happy for them."[73]. How does that look to the grandkids? Mommy got high with uncle Hunter and cheated on Aunt Kathleen? Biden's grandkids think Jill the Grand-mom and Joe the Grandpop are cool with this? My family is ruined because of Uncle Hunter and his drugs. This is what a cheating couple says when they cheat, "we are glad." Save our country's soul from the disgusting Trumps.

The Trumps are not deceiving and sleeping around with each other, and it probably was going on while Beau was stationed overseas. His brother was being lied to, and his parents were cool with it. This is why when you question Joe's soul; you can understand his lack of respect for your family and its future. His family is full of lies, cover-ups, and guilt trips. Funny though, Joe Biden believes in an eye for an eye, just like a good Catholic, just like a person who spends his days in a pissing contest with everyone. So, what does he say? If I cannot have anything nice, I will ruin it for all of us.

His family is an after-school special on the Playboy Channel. His core values cannot be taught to his grandkids because there are none. Please do not lecture me on marriage, faith, love, or family. Total lack of morals and respect for the decency of our country, which was founded on religious freedom. A "true" fake ass Catholic. God did not notice Joe's lack of marital vows; he did not see the lies and the lack of respect for marriage before the eyes of the lord. I did not do it, do not be mad at me. I am just telling all of you who acted like Trump and Trump supporters, you know, the deplorable. We are who you said we are; we are deplorable! Deplorables that sleep around in the White House, the despicable that gets high and sleep with their dead brother's wife. Deplorables? How about you are the "Deplorables" instead of Democrats. I like the sound of that.

Learn about the animals you vote for and how you will be treated when a politician does not even know how to treat his own dead son's wife, his poor Beau. Just like Judas denied Jesus three times before he was crucified. Joe Biden has failed Beau three times as well. First, by not beating his son's Hunter ass when that went down in respect for his dead son! The second act of betrayal was by removing troops from Afghanistan in August of 2021. By disgracing soldiers everywhere, dead or alive. His son did flips in his grave. Of all the people that would tarnish a dead vet's life and legacy, his brother and his dad brushed it over. How do his granddaughters look at him? How does America see him?

Do the voters know, when they screamed that Trump is a pig, a liar, and a scumbag, did they know? Joe Biden has tarnished Beau's legacy and life by letting your son Hunter be a bigger loser than you. Good one, Joe! Joe Biden said once, "that Hunter is the smartest man he knows"[74]. Then Beau most of been a stump on a log. He was the Attorney General of Delaware. Then why was he the laughingstock at the Biden Thanksgiving dinner table? Let us look at how dangerous it is to live in Biden's Delaware! Not the racial jungles or the non-English-speaking coffee guy, but just breathing, eating, and drinking the water in Delaware is unsafe. Let us look at the son of Joe Biden, a statistic in the making. Let us see the third act of betrayal, the kiss of death!

The death of his son Beau has been explained, dramatized, and revisited since the day he died. We have so much sympathy for him over the Iraq war; he died years later in his mid-forties. We cried over how he died a painful battle with cancer to the brain; his brother slept with his brother's widow. I feel bad, and Hunter gets horny. His death was sad, and cancer should never be wished on anyone.

This book is dedicated to a person who lost their life to cancer. Death, especially by cancer, is horrible, and we have seen enough deaths over a pandemic in the last two years. Added by bad decisions by governors and a lack of medical supplies has taken a toll on the population of America. The deaths of so many Americans due to Covid could have been much less, or not at all. If our Country continued with the exact pandemic solutions we had in 2019, would fewer people have died? If we followed the Tan Man instead of Joe and the science, would the death count be less today in 2022?

Just like the ifs and whys, maybe the death of his son could have been different also. The sad part was Beau Biden's death was a Joe Biden homegrown political statistic. Statistics from years in office. The makeup of statistics in Delaware on cancer deaths each year could show how bad and damaging someone's political policies have become over forty-some years. His death was a statistic from his father's careless years in office.

Forever Chemicals were not in Delaware before the 1972 election! Forever Chemicals are in Delaware after 47 years of Joe Biden in the office! In Delaware, 30% of all deaths each year are due to a type of cancer. Almost one in every three people die in Delaware from getting a form of cancer. The highest rate of those people who get cancer is who? The highest rate of cancer patients in Delaware is White males between 44-67 years old.[75]

Beau Biden lived in Delaware his whole life, Wilmington especially. He died at the age of 46 in 2015. He was diagnosed with a brain tumor in 2010 and fought the most brutal fight of his life. Brain cancer has a five-year survival rating of 34% with men. Beau fought till the end. Sadly, he was up against Forever Chemicals as a child and, in 2001, was diagnosed with a rare disease called Ankylosing Spondylitis, which affects joints and the spine. [76] It is an exceedingly rare disease; most doctors are still unsure of the leading causes. A protein in your body tells your immune system to fight bacteria, causing harm to you. These bacteria can come from pollution, chemicals, and even Forever Chemicals. After studying this disease, science shows that genetics and your environment may lead to the disease. So what environment are we talking about? The disease affects the lower back, joints, bowel movement, tiredness, and loss of appetite. That sounds like half the people I know! So, after doing research, I found out that the disease is sometimes hereditary or from your environment.

The gene is called HLA-B27, the antigen that creates an autoimmune concern in sick and healthy people and affected men primarily in their early thirties when Beau got it. An autoimmune disease is when a person's immune system attacks their cells. Not the best case to be in when you have a terminal brain tumor. The spine is tragically affected when you have Ankylosing Spondylitis, and the spine is connected to the brain. Also, when you have the HLA-B27, you have a weaker immune system to fight off diseases and create more White blood cells. A low White blood cell count increases your risk of developing a potentially life-threatening infection and losing the fight against cancer and other diseases. These cells are made in the bone marrow and travel in the blood throughout the body. They sense infections, gather at the disease sites, and destroy the pathogens. When the body has too few neutrophils, the condition is called neutropenia.

This condition makes it harder for the body to fight off pathogens and defeat cancer with treatment. He was fighting a losing fight because his immune system could not remake what the chemo was killing. The number of people in Delaware that die from cancer is staggering. The number of people in Delaware with cancer who suffer from Ankylosing Spondylitis is outrageous.[77] One in four people in Delaware have Ankylosing Spondylitis, which is twice as common in White adults than other races.

Having HLA-B27 might have an increased chance of catching Leukemia, a type of cancer. In the 1990s, Delaware ranked second with the highest cancer rate and mortality from cancer. White men are the highest death rate % of Delawareans that die from cancer. His son was a self-made statistic. Delaware has been the highest in the country of cancer rates for decades.

In 2009-2013, 52% of all cancer patients were male. Caucasians were 82% of all cancer cases. A statistic that I am in too. A White male between 44-67, just like Beau was, I lived in the tri-state area as a kid just like Beau did. Will I be the following statistic like Beau was? What is the fate of other people who live in Delaware? We are told of the pain he went through from the brain tumor. He had Glioblastoma, a highly aggressive type of cancer. He did put up a battle before his death, but this type of cancer works quickly. The pain his family went through is devastating, so bad that I cannot believe his brother is that low. While Beau Biden's children might have needed a friend, a hand, or even a ride somewhere, the Biden's were falling apart. From the top down.

The other side of Beau is a different story altogether. Pain still exists, and it might be from a statistic his family created again. Beau went to the best Catholic Prep School in the State of Delaware. He married his college sweetheart and served his country in Iraq from October 2008 to 2009, just around election time. He served from 2003 to 2009 in the Delaware National Guard and served one year of active wartime duty in Iraq, the year his dad ran for vice president.

Afterward, he served as Attorney General to Delaware. He ran in 2006 and won by a slim margin, pushing the notion that his opponent at the time was soft on sex offenders and internet child abuse.[78] He ran on the notion that he would toughen up on crime and put an end to internet predators, domestic abusers, and especially senior abuse. Real fast, why would these be significant problems in Delaware? Did he question the Senator of 46 years why these are the main campaign promises to the people of Delaware? The same people your father served for 46 years. Is anybody asking why those would be the leading running platform during a campaign?

As Attorney General Beau Biden was going to fix the challenging crime problems of Delaware, a state where his dad was working for forty-some years, making all of these problems exist and go on! It is like a son taking over a family restaurant and changing everything broken. So, he won the 2006 election, and he pledged to be firm on all sex offenders and rapists. Then only after 2008 did he forget what his campaign ran on and what he promised the people. The apple does not fall far from the tree. Again, a DuPont was in trouble. The heir of DuPont that Joe Biden helped create raped and abused his daughter.[79]

Beau Biden's office was in charge of the case, finally a chance to make a real difference and set an example that sex offenders, any sex offender, will pay. A chance to make good on a campaign promise too. C'mon man, it's a Biden! No matter how rich or poor, a crime is a crime; that is what he ran on! Attorney General Beau Biden also had his children at this time, and he had a daughter only a year older than the little girl that was raped and beaten by her father. A DuPont. His other child was two years old at the time. A year younger than the girl raped by her father! What did the righteous defender of freedom and sex crime vigilante do?

Absolutely nothing; he lowered the sentence to probation and blamed the judge. The assistant prosecutor assigned by his office blamed the lack of evidence and witness credibility.[80] The evidence was a three-year-old torn from front to back and bruised; the witness was the girl's grandmother, who bathed her and took care of her. The same witness reported it to the police and told them to save that little three-year-old girl. So, when I see crocodile tears run down that older man's face, is he thinking about Beau or that three-year-old girl who was raped by her father and got away with it because the family was a friend of the Bidens? Karma is a Bitch, and God does not like being played with, so when you tell the world that you will end rape, sex offenders, internet predators, and abusers of all kinds, then you better actually mean it. Do you think a Catholic priest sex offender is going to Heaven?

Somehow Beau won re-election in 2010 after getting a childhood rapist off free. The DuPont heir paid his fine for raping his daughter, pleaded guilty to a charge of rape in the fourth degree, and paid a fine of $4,395. Beau won re-election because the DuPont Unions voted for the independent candidate during the primaries, so there was an obvious choice when the election came. We all know the Biden name. The water in Delaware must give you short-term memory. Beau Biden might have been a hero to some, but even his brother did not respect him; why should I? I swear to God everything I am writing is there in black and white. Do not believe me? Look it up. Do not get mad. Vote out liars and scum. Or God will take care of it, your choice!

The following family member is Hunter Biden. Should I end it there? Every family member of the Biden family has some controversy. Joe Biden's first wife's accident still raises questions. Still, no police report can be found, nothing. To Jill, was she married when she meets Joe, was she the babysitter who Niele Hunter feared? Did she lie and cheat on her first husband with Joe Biden? The brother got in a car accident and never paid the court-ordered requirements. What about Hunter and his laptop? Did Beau do many favors for criminals?

Could it be on the eve of 9/11, he let terrorists free and gave away a military base full of weapons? Again, I did not do anything; I was not on the floor looking for parmesan cheese. I did not get in trouble for stealing before the 2020 election. I am not Joe Biden's Niece![81] I was not there when his wife and daughter died. I do not know why he says one thing, and the truth is something else. I do not understand why he hates America! He has so much pain and so many cover-ups! He has made his destiny, punched his card, and prepared his own life. Because if anything a Catholic believes, it is life after death, in Heaven. Your actions on earth give you acceptance into Heaven.

Why is there so much controversy following the Bidens? Why can he never answer a question or even hold a simple press conference? They are all pre-made questions and answers, all setups like the debates and Chris Wallace. No looking America in the eye and giving us your best John Wayne stare. He will not do it face-to-face or eye to eye. We got the best of Joe Biden as a political figure 50 years ago. It lasted one year, and power, greed, and anger took over. He was acting like a movie villain that we did not know existed, hidden in the shadows or hides in the basement, ready to take out the weak and vulnerable. Joe has followed the footsteps of a group of men who have seen the darkest days for the Democratic party. He followed a plan of a bunch of angry old White men who were about to lose it all in the '80s. Creating damage control and recruiting young Democrats, they grabbed Joe when he was young, and he never had a chance to take a breather or even tell the truth. Joe was a statistic of the Democratic party's agenda, another great son of the Democratic party.

He honed his skills in damage control while in the Senate, as vice president, and today's president. Never give the truth, never answer a question, or be honest about a drone strike. He has learned and mastered the art of damage control. So much so that it has entered the home. Damage control on everything that happens. There is a saying that every story has three sides, yours, theirs, and the truth. When they hide the facts and damage control the situation, what three sides do we get? When they damage control a story, the liar becomes the media, the president, or even your neighbor.

The story has three sides, the truth, the lie, and the spin. Yours, Thiers and whatever they can make you believe. I do not need a mommy daddy government; I do not need to feel bad for a politician because he has suffered personal loss. That is called LIFE. You cannot damage control life. Life is wrought with the truths of day-to-day challenges. We face a lot as a growing nation still under 225 years old.

We have our troubles and pains in our own lives. No one wants a son to die of cancer; God forbid, so why not stop Forever Chemicals? No one wants a child addicted to a drug; God Forbid, so why not crush the drug cartels in Mexico instead of gifting them young, innocent lives and free border passage? If you are so angry about drunk driving and your wife, why did you offer cases of beer to get a covid shot when entering the office?[82]

Why do the pains and problems that affect your family and life have to become my burdens? You have your concerns, and we have ours, so a great father, husband, and government leader should shelter, protect, and shield his flock like the God he follows. What is Joe Biden's wish for me to suffer the same pain he had to live within his family? We all suffered and lost on 9/11. Yet on the eve of the twentieth anniversary, he has led another generation into the terrors we faced, overcame, and conquered by beating them to the ground. Why are you so angry at your failures that your embarrassment trumps your love for humankind and fellow Americans? God the Father gave his only son to be crucified for our sins.

Why are we paying for your sins, why are you making America unsafe, why are you helping the same Cartels that made the drugs that crushed your family for years. Heroin dealing Cartels made your son Hunter sniff the floor like a dog for drugs; he said it not me.[83] Why are you giving a country back to the opioid selling Terrorists so they can send heroin to poison more families as they did yours. Why are we paying for what happened to your family and your life? It is almost like a selfish person who does not have a nice bike, so he steals yours and breaks it. If he cannot have something nice, then no one can. The hate and disdain that Joe Biden has for others is disturbing. What do I have to show for my mentality at the end of a long life, years of power, and money? Anger and hate because I am Joe Biden, I rode a train, and I got paid to spend your money.

It is a scary reality that we will all face at the end of our lives. When the end is near, we take inventory of our accomplishments, legacy, image, and inner peace. Our peace that this is the end, and we left it all out there. He has faulted on his duties as a Catholic, a father, a son, a president, and a US citizen. A US citizen that leaves his country better off for the next generation is worthy; the opposite is selfish. If we just become better US citizens and care more about what matters, then the world and especially the United States of America will be a better place. There will be no need for damage control. No need to Build Back Better. No need to spin the truth and lie. No need because God only sees one side to every story, the RIGHT-eous side.

Chapter 6

46 Years in the Senate & Joe's Friends

What has happened in 46 years of American history? Let us look back at what 46 years of grey hairs look like. First, just for giggles, Joe Biden's last sponsored bill before leaving Congress was the Enhanced Partnership with Pakistan Act of 2008.[84] The same country that hid Osama Bin Laden from us. About two hundred miles from the Kabul air base that the Taliban was just gifted. Several 9/11 attackers were trained in Pakistan and came from Afghanistan. This bill was co-signed by Senator Hillary Clinton, Senator Barrack Obama, Senator John Kerry, Senator Dick Durbin, Senator Chuck Hagel, and Senator Tom Carper, to name a few. Classic Democrats create a problem (Russia and Ukraine Border, Afghanistan withdraw), then be the champions to control it and save the world, like make-believe superheroes.

The same co-sponsors and sponsors of this bill are pictured in the Osama Bin Laden war room photo.[85] Hillary Clinton has her hand over her mouth in disbelief; Joe Biden is holding a Rosary and praying. They had no idea when signing a bill in 2008 that the country was hiding and holding America's biggest wanted terrorist? Either they all knew, and we are the fools, or this was another miscalculated Democrat "fake you out" power move. Oh yes, Anthony Blinken was there too. There needs to be police for career politicians. The other co-sponsor Senator

Lugar visited Russia in 2005 with then-Senator Barrack Obama to depart for a meeting with the President and the Speaker of the House of the Ukrainian government. The trip was to deactivate weapons from the former Soviet Union days. Where are the transcripts from that call and meeting? That was his last act in the Senate, and he has not stopped causing problems since. For who? Us Americans.

In his first act in the Senate, he signed a bill with other Democrats and then-President Carter to go against Peace in the Middle East; this led to the Yom Kippur War. The rise of Syria as an enemy to America, when did this happen in the 1970s. This conflict or war sent the same evacuation through humanitarian action that brought Syrians caught in the fighting to America. This led to more mass evacuations to America of Syrian war refugees. They all landed in New Jersey and Delaware and worked at DuPont in the '70s and '80s. I have relatives of Syrian descent who lived along the Delaware River and worked at DuPont. He is doing it again, we have created a reason to evacuate thousands of people, just like when he was vice president, and all the refugees went to the Minnesota area. This was not by chance!

The people of Minnesota elected their first Muslim-born female as a Congressperson. Joe is doing it again with South Americans for AOC. They are sending Afghans to Minnesota and Wisconsin areas. Our politicians are settling foreign people in crucial red states to change the vote.

In 46 years in the Senate, he has voted, sponsored, and co-sponsored thousands of bills that changed the world. When you go to the bathroom, if you do not wipe when you are done, you might smell like poo! So, after 46 years in the Senate and not once wiping after doing number two, you stink like shit! When Trump ran for office against lifelong politicians Hillary Clinton and Joe Biden, they accused Trump of problems they created. Lifelong politicians blamed the person who supported them in every election. They used Americans' self-hate and lack of education against them. They never showed you why they were the best choice for you and America's future; they just showed you their opponents' faults, never being the best qualified, just the best at spinning the truth. America is best when politicians come as a toy in a happy meal. A piece of crap toy made in China.

It is like a small child with a million dollars and his future in his hands, and he goes to the casino and bets it all on red. When you vote, you vote to let a person control trillions of tax dollars that only people who live AND work in America pay. Only taxpayers should vote. People might work but do they pay taxes? Should they be able to vote for a person that will be in control of your taxes or our combined money? I pay taxes for roads, schools, hospitals, police, firehouses, and ambulances. Why should non-tax-paying citizens use that for which I pay? If you buy a car, does the whole neighborhood use it? When you order a pizza, does the delivery driver get two slices?

Politics are not just red, blue, and independent. They are like giving someone keys to the country. If they never had a license, the ride would be bumpy and fraught with danger. It is all right not to get in the car with a drunk politician that lies, steals, and cheats. Even if he is your friend and brags how he got away with Chappaquiddick, tell him NO! Even if your dad and his dad before him are all best buds, and it is a legacy to get in the car with someone who has no control, just say NO! You have the right to make a politician do what you want. When one screams slander, then they are covering up their weakness.

Imagine a College Football Draft, each player, instead of a highlight reel, had a videotape of all the bad plays from other young players entering the draft. What if the coaches only pointed out the losing things about a player and why they are horrible? What if they asked for stats, and he just gave them stats of all the dropped passes of other players? I might not be the best or even suitable, but that mentality is more detrimental than my lack of talent. I might not be a number one pick, but he is number two. Imagine how sports would look! This is not a high school prom voting committee. Every election, your taxes, health, future, and country are under attack.

In 46 years in office, no one noticed the problems that kept harming Delaware, after 46 years. He was elected in 1972, 78, 84, 90, 96, 02, and 08. No one took the keys out of his hands and looked at what had happened. Has Joe ever really won an election on his merits? Has he ever earned the job? Was he the best choice for Delaware or even America? In 46 years as a Senator, why Build Back Better now? What, were you not building better back then?

The slogan Build Back Better sounds like a young first-time Senator from Chicago who must change the landscape of Democrats. After decades of abuse and damage control, I will save us all. After 47 years in the public service, I will save us from a businessperson! Does that sound correct? Joe has been in office for more than 46 years; we should have been building back all that time. What has he been doing for 46 years? What has he voted on in those decades? What has he covered up over those 46 years in power? Power over your health, money, and taxes, and most of all, control of your family's future. What has he been doing before becoming vice president and president?

Was there ever a time in Joe's career in Delaware that he was ever loved like Trump was? Did the people of Delaware ever love their leader, their Senator, and what he did for them? Was Joe Biden a good Senator for Delaware? One of the first things Joe Biden voted on in the Senate was the vote on redistricting voting areas. This was a way the loser can always cry foul; we now know the place that lost: not fair: redistrict it. It has been argued that redistricting is a core function of legislating. Then why did it not start until one hundred years after forming our country?

Since then, Democrat presidents have held office longer than Republican presidents. The same goes for the House and Senate, and redistricting still comes up. If redistricting was a way to keep them in office, it should be stopped. This is one of the first bills that Joe Biden voted on; this was a start of a lengthy career in political politics. When Joe Biden votes on anything, it is either for the good of his party, the particular interest group he represents, or himself; never what is best for all the people he serves. A particular interest for special friends gets guaranteed votes. Joe Biden is the most-liked and un-liked president in America today.

This chapter became the most important chapter of this book. As I kept looking back in time, the same names would pop up. This one helped Joe, served with him, supported him, scratched his back, and so on. Then it started to make sense and became evident. Joe has been groomed just like he has been grooming others over the years. When you look at what the world has come to, you wonder, is it more extensive than what I am reading? Is there somehow more to the picture than Joe's hate for America. Is this Global, and are others involved? Are we sheep for the slaughter that is being played? Are we going to die like a statistic like Beau from the causes of the powers that be? Are we going right back to a monarchy and a one-party rule? So, as I typed away and dug deep, I Noticed one name that kept coming up. LBJ!

Lyndon B. Johnson led the chain of command through the years. From Johnson to Kennedy but not John's frustrated brother, Teddy. Then to Carter, Mondale, Clinton, DuPont the Governor, and Joe Biden. The Democrats need to be the rainbow coalition of voters somehow. It started by tearing down a little piece of America one by one. They were the backbone but never got recognition. Joe's heroes have been your worst nightmares.

These men decided long before they would never keep control of a country unless they monopolized the people and the power. This crew has more skeletons in their closets from assassinations, car wrecks, and mysteriously dead bodies than the Grimm Reaper. They have changed the United States from prosperity and freedom for all to "you ungrateful Son of a Bitches". When they claim to have given everything, it is not enough because the effort from these politicians is not from the heart but the angle of deception and authority allowed. When they do not give a shit in another term, they never win the hearts of the voters. So, they must make it, so the system does not fail them.

It does not forget those that "serve" them either. A politician is a civil servant. Serve the people and when done, move on.

This chapter was exhausting to write; it took so much out of me because of civil servants' harmful, greedy, selfish, and thoughtless actions. So many Americans and people worldwide have suffered. Not just wars or death or even a pandemic. Financial debt, generational debt, unhealthy living due to pollution, the start of anti-American propaganda, wars, and conflicts over and over. The Democrats have a problem of only doing damage control after they cause the problems. They start the fire and then heroically the first ones there to put it out.

Like when I was a kid in a small town, we had a volunteer fire department. Well, one summer, there were a string of fires, and ironically this young teenage volunteer firefighter was always the first to respond. He was a hero, knocking on doors saving lives, running into the fire to fetch the family pet, basking in the glow of being the neighborhood savior. One night after a baseball game, another fire started across from the ball field where he lived. This time the fire beat him. He was the one creating all these fires in this small town. He set the house next door to his parent's home on fire. The container of gas he used caught on fire while he was starting the blaze. He lost control, and the fire he began started to travel next door. The fire was racing from the neighbor's house across the lawn to his parents' house. His parents were sleeping at the time, and he panicked and rushed in to save them. He never made it out, and nobody did that night because the gas can explosion so severely engulfed the neighbor's house by igniting between the homes next to the gas lines entering from the street. What made it worse was that both garages were on that side as well. Gas cans, propane tanks, and lawnmowers ignited, causing the blast even bigger! The hero could not put out the fire he started this time. The boy had played with fire too many times.

Let this be a lesson to everyone who votes, lives, breathes, and should be paying taxes. Know who you vote for because someday it may be your house in flames. Joe's heroes have started so many fires and burned so many homes down with families in them. Wars, fighting, division, and anger have fed Joe's bros, and they all earned the silver medal of shame. However, this time the flames have grown too large. The fire has spread to schools, classrooms, and kitchen tables; to your house and mine. The smoke does not even have time to clear between one inferno and the next!

If you have made it this far in reading this book, I know you will stop and say, "that son of a Bitch" by the end of this chapter. What a son of a Bitch? The information I am about to tell you is accurate. If you do not believe me, get up and ask someone older than fifty or someone not wearing ear pods. The following is accurate, and this is why so many Americans struggle day after day. Why does the Left want to change history? Why does our government make it so hard for us to succeed? Why do they not even give a shit about you?

If you know someone who has struggled with credit card debt, then guess what, you have Joe Biden to blame. I know you thought this was the chapter I told you about when he ran into a burning building and saved the orphan children. Well, he never saved orphans, but he did start credit card debt! Of course, I could lie and tell you that Joe Biden and Pony-Boy went in, repeatedly, and saved them all; even saved the puppies. But that would be damage control, not the truth, and as Americans, you deserve the truth.

In the 1980s, when Miami Vice was the hottest fashion statement, America was on top of the world. Ronald Regan stopped the longest war in America's history, longer than the 20-year Afghanistan war. The Cold war with Russia stemmed from WW2. The market and the banks were all pro-American, and the country as a whole woke up every morning screaming USA, USA. America was distancing itself from the rest of the world.[86] What does a politician do when his state is being pumped with Forever Chemicals? Create a credit card Empire with the culprits to hold

Americans down for the rest of their lives. Credit card debt, credit card fraud, and credit card forgiveness. All stuff that the US

Government should have nothing to do with but somehow did. Why would a Senator from Delaware and a Republican Governor from Delaware named DuPont want to start a credit card Empire? Because they knew it worked, it had worked since before slaves were freed in America![87]

In towns in the South, like Buffalo City, NC, after the Civil War. After freeing the Slaves, they had no money or way of starting a life in more expensive Northern territories. So, they started working for the slave owners but now got paid and could spend their newfound income at the county store, owned by the plantation owner, or buy meals during unpaid work breaks at the boss-owned diner.[88] In the years following the Civil war, slaves faced new and challenging problems now that freedom rang. They had money, but the wooden nickels only could be spent at certain stores owned by and profits made by their bosses.

In the early 1800s, Delaware's DuPont gun powder revolution was hazardous work. The employees of DuPont were paid in company money back in the 1800s when they were the biggest suppliers of gunpowder in the US.[89] DuPont became every employee's employer, lender, bank, and accountant. They were supplying ammo for every war from 1810-to 1910. If your son was killed in a battle between 1810 and 1910, it likely involved DuPont gunpowder.[90] They were so powerful that they bailed out General Motors. They controlled the government officials, and with payoffs and buyouts of weaker competitors, they even controlled towns. This was just the beginning of employees on the credit borrowing system, the ideal that sparked credit card prison for so many Americans. Borrow money that you do not have! You spend freely, but you never get free from payments.

Commercial after commercial, are credit cards ads with annoying overpaid actors asking what is in your wallet? Then the next commercial is to check or change your credit score. You only have a credit score from taking on debt from creditors. Every time you go into debt, you create a credit score. No debt or financial obligation;

you should not even have a credit score. If you have no credit card, you never have debt or even a credit score. Are you following me so far? The way to have a good credit score is to be consistently in debt and pay it slowly over time. You pay off debt like cars, mortgages, and loans to keep a good credit score. When I waste money on my credit card, when I buy more products, when I build up debt by owing people and creditors money, my credit score goes up. Wait a minute! That does not seem right. Why would that famous spokesperson lie or deceive me? They must be in debt too!

When you open a credit card and cannot pay it off, you enter a long-term relationship that starts sweet, and then month by month, you get used, abused, and cannot seem to part ways despite years of mistreatment. The problem with credit cards is that you are paying for stuff you cannot afford in your budget. Using money that you do not have. Then the product that you do not have money for, to begin with, now costs you even more due to added interest rate. As soon as you use a credit card, you go into debt. Paying the monthly minimums and accruing often exorbitant interest rates is burying you in debt. Very few people use a credit card then pay it off before the first payment is due. So very few people have the means and willpower to do so. Most Americans pay the monthly payment, so they do not get late fees, go into (oh no) lousy credit, and then debt snowballs out of control.

So, when you use your credit card and do not pay it off, you have to pay that back, and then extra money called interest. A loan shark in NY has the same payment plan, only at lower interest rates! The credit card company breaks your bank and your credit score rating. While the loan shark breaks something else when you fail to pay, both are very painful. Most credit card companies have an average interest rate of 16-19.5% in 2022.[91] Almost 20% interest to borrow money. So, if I borrow $100 and pay it back in payments, I pay around $120 to pay it off the next month.

Today, you pay far more for products when using a credit card, like the convenience charge a gas station adds for using a credit card, only worse. So, if you bought that shirt when it was 10% off on a credit card and paid it back slowly as a minimum payment plan, you end up paying more for the shirt than the original price. Credit cards are a significant problem with every generation, College students, the struggling middle class with growing families, and even seniors who never planned financially for the future. The credit card is a fraud. You, I, and the government all spend money on credit we do not have. How did this happen, and Americans did not do anything? What evil government created credit cards? What wholesome American would allow banks and debt collectors to call your house at 5:30 pm during dinner time. Who would do this to America?

Joe Biden and his friends in Delaware are the winner's ding, ding, ding, and guess who the losers are? In the 1980s, during the Cold War with The Soviet Union, which we now call Russia, America reached a financial growth under Reagan that had never been seen before then. And not since then until Trump was in office. Reagan moved America far ahead of other countries by simply making the "America First" policy. This led to better jobs, better vacations, and more spending. The spending boom was on non-essential stuff like sneakers, sports cars, boats, well, you name it, it was happening during the '80s. The government noticed tax revenues coming in each month on business sales. The government needed to cash in on this new American business empire. States all over the country had to sell their location as the best state to do business.

The state of Delaware from 1970 to 1990 changed from farmland to an economic boom of companies. Biden and Governor DuPont changed the sales tax to 0% so businesses could build corporations up and down the highways.[92] Why? To beat out other competition, or US states for the credit card company business. They made Delaware farmland into a corporate business utopia. Remember Trump and his corporate America Wall Street friends. Joe Biden was a member first! They courted banks, credit card companies, and big businesses to Delaware through tax cuts, deregulation of environmental practices, and dropping the sales tax rate to 0% on all in-state purchases. People sold off their 200-acre farms, and industrial parks showed up throughout the state. Farms are pretty, but the tax revenue for the government is far better from a high rise with three hundred companies in it. Plus, those high rises grew upwards in a much smaller footprint.

The tax breaks and corporate kickbacks made Delaware a prime location to move a corporation to. The biggest company winners were the credit card companies. They made out better in Delaware than any other state in the US. Not having sales tax and fewer corporate regulations would allow credit card companies to charge whatever they wanted in interest rates—starting a never-ending payment cycle called credit card debt. The DuPont's were Governors, Senators, Mayors and worked on the Biden campaign for Senate.[93] DuPont employees staffed Biden's first campaign. They have been friends scratching each other backs way before the credit card transgression. This friendship or alliance allowed Biden and DuPont, the Senator and Governor, to make up the rules as they went along.

Since the corporate laws are so relaxed in Delaware, all the companies from the bordering states moved to Delaware or incorporated in Delaware. Delaware made it easy and legal through local politicians to allow banks to charge any fee they wanted, foreclosure on debts owed, and set any interest rate they wanted. While the United States was recovering from the Jimmy Carter presidency and his failed policies, people started to create budgets and tighten up their wallets like the generations before them. Biden and his friends found a way to make things worse again.

During the Trump years, the bottom 40% of the population's wealth grew the most. Then under one year of Biden in 2021, the ten wealthiest people in the world doubled their net worth. Enough said, folks, looking out for the big banks, big corporate money, and his donors are Joe's number one concern. When states were trying to find income, Delaware was in an economic boom by removing regulations on corporate America. The age of Politicians and banks had begun.

Through the '70s, the '80s, and '90s, Biden helped make legislation that helped banks grow as big as they wanted, creating an unfair advantage to consumers who had no voice or protection in DC. The banks and corporations had a friend in DC, the companies that poured into Delaware from the late '70s to the '90s, had Joe Biden watch their backs and fatten their wallets. A local boy from Scranton, PA, a president for the people, did this. Why? Because he loves Americans, of course! He and his buddies in power knew exactly what was going on, how they were affecting the lives of Americans and did nothing to help but everything to stay in control. Biden was so easily swayed through financial and political gain.

Joe Biden allowed American families that use a credit card as a safety net or a way to live day to day to be forever in debt. There is that word again, Forever, and it seems like everything Joe Biden touches has a forever price tag effect. Giving banks the power to charge whatever they want, foreclose on whatever they want, and pay no tax or regulations for the damage they do. He made laws to get the wealthy more prosperous and made the poor stay in debt. A bank executive will and should find a way to make the most money for their company; that is the purpose of free enterprise. When politicians change the rules to help banks crush the soul of hard-working Americans, that is criminal.

Forget Afghanistan, the 2020 election, the pipeline making us energy-dependent on Russia, forget the fact that his vice president called him a racist for creating laws that kept her Black and poor as a child! Forget the fact that he, too, has made a career of smelling, sniffing, grabbing, and getting too close to women who are not his wife. Forget that he just gave the terrorist planes to fly them into buildings, this time without hijacking them! Joe Biden gave United States military planes and weapons to the enemy. Ukraine asked the US for anti-defense systems against Russia and received none!

Forget that he lied and plagiarized his presidential speech in the '80s. Forget all these facts for a conversation about treason and impeachment. The credit card laws were made in Delaware under Joe Biden's watch so he could go from a Senator for the people of Delaware to a Senator for the banks and greedy money. That alone is calls for impeachment and jail. Today is no different; who did he name to be the Senior Advisor to the Office of Domestic Finance at the US Treasury. Another DuPont, by marriage, Darla Pomeroy, an heir to the DuPont family fortune.[94] Again, he hires friends instead of the qualified person for the job. Anthony Blinken, an Obama hire, now hurts Americans and our children's future. More than half of Joe's staff are ex-Obama friends or ex-employees.[95] It makes no sense, and who gets hurt, the American people!

Joe Biden fought his whole time in the Senate for big Banks, co-signing bills that made laws for the banks of Delaware to go across the country. Bills that allowed banks to open Mega branches in every state, open up multiple banks in one concentrated area to compete and ultimately crush smaller banks. They made it easy for banks to monopolize the market and change the rules on banking from state to state, favoring big money. He could not stop in Delaware; he helped pass laws so other states could relax regulations and banks could charter branches from state to state. Operating in the same destructive way they worked in Delaware was now nationwide.[96] Affecting every American with a forever credit card, a forever credit score that is a shackle putting America forever in debt to foreign banks.

Joe Biden's bad economic education of how money works have harmed America forever. You do not let people borrow money they do not have; it is a bad financial idea. That is irresponsible and not even a politician's job. A bank does not loan money to just anyone. He learned this from his big-money friends that ran Delaware. Instead of stopping the crime and helping Americans as a civil servant, he masterminded the crime, and now we are doing time. The credit card system did not start with Joe Biden, but he made sure it expanded, exploded, and that it will never go away. Everyone gets a fake credit card in the mail, though! Is Joe Biden telling the truth, a politician for the people against the evil Republicans?

Joe Biden not only harmed the health of every American living in Delaware while in office for 46 years. He also damaged generation after generation for creating a system in Delaware in 46 years that will affect Americans financially forever. Joe Biden will leave his legacy on America one way or the other. Forever Chemicals, forever laws that harm Americans, forever bad foreign policies, and a forever effect that will leave a bad taste in our mouths.

Joe Biden campaigned on ending Heroin addiction in 1972 while running for Senate. He had newspaper articles made up slamming his older opponent.[97] Caleb Boggs's generation wants to cure polio; Joe Biden wants to end Heroin addiction. What do you think of his track record? Should we ask Hunter's wife and kids? What would have happened if Joe Biden fought heroin dealers and stopped big business and their greed. There would be far less financial debt or financial heartaches for over two hundred million Americans.

What if Joe kept to his Catholic roots as he did early in his career before he flip-flopped on abortion. What would have been the downside? Unborn babies would now have a voice and a chance in Delaware. What if Joe fought back against the chemical dumping and creation of Forever Chemicals? People's lives would be healthier. Maybe his son Beau would have lived longer too. What if Joe fought against crime, drugs, and the nepotism that plagues Delaware? Maybe Hunter would not be vacuuming the floor with his nose? Perhaps if Joe had taken the righteous path, he could have saved lives and captured the hearts of Millions. He could have kept the streets and Hunter clean and not embarrassed his family and the entire United States and made a mockery of addiction. His sons would have had better, more healthy lives. If he had been American first in his life and the way he handled politics, then what would have happened? Where would we be as a country, building back better after years of disgracing ourselves? Building back better after years of damage to the environment. Building back better after years of doing the wrong work while on the job. Facing the end of life, and now it is time to fix all your faults, in your final hour? A little late to Build Back Better. Rome was not built in a day, and Biden cannot fix 77 years of neglect, corruption, and lies in just four years.

We can never Build Back Better from Forever Chemicals, forever lies, and giving billions of weapons to the enemy. We will be building back better after you leave. After Obama, Carter, Clinton, and any politician who just does not care about anything but themselves and special interests. The same selfish people in life that cut you off and flip you the bird are now in power and flipping the US the bird every day. There should be no need for a politician of the Democrat party, the party that is the oldest elected party in US history, and a politician who has been in office for over 46 years, to say Build Back Better. Where were you all this time? Build Back Better from what you broke down? Why do we have to Build Back Better? Is it because you have been in power tearing us apart for generations? Build what back better, the racist ways of the Democratic party past? Build Back Better, a pure damage control statement from the Kings of damage control. Make a problem, blame someone, then pretend to fix the problem.

Obamacare was a good example, more than 46 years in office, and now suddenly you believe in Universal free health care? Sir, no offense, but you spent more than 46 years allowing chemicals to kill 1 in 3 people in Delaware, and now you try to offer free health care. Building back better from the Forever Chemicals dumped during your watch. Building back better will never happen where Forever Chemicals were left. There is no building back from Forever Chemicals. There is no building back from cancers in our drinking water. The Democrat party hated Trump because he did the work. He was an employee for Americans. Joe got elected, and now we owe the Biden family our lives? Even after you have gone, your legacy will remain for poor decisions and your Forever Chemicals. These things will always remind us of Joe Biden.

He follows the wrong lead on many issues then flip-flops on voters and his constituents to push his agenda. In other words, his foot is in his mouth, and he stepped in shit. The handling of the pandemic, blaming the unvaccinated, fining those who will not get the shot. He is not enforcing the laws on Illegals crossing the border or fleeing countries where Covid runs rampant. He is only allowing it to permeate our communities over and over again. However, he pushes fines and regulations against Americans. Only if he could be human and just tell Americans the truth. Joe Biden needs the mandatory laws to get Americans vaccinated! Joe Biden knows the throngs of unvaccinated refugees he let in this country will infect you! It will make a new super-strain of viruses, killing even more Americans.

He did the same thing during the start of the AIDS pandemic in the 1980s. If you look up the definition of AIDS, it says an epidemic, but that is wrong and discriminatory. AIDS was a pure example of how America faced an epidemic that may have disproportionately affected one group at the start. Still, like most viruses, it mutated to impact other groups in the population. Since the CDC named AIDS (Acquired Immune Deficiency Syndrome) in 1982, 21.8 million people have died of the disease. In the beginning, the original definition of the term AIDS was an epidemic. Why?

Because in the beginning, AIDS mainly affected White homosexual people. It was not until 1984 that they named HIV (Human Immunodeficiency Virus) a worldwide threat, which led to a new definition. AIDS might have started with just one type of group, but since 1982, 4.3 million children under age fifteen have died of AIDS. Some were born from mothers with the virus and must take medication lifelong to treat the virus. The central part of the story is that we thought only homosexual acts could give you AIDS, so closed-minded and not scientific at all. We now know so much more about blood transfusions, drug use transfer, and, most importantly, medical treatments to end the fight against AIDS.

The virus hit America hard in the early 1980s, and politicians did what they did best, point fingers and blame others.[98] When the disease hit, a doctor first discovered it in San Francisco, California. California was dealing with a specific population that it seemed was the only group dying from this horrible disease. It was not until a boy was diagnosed with AIDS from a dirty needle during a blood transfusion that Americans, particularly politicians, noticed. Then in 1986, the AIDS virus was affecting Black people, Latinos, and newborns, who made up 90% of all AIDS cases. It was not until 1989 that the HSRA (Health Service and Research Administration), a US government agency located in Maryland, finally created funding for research on a cure after millions of people had died. This US government-funded agency is responsible for all studies of diseases affecting the United States and other countries. The budget in 2019 for the HSRA was over ten billion dollars, and they also got a 9.9 billion in federal grants through lawmakers' loop poles. In 1989 the HSRA was finally granted funding to help find a cure for Americans.

The Ryan White foundation was made under President Regan, named after the 14-year-old boy who died from a blood transfusion. The bill would be called the CAREs ACT and was signed in 1990 after he died a week before his high school graduation. Why did it take so long for a smart, scientifically sound Congressional act to be signed into law? Finally, in January 2020, the US government passed a bill worth $119 million to halt the epidemic of AIDS in America by 90% before 2030. After 30 years of political volley balling and millions of American deaths, Trump passed the funding needed. So, we can do it. To cure a devastating disease in society, we just need to work together. How many Americans had to die before this would happen?

Just like the unvaccinated people are blamed today for killing Americans, the AIDS population was attacked and ridiculed for years as dirty, unclean, and a walking disease. The people with AIDS had travel restrictions placed on them; they could not go to some schools, work or even live in some apartment buildings.[99] We just went through a pandemic where we had to wear a thin mask that would supposedly stop an airborne virus from killing us. AIDS was only transmitted through sex, needles, or blood, and maybe through saliva tainted with blood. We know, yet many were disgusted with the possibility that someone with AIDS might be near them. The Covid virus could kill you with a microscopic droplet of air; AIDS needs to be in your blood. America despised and looked down on the sick with AIDS; the politicians could not decide if the disease was staying or a rare curse from God.[100]

The HRSA during Covid fumbled the ball again during an epidemic in the US. The agency has shifted from caring for all Americans to now, and I am quoting their website, "Ensuring Equity in COVID-19 Vaccine Distribution, Engaging Federally in Qualified Health Centers. The Health Center COVID-19 Vaccine Program, a partnership between HRSA and CDC, has begun".[101] That is their mission statement, the only problem, just like AIDS, Covid just does not affect one group of Americans. Focusing on the political low jab or even damage control for failed local politicians does not stop Covid. The poor die just like the rich die.

Another political talking point that a "Think Tank" told a politician to say. Blame game during a time of need. A medical health agency blames patients before treating them. Politicians use Science for political points instead of information to help their country. The Covid virus can be transmitted through a simple cough in the air, and it can kill you. Somehow, we still managed to go on with our lives and deal with unvaccinated people. The AIDS virus had to be transmitted through blood and physical contact or sharing needles; we acted like a person with AIDS had a plaque. People's image of a person with AIDS was like a person with Leprosy from the Bible. Why were we so afraid of what we did not know? Misinformation. Much like "But if Donald Trump tells us we should take it, I'm not taking it.". [102] that is what Kamala Harris said when asked about taking the vaccine in 2020 before the election. Did she still take the vaccine and the booster? Even though she pushed misinformation and showed divisive political ways?

The people Joe Biden looked up to as a young Politician are the same people that have created a divided, unfair, and angry America. People like Bobby Kennedy, the statue of a head behind Joe Biden in the Oval Office. People like Kennedy's let a pregnant woman drown in a car as he ran away and did not report it till the following day! Ted Kennedy was a mentor to Joe Biden. While Kennedy's father was the biggest bootlegger during the prohibition era, the Kennedy boys fought for social justice. Their dad fed America alcohol from Cuba, undermining America during prohibition. John F. Kennedy also approved Bobby Kennedy to spy on Martin Luther King Jr by phone tapping. Biden retreats from war, as Robert Kennedy defended his brother JFK for staying in Vietnam while running for President against Nixon.

Joe Biden won the presidency and traveled to Georgia to see his old-time ally, Jimmy Carter. Maybe the most harmful president to America's future besides the Joe Biden and Barrack Obama era. No other president in America's history had done more harm to his and other countries than Jimmy Carter. The similarities of both terms and ways of getting elected are remarkably similar. Jimmy Carter ran in the 1966 and 1970 Georgian Governor's races. In 1966 he ran against Lester Maddox, a Segregated Democrat who would not allow Black people to eat at his restaurants [103]. Jimmy Carter knew the only way to beat him and get the segregated South's Democrat Governor nomination was to be more pro-segregation than his opponent.

The Democrat party was the racist South voters from the days of slavery. To win their vote, Carter played to his old Southern boy roots. Similarly, Joe Biden ran on a set of empty promises that the people who voted for him and believed him. They both ran a race to win the old White racist vote; Carter and Biden used the same political, racial division game to win the presidency. Carter ran every campaign the same, "I am a nice guy," but I will slander my opponent any way possible to win. Carter ran heavily on being a boy from the South, even keeping a confederate flag in his office.[104] In 1970, he finally figured out the political game. Say one thing and do another. He barely beat out Carl Sanders, a fellow Democrat who Carter painted as being "ultrarich" and a friend of the Democrat "establishment." He used racially fueled promises in the ultra-White Democrat Georgia to beat him. He even went as far as to criticize Sanders for supporting Martin

Luther King Jr.! Perhaps his lowest ploy, Jimmy Carter supporters, handed out pictures of his opponent with Black Basketball Players to dissuade White voters. ([105] Carter knew the only way to beat his opponent and get the segregated Southern Democrat nominee was to lie for the vote.

Joe has learned from the ninjas of politics. The Clintons, the Bidens, and the Obamas. Elected politicians and civil servants are now all wealthy royal families of power after becoming servants of America. From taking on an oath to protect and serve the people's best interest to owning millions of dollars of property and having wealth and power. Autocracy, monarchy, and the ultimate ruler. When did taking a job as a politician means the ultimate key to wealth and power? Who is working for whom? Joe Bidens' beloved past politicians have done nothing more than creating an absolute rule of power and a path to stay in power. I keep showing you, in this chapter, the flip-flop campaigns that only a lazy person would appreciate. Never put in the work, never really doing good, just all talk and no hustle. Joe Biden said it by accident, Autocracy rule, a Democrat one-party rule.[106] He slipped and told us the game plan of Democrats, control the vote, and control power. It is not like he does not know how to fight or stand up for what he believes in.

He believed in making sure the banks that made him rich would never be too big to fail in Wall Street. In 1999 when Bill Clinton was already in trouble with Monica Lewinsky and on a spiral down spin and not only fighting the press but fighting Hillary. Joe Biden's banking friends asked one more favor while the Democrats controlled everything still! During the Great Depression, the banks failed, and people lost everything because there was no safety net. After the Great Depression in 1933, Congress passed a bill to secure investors' money, so Wall Street could never gamble away your savings. Bill Clinton and the rest of the Democrats in the pockets of big money made sure their bank friends were taken care of. Some Democrats even argued that the brash young Biden was out of line with his vote.

The vote was not securing Americans' money but assuring that big Banks would be too big ever to fail.[107] The repeal of the act that stood since 1933 would allow the separation of commercial and investment banking, preventing securities firms and investment banks from taking deposits. Some commentators and critics have stated that the US Democrat President Bill Clinton and the Democrat majority led Congress to repeal the affiliation restrictions of the Glass–Steagall Act was a fundamental cause of the financial crisis of 2007–2008.

Showing that one mistake leads to another and another. Congressman John Dingle said this about the Act:

"I think we ought to look at what we are doing here tonight. We are passing a bill that will have very little consideration, written in the dark of night, without any real awareness on the part of most of what it contains.

I just want to remind my colleagues about what happened the last time the Committee on Banking brought a bill on the floor which deregulated the savings and loans. It wound up imposing upon the taxpayers of this Nation about a $500 billion liability.

Having said that, what we are creating now is a group of institutions that are too big to "fail." Not only are they going to be big banks, now they can be big everything because they will be in securities and insurance, in the issuance of stocks and bonds and underwriting, and they are also going to be in banks. And under this legislation, the whole of the regulatory structure is so muddied and confused that liability in only one area will fall! Taxpayers will be called upon to cure the failures we are creating tonight, and it is going to cost a lot of money, and it is coming. Just be prepared for those events."[108]

This action and passage of a law overturned a safety net for Americans that was put into place long before Joe Biden was a Senator. The effects of him and his friends passing this bill will ensure riches for the wealthy for centuries. He is not taxing the rich in his new tax hike. Build Back Better on the sweat equity of poor people. When Joe

Biden entered office, he was making under $75,000 a year in 1972. After 50 years in office, Joe Biden's net worth is over one hundred million dollars. How does that happen? My friend's compound interest is not even that powerful! Is that how being a politician who serves the rich makes out?

How often will we hear a politician from the left say tax the rich, the middle class is hurting. Then you see them at the Met Gala, at a $30k ticket event, a Senator wearing a dress that says Tax the Rich. Please tax the rich, tax the actors, tax the movie stars, tax the athletes, and tax the super-elite! You remember how they campaigned and tore down Trump. Every actor, musician, and athlete said he was not going to the White House. They are all rich, and they are all ready to be taxed. You are telling me that they voted to tax the rich guy? They except always being taxed by another fellow Democrat.

Start with you, Hunter, the Clintons, and the NFL players who kneel. Tax them all, please, and then when they raise the price of their products, the consumer pays the difference. That is called Inflation, another thing you learned from Jimmy Carter. There is no tax on the rich; there is no tax on the wealthy elite politicians; no tax dollars are coming in from the ultra-rich "civil servants." Please stop the lies, the game, and the spin. Do not tell me what you will do; just do it. The Obamas just built a $33 million home; please tax the rich. Start with every politician who is worth over $ 50 million. Do you need a list? Open your phone book, digital or old school paper! Better yet, go through the list of who bought an "Authentic Hunter," it is full of stupid-rich people buying "world-class art." Open your contact book for us, Joe; it is full of names of people whose pockets you have helped line heavily. Start doing what you say and tax the super-rich, the political elite; let us see what happens next!

Chapter 7

Their Playbook on How They Did It

This book was not made from hate or anger. It wrote itself; it simply reports on the past in which I grew up. When I type and say things repeatedly, I ruminate about the steps we need to take back our country. Too many steps back, and I worry we will never break the cycle. I wrote this book to help educate people on why we need to have voters show ID, tax returns, and IRS proof before voting. The simple act of showing ID to verify who you are is not unheard of. The civil action of showing ID occurs every day when you log into your computer, pick up a prescription, or even be pulled over by the police. I must show ID to buy a beer for myself seems normal and makes sense. I must show an ID to vote for a guy who might use a nuclear weapon should be mandatory. Taxes are what make America the greatest country in the world. Yes, a Republican said taxes are the greatest thing in the world. Not high taxes, not low taxes but taxes. A Fair tax is a way to grow a great country. Everybody pays their fair share, a saying you have heard before. Not Socialism fair share while you are handcuffed on your potential earnings.

To keep Americans satisfied and safe, we need things like roads that lead to a hospital, school, mall, restaurant, or dentist's office. These things we take for granted, called roads, can be smooth and well managed or rough and poorly maintained. Rough roads cost me more money on my car, tires, and gas. Stopping and going and avoiding potholes, this road needs repairing, causing expenses to the town, the county, and the state. Taxes pay for that road to be smooth and well maintained, so I can get where I need to be, and I do not need to take my car to the shop for repairs or get new tires. Money from taxpayers pays for that road's repairs. Not giant bills from the federal government to fix highways and bridges. Local taxes pay for roads and bridges.

Let us say, one particular year, a new wing needed to be built on the public school because of an influx of illegal migrants that were placed into your community. They must make a separate classroom to teach them in their language, and then you also need to find teachers to teach these people from another country. They live here and go to school, church, and hospitals just like you. The one problem is they are here illegally, not contributing in taxes, and are getting money from the state or the US government to help live their new life in America. Not paying taxes, but still accumulating money, getting wealthier, and using the resources connected to that highway needing repair. The township is strapped this year due to the added cost of the classroom in the school! The money will have to come from raising taxes on the people in our town. They cannot take money from the school, the police, or firefighters to fix the road.

You have seen what defunding the police does, stealing from Peter to give to Paul. Instead, it was stealing everything from Peter, Paul, and Mary. Crime rise has a reason because the towns are sending funding from police to fund new classrooms for immigrants. The defund the police movement backfired and only created more crime, go figure. It is almost like people do not think and do not know history!

When they built NY City, the first thing they did was hire one million police officers. Does that sound right! No, they built roads, houses, streets, schools, then police officers, and then police stations were planned for and funded. Then as the centuries went by, America started to think we needed more police officers, way too many crimes, and too many criminals. More people meant more crime, so what is the need for defunding the police? Backward mentality! So, what happens? Neglect becomes the norm; Americans and all citizens suffer due to a lack of funds to fix problems that plague taxpayers. Crime gets so bad that people are killed for no reason at all. Murder and muggings are on the rise. Is this the new norm?

When you allow people to take advantage of honest taxpaying citizens, then the citizens become the victims. The criminals become emboldened, superior, and arrogant. They use the same resources but do not pay taxes to keep the resources going. So, slacking and depreciation of America takes place. The money to help them relocate to America is taxpayers' money; the money to build the new wing on the school is taxpayers' money. As an American citizen squanders to live, the politicians hold some up higher. These create natural division, hate, racism and shape our problems today. The problem is they do not pay their fair share of taxes. The answer is that the rich should pay more; we all pay, or people have to get out!

If you had ten people living in your house, and only five work and five stay home all day and play video games, the five that work pay for the other five to eat, sleep, and live in a beautiful community. How long till the five workers tell the five slackers to get out? Being an American does not mean just living in this country; it means contributing to something better. Are you letting the kid next to you copy all your answers and not say anything? When he receives the full scholarship, and you do not, is it fair then? If we all paid taxes and did our fair share to keep our community and its resources available, we would not need to Build Back Better.

We would not need nine trillion in infrastructure bills and aid to millions of undocumented immigrants. I am not taking from their children; why are they taking from my children? I do not ask for your handouts; why are you giving handouts with my money? Being an American is not asking what your country can do for you anymore[109]. It is asking the world if they want to live here for free. When is my land not your land? When is America the ground for the people that care for America? How many people in America do not love America? How often will we play "good cop bad cop" with our children's future? How many generations of unborn Americans will have to pay for other countries' populations? What playbook should we follow now?

Defeating the Right and staying the course of damage control, never knowing what the news will tell me as I wake up for a stimulus check hangover every day. Or, maybe we could try this for our children. Let us try the playbook where I go to sleep knowing I live in the greatest country ever known, and when I go to bed, the people in charge have an America First agenda while I sleep. Whatever I vote, Republican or Democrat, the goal moving forward is America first, or we have failed our future generations. The generations that are doomed before they begin. What playbook do we use to secure the Greatest Country Ever? I hope it will be an American playbook!

When a politician runs for office, the first thing they should say is-- nothing! Absolutely nothing! Imagine that you are on a job interview, and you walk in and start rambling on how you will build this business better. We should be asking the questions, not Chris Wallace; we are hiring them, they should answer what we want. A politician works FOR the people; politicians get a job to work FOR the people. This statement is where we start from here going forward. The difference between now and 1980 is that when I went to work in 1980, I went to work to better myself. Never getting all that I wanted, but still being a productive member of society. Paying taxes, working hard for my job and my money, earning all that I have, and most of all being appreciative for what you got.

Working today is a chore; it is seen as taking my time away from more important things, like the internet and my phone. Today workers get upset when you come to their drive-thru window to order like you should go home and cook for yourself. The people do not understand the purpose of being there at work and contributing to something more significant than yourself! Working not just for a paycheck but for a purpose. If you do not make work meaningful and try your best, then I do not come back to that drive-thru window or that store. The store loses profits. Eventually, the manager cannot keep many on staff with no income due to evil workers. Then someone is laid off; the employee gets angry at the course taken, they scream and post a nasty comment online about the manager. Then they still bad talk the store that let them go, creating more lousy publicity and profit loss for the struggling business that let you go. Then your so-called friends or co-workers who got you the job now start losing hours every week due to lack of sales from bad reviews. Then years go by, and you apply for a "real job," so you say, and they check your internet footprint and find out that you are the one who got their favorite breakfast spot closed down. You cancel cultured a small business due to your lack of effort and caring about your job. The new job does not hire you because he misses his bagels, and you are still angry at what? Yourself, or someone who would not hire you? This generation has been lied to, and now they are finding out the hard way how life and jobs work. Not everyone makes six figures; it is ok!

This nonsense started when Barrack Obama said," you didn't create that, you didn't start that, it has already been done for you"[110]. That statement from Barrack Obama was a classic politician lawyer, and I am trying to get into your pants line. You are beautiful, but with my help, you could be the best. A pick-up line that a sleazeball uses at a bar at 3 am. Nice drawing, but did you see my kind of line. That sandwich is good, but did you see how they made it. You are just a carbon copy of someone else no matter what you do. A politician created the pissing contest to unite and vote for a failure. If you fail in your life, do not worry; it was done for you by a politician! An actual politician line that never says what he means, never says anything meaningful, but just leaves you feeling a little less secure after he is done. I can try, but for what. I can do it, but why it is already finished. I can explore, but what is left to find.

Are these the words of the most inspiring men of our history? I think not. These are the words from a politician planting the seeds for a Socialist Society of America. Try hard? But for what reason? You are all the same. These words come from a person who could not accept that he would not be who he is without this great nation of ours and the people inside of it. Words from a person who does not want life to get any better for you because I am on top and let me stay that way. Words that inspire you do not start with "you did not." Comments from a person who cannot understand or accept that one President made life better today than yesterday. Trump did not create Tax-cuts; they were done for him.

Obama created a friendship with Bill Ayers, a person on the FBI's most-wanted list.[111] You created that, not me! The fact is, America has been working to create a better society for all. We did work together with Obama; we were not divided, that is why you were President. We are building back better every day. That is why you, a child of a single mother, had a chance. We are compassionate people with flaws but still gracious enough to help a single mom raise a president. Coming from a person that broke so many barriers and hurdles to become the first Black President, then just shit on all the dreams with a statement like, "you didn't start anything." The acts of these politicians inspired me to author this book about corruption in politics, which went on for generations.

Do not worry, Obama; the crime has been done before you. I will not write about the lie that the Republicans are the party of slavery and hate in America. Do not worry; many politicians tried to divide America the same way before you. I will write about how your vice president poisoned his state and its people; then, he used and poisoned you. Do not worry. You are not the first politician to pretend to be earth-friendly. I will write about the fact that every skeleton in Joe's closet is coming to life, the freaks come out at night, just like the Democrat voters in 2020. Do not worry. You are not the first Democrat president to hold secret votes behind closed doors in the middle of the night.[112] Do not worry. Other politicians meet behind the media eye.[113]

Bill Clinton and your former Attorney General did it; the reporter who broke the story wound up dead![114] Ouch, that most of been a big meeting! The Democrats learned this trick from the slave-owning Democrat leaders of the Confederate party. They did it too![115] Do not worry. You are not the first, but please God be the last.

To set up this next part of the book, the flow of actions by Barrack Obama, Joe Biden, and the Democrat party over the last 12 years have been building a damn for freedom. The decisions made to hire certain people, pass specific laws, change America's policies, and chisel away at statutes that show The Democrat's past. Lookout Lady Liberty, your next! They have put people in power of certain parts of society that look harmless but harm us all. Take, for instance, the Department of Education. Sure, it teaches the youth of America. It keeps them off the streets and in sports, activities, and character-building skills for the next stage of life.[116] How does having a solid public school system and a good education for every child affect everyone? The foundations learned at school, throughout every level, are essential. US students spend more time in class than their international peers.[117] Why are we ranked lower than other countries in learning? [118] The classroom becomes the second home for some children, a guardian or foster parents, or a babysitter for others. It is a place to eat, it is a place to learn, and it is a place to be safe.

The United States has seen what happens when the wrong people control a school district. The cycle of problems worsens, and when the shit hits the fan, it looks like the public education system does now. The damage is done first. Then the cover-up occurs, fighting and division ensue, and the damage control begins. The cycle repeats until the whole thing blows up like Loudon County, VA[119]. Every decision made by teachers' unions, local leaders, mayors, police officers, and politicians affects us all. The people placed in the power of elections created the same problem for American voters in 2020.

We expect and deserve to have competent leaders. Now we have to deal with the consequences of inferior appointees. They are hiring friends to control the vote, the malicious slandering campaign, and what ballot you will use. The people appointed by Barrack Obama and Joe Biden while in office have done the same thing for the US Election Assistance Commission. Hiring and selecting friends has now damaged your way of thinking about America's elections forever!

The US Election Assistance Commission needs an employee yard sale fast. People like Christy McCormick, who in 2014 was nominated to fill a key Administration

post.[120] Appointed to the office by Barrack Obama to change the voting status quo. Before this position, she was a Senior Trial Attorney in the Voting Section of the Civil Rights Division at the Department of Justice.[121] She was appointed to be the Rule of Law on Iraq elections from 2008-2010. She also oversaw a 12-day election recount in Iraq during their 2010 election. Christy McCormick did what her boss asked her to do. She was appointed in 2014 to work on the US Elections Commission with Matthew Masterson for her dedication and hard work. The hard work, long hours, and doing whatever they asked paid off.

The two appointees would take on the crazy election cycle of 2016, where she was criticized and even told the Republican GOP that the fake Russia hoax was "unreal." McCormick wrote that the claims were "deceptive propaganda perpetrated on the American public by the Obama administration."[122]. She would play the Good Cop while, on the other hand, Matthew Masterson never forgot the hand that feeds him. He overloaded McCormick's team during the 2020 elections. He cut funding and staff by almost 50% but told the United States that the US EAC had total control.[123] She was the one the public knew. While she played her part, McCormick was doing her job, telling reporters that they were working overtime to have a secure election. Great Job!

Masterson went on to his new career but still told Congress and the world about disinformation.[124] While working for the US EAC, the former Obama appointee set up the "LIE." The powers that be controlled the election and the appointees played their roles perfectly. The term, it takes an island to raise a boy; well, it took chains of islands to steal a LIE! Please, read on.

Where to go from here, that only taxpaying Americans can vote. How about we just start at securing the vote first. You must show your most recent tax return filed, and then you can vote. Not for identification but because if you do not pay taxes, you have no say in what politicians do with our tax money. Remember when I said the first thing a politician should say is nothing. You work for the people, hear their problems, concerns, and complaints, and go to work. Creating new laws, voting on rules, and passing new bills should be necessary, not a once-a-month fight for the Fox news network. Will it get enough votes? Will they be able to sway two more Democrats to avoid a revote? If 75% of the Senate does not agree, then maybe 75% of the population of America does not either. Not 50/50!

How about you ask the people to vote on what bill to pass? It only affects us, the people. Taxes fix the road that you drive to work on; taxes are what makes our school be built; taxes are what puts gas in fire trucks as they come to save your life. New bills, laws, and taxes should make every American sit up and take notice. When politicians get together and hold meetings when they are not in power, you should be worried. In 2017 when Trump was going through his first impeachment trial, a Hillary Clinton worker lied.[125] The Clinton's co-started and co-owned Skolkovo, a company in Russia.[126] It is considered the Silicon Valley of Russia. A place where all the "Hackers" can learn their skills.

So, during that mock trial, the Democrats knew it was a phony hoax; they used their smoke and mirrors deflection method and painted Trump as a Russian Spy. Hillary Clinton stood in front of America and said that Donald Trump had ties to Russia.[127] She blasted Trump because an interview with Larry King aired in Russia. In 2018, two of the top three prizes in a Russian reality TV show that followed the fortunes of Russian tech startups went to residents of the Skolkovo

Foundation. So, one is a puppet for Russia, and one is a supporter of Russia with help from Anthony Blinken and his wife, working for the Clinton's, then Obama, and now Biden![128]

They hired an inner circle of friends to control anything they wanted. Crime by defunding the police, oil prices by cutting the pipeline, drugs, and cartel supported immigration because of stopping the wall. They decide what disaster makes them have a job to clean something up. When McCormick holds a voting meeting, we better notice and fast. When they talk about voting laws in 2017, that means there must be a disaster coming. Why? Then we have something to clean up, a Democrat-made disaster. They will create a catastrophe, Russian collusion, then hold a think tank and fix their made-up disaster.

They changed how technology and voting are done in the US.! While the US was worried if Russia voted for Donald Trump or it was real red-White-and blue-blooded Americans, the Democrats who lost the election were planning future elections. The technology of voting and how it can be "better." Folks, this article I found, and you are about to read, stuns me. While Russia was being blamed for interfering, the Democrats, who were not in power, held meetings on disrupting future elections.

They knew the hoax was fake; they started it! As a smokescreen to hold underground meetings on elections. Trump says the "Lie" and half of America still has questions about the 2020 election because of misinformation. I read this, and I wonder, wow, if only they put in this much work doing things FOR the American people. Who needs voting reform, the voters or the politicians? When they just defeated the Republican nominee by the most votes in America's history, the next step is to change how we vote?

This is why the Americans, not just Republicans, are so upset; why January 6th took an ugly turn; why Americans do not believe in their government anymore. If this is what they do while out of office, imagine what they do in office. When you are done with your civil servant duties and time allowed to serve, then you are out of politics. This is why our country today scares so many Americans because of meetings like this.

How to control the Voting in America 101: Class is in session! When Hillary Clinton lost the election, Americans were not surprised, but the Leaders were not surprised either. They had seen this before, with Nixon, Reagan, and now Trump. Before the 2020 election, Trump had the most votes ever. So, what do the Democrats do best? Damage Control. Make it, so we go total technology voting with no record of voters and no identification. They blame a foreign country and find lawyers to debunk all claims against them. And whatever they do, manipulate the process never to lose again?

Autocracy, like China, Russia, and other powerful Communist countries. Like the elections held in Iraq in 2010 that Christy McCormick was overseeing, it took 12 days to do a recount. Twelve days to find out who was president. Even the elections of 2020 in America took three and a half days to find out the winner.[129] We have become an Iraq! Like in the movies, the stars shine and stay together in the sky, the extras die off one by one with no sequels. We are all just extras to them. A vote, a number. Even if we decide to vote for our country and values with our hearts and minds, does it matter? Does it count? The same ones who cried foul with Trump did it when Bush Jr won. The ones who called Foreign Interference did it when Nixon won.[130] The lie they tell you is the lie they tell themselves when they lose fair and square. So, when the lies run out and the excuses do not work, they just rig it where they cannot lose.

This conference was put together three years before the 2020 election, before the Covid shutdowns, before the second impeachment trial. They knew the first impeachment trial would not work, so they kept digging and produced another. To change, manipulate, secure, debunk, and set a narrative that we all are crazy! This is what non-elected officials do during non-voting years to make voting "better." They knew the importance of the mail-in vote before it became an issue. They knew that they would need more technologically advanced voting systems before the pandemic; they were sitting and waiting to be used. They knew that there would be a significant uptick in the mail-in votes two years before the pandemic. They knew the outcome before the American voter. The American taxpaying voter never had a chance to be heard.

Well, when you see these names in the news, read an article in the paper, or catch them on some talk show bashing the January 6th "rioters" and former president Trump. They were at this meeting and knew all this back in June 2017 because Biden, Obama, and Clinton knew they would not lose again! Next is a file from the minutes and introduction of the meeting. This meeting mainly was Democrat officials, two people who attended are now dead, and almost everyone involved now has a position in the Biden presidency today. If they did not hate Donald Trump, then maybe this would be no big deal, but the politicians told us how they felt. Every time they can![131]

This next section is an excerpt of the minutes taken during an election rehaul set by Barrack Obama, Joe Biden, and all that work for him now. Including the ones behind the scenes putting people in the White House then, now, and in the future. The names in **BOLD** lettering only work for Joe Biden now. The words <u>underlined</u> and in **BOLD** lettering worked for both Obama and Biden. <u>Underlined</u> words in **BOLD** and with **Asterisk*** worked for Clinton, Obama, and Biden. This is an actual document taken from Congressional records.

Why have a public record breakdown? This election committee meeting was passed in 2014 by the Democrat ran Senate and was set to take action when the wrong person was in office.

(Sentences in *Italic* are descriptions of the attendees and presenters by the conference committee. To show where and who they work for.)

The presenters of this Voting Technology, Redistricting, and American election overhaul were mostly appointees by Former President Obama and Former Vice President Biden. All the presenters and sponsors are all former or current employees of Democrat politicians. People at this conference have worked with Senator Chuck Schumer, Ex-President Barrack Obama, Ex-Vice President Al Gore, and his former running mate in 2000 and 2004, Joe Lieberman.

The Future of Elections: Technology Policy and Funding Conference [132]

June 14-16, 2017

Abridged Speaker Bios – Listed in Order of Presentation

Wednesday, June 14, 2017

Welcome to Elections Technology 101

PRESENTERS:

Wendy Underhill, NCSL

She is a State Legislator; what does that mean? How does someone become a state legislator, are they elected, appointed, or try out for the job? What are the qualifications to be a state legislator, and why is she at a Democrat-funded, Third Way[133] Technology Conference on Voting? She is the Director of the National Conference of State Legislatures and the head of the Elections and Redistricting Program happening in America. This group finds where the vote is unfair and changes the demographics to fit a needed void by education level, color, race, and sexual orientation. Her articles in magazines tell a different story.[134] She talks of ballot harvesting before it became a thing. Amber McReynolds[135] and Wendy Underhill trademarked the phrase, mail-in ballots, folks.

They create the image of hate, racism, and ballot fraud. Or we could just end it all and show ID! Showing an ID to vote is not racism; people that vote with racist intentions are racist. When a person says I do not see a politician, which I can relate to because they are not of the same skin color, that is a racist statement. The idea of American freedom and power is not on a color chart in a classroom. It is burned into your heart, mind, values, and your actions. Why is she the first presenter to a bi-partisan election conference?

So, how does redistricting help Republicans as well? She was appointed to work for and help this country by doing interviews about disinformation that she helps start! Well, Wendy's forgotten her oath to the constitution but never to her Democrats. Redistricting is a crock of shit; if a politician is suitable for the people, no amount of redistricting can stop a landslide. Redistricting the voting lines keeps the voting machines from allowing a blowout victory.[136]

RCV VOTING might help, a four-tier voting system. Did you know four presidents ran last year? Trump ran against Hillary Clinton, Barrack Obama, and Joe Biden! The voting machine will always use a four-tier voting count until the front runner receives 60% of the vote. So, to stop that from piling up and having a clear win, they redistrict an area where the votes will always stay close. The voting machine counts will always be almost a dead heat when voting. We saw the 48% to 49% game all night during the election. They keep it too close to call and always in the margin of error or the recount allowed margin.

For three and a half days, the vote count was never more than a 2% difference in the lead. Due to redistricting, the machines are always too close to call, allowing the four-tier voting system to work. The RCV voting tier can only work if the race is too close to call. Wendy Underhill has been involved in your elections, your country, and your way of life for a long time. She has worked for the US government since 1984, yet not much can be found online about her work history or personal life. Everyone at this conference stopped using Twitter, Facebook, and all online social media from 2015-2017 to today or wiped their information platforms. So that just makes me hungry for more.

Wendy Underhill has been controlling redistricting in Colorado. To show you how it works, let us look at Colorado's voting demographics. The population of Colorado is changing, and the demographics are changing. The reason you leave your homeland and come to the greatest country in the world will never change. The land of the free and the home of the brave! Redistricting allows certain people to stay in control. If we all believe that America is the greatest country globally and its people are the best, political parties should not matter.

If we love America and what it stands for, we all should believe the same way about our country. They need to control the vote outcome and push their way of life on you! The race riots, stealing up to $1000 without legal action, defunded police, or lack of, like a corrupt third world country. Add high inflation, poverty, more significant divides between the rich and the poor, and you create crime and hate.

A year before Covid began, the Democrat friends set up a way to use technology to hide votes, cause chaos during pandemic voting, and secure their victory before the battle even began. Why would voting technology be on your mind after the 2016 election with Russian collusion?[137] The fake Russian collusion should have sparked a major security conference and overhaul of our system. Voting laws should have gotten tougher; if we had fake Russian voters and hackers, stricter security measures should be implemented. We should have had conferences to buy secure machines, hire adequate security, hire anti-hackers like John MacAfee, who volunteered and offered when hearing of such a conference but was declined.[138] He was told no and was chased out of America over Tax Evasion. Then, he was found dead in a jail cell, killed just like another influential man who knew too much, Jeffery Epstein. What did she enact after the so-called 2016 flawed election? The "Motor Voter" system.[139] A system that made voter registration even easier for illegal immigrants, so much that even she admits fraud due to the motor voter program. The system failed, and a computer or human error turned mostly un-registered voters into legal US citizen status by accident.

NO person in America believes that when a country is attacked during elections, the following election cycle during a pandemic of all years should have fewer regulations. When a cow farm delivers milk, and thousands of people get sick from unclean utters before milking, causing babies, children, and the elderly to die, do you think the FDA lowers utter cleaning standards nationwide shortly after? No, they increase regulations. They improve health sanitation. Why would this be on the concerns of Obama/Biden during their last few months in office to set up a commission on voting after they leave the White House? Is Wendy a registered voter, what party, what flag does she salute, and what soldiers died for her freedom?

Maybe this conference should be held at Arlington cemetery. They can sit on the gravestones and do their meeting there. I mean, you might as well trample and spit on the graves of the soldiers that died so you can come to this country and live the way you do. Maybe seeing the death and funeral of a true American, then perhaps you can understand why this country is so great, and ask yourself, what are you doing. Publish an article on how you are changing voting in America. Call Fox news and be on the "Five" and bring maps that point to where you redistrict. Tell people what and why you went to this conference, at least be honest to America. Joe Biden and Barrack Obama hide behind you, and now you will be the face of voting corruption in America in 2022.

Redistricting has a new definition. Redistricting means redeveloping a new country to fit your demographics and crush anyone in your way. You did this, not me; you were the main presenter in a

Democrat government takeover of our election system with the help of Barrack, Lieberman, Biden, China, Russia, the Third Way, the media, and all who attended, presented, and knew about this Think Tank. Well, guess what, think again!

Co-Presenter

<u>Matthew Caulfield</u> THE THIRD WAY GROUP *(140)*

To understand Matthew, you must look at where he learned the truth about elections, the Wharton School, which even shames its Alumni. Matthew is a Jersey boy, growing up near farms in South Jersey. That part of Jersey has farms, beaches, hardworking Americans, and his area especially has seen an uptick in foreign population growth. So, getting the past behind him and finding a fresh start will do any Jersey boy good. He came from South Jersey to the Wharton School of Pennsylvania, the school where Warren Buffet grew to be a financial mastermind[141]. The school has had a lot of political alumni.

The great mayor Mike Nutter of Philadelphia, the Governor Phil Murphy of NJ, US Attorney Rod Rosenstein[142], and former Trump advisor Ivanka Trump. Many famous presidents from other countries walked the halls of Wharton, including the ex-president of Argentina, who was later charged with spying on submarine families, espionage, and illegal surveillance.[143] The CEO of one of the largest supermarkets graduated from here; he also inherited a 10-billion-dollar business and still makes fortunes on it today. Ironically, the same supermarket chain took Mike Lindell's pillows out of his 300+ stores for supporting a fellow Wharton Alumni, Trump, during 2020 and still today.[144] He was sent letters from customers asking why is he making a grocery store a political environment[145]. He even went as far as promoting mail-in ballots before the election.[146] Went as far as to send letters to Chief Justice Hecht and members of the Supreme Court of Texas, urging them to keep lockdowns during voting in 2020. Wow! An owner of a Super Market Chain who wants to keep Covid Mandates! How much is ground beef a pound right now in January 2022, $4.74lb on average? All the hate makes sense, and beef went up in price again in 2022! That makes good sense!

Another Alumni of Wharton was the only man in Major League baseball to believe and respect Pete Rose. He stood by his friend and even Inducted him into the Cincinnati Reds Hall of Fame himself. Shrugging off the haters, Tommy Lasorda was never thrown under the bus by fellow Alumni or The Wharton school elite. He was a suitable donor. Of course, the baseball field at Penn is named after him because of his generous gift. What do they teach, something so extreme that a blue-collar White boy from South Jersey would enroll in an elite school and come out having hate and dislike for a guy that is just like him?

Matthew Caulfield never checked on other Alumni; he never did articles and a Podcast on Apple.com with Politico about other past political alumni.[147] He never dug into election machines until after 2016. He never did a story in any media form about joining an Obama/Biden funded, elected, and appointed a committee on how to change elections with technology. Matthew Caulfield went to school for one thing and got a degree in dirty politics. The whole thing about everything that comes out of his mouth, his supporter's mouth, all has a distinct "twist" or, in other terms, not the truth at all.

The Wharton School has many famous names in the world today as alumni. Elon Musk, Donald Trump, and Dr. Oz are a few who get little respect. There are stories in numerous papers, web blogs, and even school emails downgrading their success at Wharton. Students like Matthew Caulfield do interviews about alumni, devaluing their educational success accomplishments and pointing out how they transferred from other lower-end universities before entering Wharton. It explains a lot, Elon Musk still donates a lot to the school, so they do not mess with the hand that feeds them. On the other hand, is it a straight-up fight? They have asked Dr. Oz to renounce his alma mater; they have mocked him on his articles about health and wellness.[148] Just like Mike Lindell, if you opened your mouth and showed support for Donald, you were in the cancel culture claws. They smeared him during Covid on the claims that Trump supported. In 2018 Trump nominated Dr. Oz as a slap in the face to the University. Maybe that is why Dr. Oz is running for Senate in Pennsylvania but lives in New Jersey. Then we have Donald Trump, maybe Wharton school's biggest name ever, the only US president from there and once major donor when the school needed it. It was like as soon as he ran for President, the school turned its back. They did not turn their backs when he donated money in 1984 and again in '87, '90, but in '91, the relationship soured.

That year four Alumnae's Plaques were stolen from a Hall on campus.[149] No one was formally charged, and Trump's plaque was the only one that was never replaced. All were stolen, but only three went back up. The Dean at the time, Thomas Gerrity, never accused anyone, and just like that, the Wharton School of Business no longer respected Trump. The narrative of Trump at the Wharton school of business is still the same today. He never worked hard; he transferred from another institution, and his father gave him two million dollars; he never worked hard for anything. You know the story money grows on trees, and everything was served on a silver spoon.

Matthew Caulfield joined a political think tank group called the "THIRD WAY," also known as Clinton Democrats or Centrist Democrats. But mainly, it was a CENTER LEFT DEMOCRAT group that was started in 2005. The founders were John McCain and Joe Lieberman[150]. When they started the group, it was to tackle gun laws after James Brady was shot and paralyzed, saving President Reagan. Joe Lieberman lost the 2000 and 2004 elections with running mate Al Gore.[151] They became the laughing stocks of politics, Al Gore for his climate change fear tactics and Joe Lieberman for being too Conservative for some Democrats.

They combined the Gun Control Group started by McCain and Lieberman (Americans for Gun Safety) with this election think tank and began the US THIRD WAY.[152] The new founders are all Democrat-appointed! The Third Way was campaigning for Barrack Obama; he used the Third Way to lobby and manipulate the elections from race games, poverty lies, and false acquisitions. After watching eight years of Reagan, then Bush Sr., they saw what a Republican could do for this country.[153] During Trump's presidency, he faced impeachments, pandemic viruses, corruption, lawlessness, and worst of all, another racial and political civil war! Is this what a think tank does? What did they think up for 2020 during the election? After reading Matthew's Politico article about Trump and the elections in 2020, I now understand what they stand for.[154] Let me take a shot: manipulation, Race riots, Antifa riots, calls of Defunding the Police, College, and University brainwashing, and worst of all, allowing foreign money to buy out America. The group started after the 2004 election. The Third Way was financially, publicly, and politically supported by such politicians as Bill and Hillary Clinton, Joe Lieberman, and late Senator John McCain. All non-supporters of Donald Trump. After the 2004 election and the loss of Al Gore to George Bush Jr., the think tank was born. After Hillary Clinton's loss to Trump and after being promised eight years earlier by Barrack and Biden that she was next[155], the hunt for RED Trump started way before October.

The think tank has been sitting outside voting polls for years, taking pre- and post-ballot votes from voters.[156] The THIRD WAY is good at brainwashing intelligent young students, just like Matthew Caulfield. They made political news by repealing the work of past presidents and politicians and renaming them but keeping the bill the same. Classic politician playbook moves from Obama, now done nonstop by Biden. Joe Biden halted the wall on the border with Mexico, magnifying the female health, drug, and crime crisis in South America. He stopped the pipeline and energy independence by crushing that job sector and costing us much more on a gallon of gas, and now we buy more dirty unrefined foreign oil than ever. Dependent on OPEC![157]

We secure a terrorist region with 2500 men and keep them in the hills, away from innocent people. We remove our armed forces, and they take over an American Air Base! The Taliban now own half a country $800 million worth of weapons and a $5 billion Air Base.[158] This is not a playbook for success but an immature pissing game in the wind. The "No Child Left Behind Act" was renamed by the left. The same program was just renamed and called "Every Student Succeeds Act" by Obama and supported by the Third Way.[159]

These Third Ways founders consist of people, like a Senior Advisor to Andrew Cuomo. Johnathan Cowan worked for Andrew Cuomo and has openly shown support for Joe Biden.[160] He has even said things like, "Look at his career (Gov. Cuomo), look at his work in New York." "He is laying out a model for what it means to be a 21st-century Democrat. Our party is in a deep hole. You have to look around and say, "Who is succeeding? Who is doing it differently?" that is an actual quote from a Third Way co-founder, Johnathan Cowan.[161]

We all know how the ex-governor feels about Donald Trump! Another co-founder is Jim Kessler. He was a Legislator and Policy Maker for Senator Chuck Schumer.[162] Chuck Schumer has shown his dislike of the ex-president almost daily during his four years.[163] Jim Kessler helped Senator Schumer with his book. He has helped him during the mock impeachment trials, pretending to have evidence and keeping America informed on how wrong Trump was.[164] Another co-founder, Nancy Hale, has done interviews and news articles about Trump and his "voters," calling the group "safari-like." [165]

You cannot have a think tank without a Clinton-era relic. As Deputy Assistant to the President for Intergovernmental Affairs for President Clinton, Matt Bennett is another Third Way co-founder. This one stands out; he worked for Clinton/Gore and served in Al Gore's office during his tenure as vice president. He also served during Al Gore and Joe Lieberman's two failed attempts at the White House.

He is also a Tweeter, tweeting on January 22, 2022, his opinion on Aaron Rodgers and the unvaccinated! All of the founders of a Bi-Partisan Think Tank Mission Statement say to "Help the Middle-Class Succeed" (I swear that is what it says on their website).

Somehow, they have become a political juggernaut. They all have worked for Democrat Politicians that openly and publicly show their dislike and hate for Donald Trump. They ran the Democratic 2016 election, and after the loss, they swore to be back in 2018 and 2020. In an interview in December 2020, one founder told Politico that he has no fear of a Biden losing middle America. All the think tank founders are not Trump fans, and Trump loves America!

No wonder Matthew Caulfield would go on to college, go from one direction, and now be the voice for a lost generation. This is not politics; this is years of planning a scheme. This propaganda think tank only thinks of one thought to settle the score of a political loss in 2004. Since the Al Gore defeat, the Third Way has set in motion a plan never to lose an election again. Media propaganda, College misinformation, and agreeing to unleash a virus on Americans to kill off the elderly, mainly conservative wealthy voters, the greatest generation had to fight one more war! If they can influence the young by changing history books, replacing the narrative to Republicans being the Black slave owners and still racist to this day[166], they can swing the votes their way.[167] After two failed impeachments, a covid virus pandemic, racial riots, debunking crime, defunding the police, unprotected borders, and mass hysteria on everything the Left media puts out.

The Third Way had one more way to win; the Third Way was in their name. The first way is being a great American politician, which is not happening. The second way is by using your opponent's weakness against them, which did not work; Trump was elected by a landslide, listened to the voters, and kept his promises. Which only left them the third way, which was to CHEAT!

The article in Politico on 6/25/2021 shows how Matthew Caulfield felt and eventually searched far and wide to find anything on the Voting Machines that his fellow Alumni Trump swore had malfunctioned. He would find out what a voting machine does, the cost, what it looks like, and even how it processes. He was going to investigate and figure out what the "Big Lie" is all about. So, America, Politico readers, University of Pennsylvania and Wharton students, Alumni, and America can finally rest. Trust Him; he is a member of the Third Way!! He swore in the article that the machines are better than when Bush Jr. won and are better than when Trump won.

Since before the 2004 Al Gore loss, the United States Government has had an agency that monitors and verifies all voting machines. Then how, what, wait, who? In the article, he said that no one could cheat in 2020 or any election since 2000. Since 2000 the US government has set up a law requiring almost all fifty states to get a certificate. This certificate costs a lot of money, coming from a particular US agency. The certification allows counties and cities to purchase these voting machines. Can only a certified voting machine be used in the United States?[168]

So, this group, the EAC (Elections Assistance Commission), was set up, and every election would be monitored and certified before any ballot is ever counted. Now I feel better! Is every voting machine certified by our US government agency? No! If you look at the map on this website, you will see that many states use uncertified voting machines.[169] Alright, calm down, how serious is it? Then who works at the EAC with Matthew Caulfield, his friend who worked with Obama and testified about Trump and disinformation, Matthew Masterson. Then four Democrat elected officials were appointed by Obama/Biden presidency to oversee verifying all voting machines.[170] Then Matthew Caulfield had to know about voting machines before the Politico interview; he worked with Masterson well before they decided to put on this conference, while Obama was still President.

This conference was put on by Obama/Biden appointed officials to work within their Third Way think tank on how finally to secure an election against a sure winner Donald Trump. This has nothing to do with the good of the middle, the lower, or any class except for the elite class. Making people think their votes count or do not count only starts riots like January 6th. Cheating the people only starts conspiracies, starts anger, and starts revolutions.

The prior "big Lie" was the Civil War. The Civil War was not about freeing slaves. It was about not paying people and making more money to do less work. In the North, you got paid as an employee; in the South, you had slaves. Would we allow the South to keep slaves and have more states with more slave power under Democrat rule when we expanded West?[171] On the other hand, the Republicans wanted to free the Slaves in the South through a war. Let the US worker make fair pay each day and expand out West as a Nation, not a conflict.

That is still the underlying problem today. Power, greed, and money rule the Political heart and core. The "big Lie' is revealed as the Democrats will kill Americans and do whatever is necessary to stay in power and have control—fighting the Republicans with pen and guns, keeping slaves, and killing fellow Americans during the Civil War. Now is just the same, fighting Republicans any way they can, killing fellow Americans by allowing a virus to enter our country, and now we are all slaves to mandates, lockdowns, and control over our lives. A think tank technology conference to control voting machines, mail-in ballots, foreign overseas voters, or so-called voters, and just in case, we still have the Third Way!

Matthew knew about voting machines long before his great interview in Politico in 2021. He was working on them with Obama-appointed Election Officials in 2017 after Trump's victory. So, when you go to college and pay money to go into student debt, guys like Matthew pretend to understand and be honest. He is not lying to me; I do not read Politico; he is lying to his peers, his fellow students in debt, his misinformed undergraduates, and whomever else believes him. The "Big Lie" is that you have been told people are monitoring, certifying, and making sure the election is legitimate. The man investigating if someone cheated on the 2020 election already knows the answer.

Caulfield, Masterson, Coppersmith, the entire conference works with and for the EAC (Elections Assistance Commission). The corruption, the fraud, and the lies that Al Gore, Joe Lieberman, Hillary Clinton, and even Donald Trump have cried about in the past, are here again. The elections that make people scratch their heads are because of think tanks like this. We do not need a think tank that encourages, supports, and pushes Americans to divide. Elections were the last thing that separated us from Communism, Socialism, and Corrupt Governments. Who will be remembered as the party of Civil Wars, division, Slavery, and Corruption? American inner cities and suburbs like Oxford, Michigan all now see what Far Left Think Tanks Do; they Kill Innocent Americans.[172]

Matthew says after the Bush/Gore fiasco, he knew he must defend Democracy. So, at 11 years old, Matthew Caulfield was interested in politics and had such a bad taste in his mouth he knew someday he would defend Democracy? Why would he try to change Americans Votes and how they should think about voting?

Matthew, here is a quick lesson; voters should pay taxes, and taxes are what voters vote on, so their tax money is spent correctly and for the best of the country. Why should you say what politicians do with tax money if you do not pay taxes? That is the money that runs this country. The road you drove to school every day while on the bus was paid for by taxes. Each summer, the boardwalk that made money for your town was built from tax money. You should only care about voting to know what your tax money (now 30% of what you make by working) is being spent on. It is being spent on partisan think tanks, not stuff people need!

The Third Way is another way a politician can hide from the truth. If you want to follow a great Politician, then follow one, do not let them hide behind fake think tanks; hide behind fake voting campaigns and hide behind the students of America. If the Think Tank makes a wrong decision, who is thinking for the President?

Wharton is more expensive now than when Matthew started school. The price of everything is going up, crime is outrageous, and the American people are at each other's throats. Is this what they were thinking of at their conference, at their Third Way meetings, and behind closed doors when they decided, they all decided to take this road. The road no American knows until now.

The Third way and any think tank political group are all just Lobbyists like the NRA.[173] The NRA fights for gun rights, and the Third Way fights for Democrat talking points rights. Their website shows you where their political interests lie, what they are thinking of, and what part of America they are tanking! The Think Tanks are Tanking America one brain at a time.

Co-Presenter

Christi Zamarripa

Why? Why would someone be so angry at people they do not even know. People have supported immigration before 2022; it allowed them to flourish in this country. Why are we now the bigot idiots? Christi has been busy holding redistricting conferences.[174] When your children could not go to school, you could only work from home; the good folks at redistricting were hard at work.[175] Why? To secure fresh voters.[176] Christi and Wendy Underhill set up conferences during a pandemic about redistricting. More than 450 people attended the Salt Lake City National Conference of State Legislatures (NCSL), held July 14-16, 2021. The one held between October 24-27 had a guest speaker named D'Vera Cohn. D'Vera Cohn works for the Pew Research group; the Pew research group says that they do not take policy positions on the front page of their website.[177]

D'Vera Cohn has a PowerPoint that talks about the changing America, a shift in demographics! Shifts in the nation's population drive redistricting, or so they say. D'Vera Cohn is an expert on how America has (and will) change, demographically speaking. Look at the PowerPoint that Christi Zamarripa used at one of her conferences.[178] A think tank that shows the demographics of America. This PowerPoint was made by a Pew Research editor and Washington Post contributor D'Vera Cohn. She has done multiple articles in the news saying Trump is anti-immigration.[179] In another article, she is quoted in numerous articles that portray Trump as an anti-immigrant.[180] She writes about Trump's hate in media outlets like the website of Pew Research and writes and does interviews for MSNBC, CNN, Washington Post, and other Left-wing think tanks. She is featured and outlines how Trump hates immigrants and has "Mexican Phobia" on a Mexican-based news website called SCIELO.[181]

So, this shows how a non-partisan, non-bias think tank for Americans feels about Trump's hate? Think again, America! The articles she writes and the PowerPoint alone show how she feels about the Republican President, Donald Trump. They want to take what is yours. We are the lazy Americans in the way. We do not work, get vaccinated, or belong in our own country. Why, because she said so! Barrack and Joe hire anti-Trump policymakers to tear us down city by city and family by family.

The PowerPoint will show you the playbook of the Democrats on why they need and want foreign people to come illegally to America. The PowerPoint is on who we need to replace, dying off populations, and what foreign countries have the most extra people America will take.

The Democrat party could use Christi Zamarripa's skills and her legal law degree to better the country, its people, and the world by doing remarkable things and acts of kindness. Like young girls being raped every day by criminals! There were an estimated 139,815 rapes reported to law enforcement in 2019.[182]

Instead, they will manipulate the American people out of everything to win. No respect for what made this country so appealing that millions leave their homes each year to come here, not only bash the people who let her family in but destroy it. The Democrat party of old White men slave owners is now the party of Asians, Mexicans, and Angry White anti- Americans. Wow, nobody saw that coming from the Democrats. The party in the 1800s was enslaving Black people and Asians and was stealing land from the Native Americans to keep their wealth and power.

The Democrat party has worn thin their opinion with regular Americans that believe in their country. They have no credibility anymore with the American voter. They will only win by disinformation to untaxed youth that will learn about their country through race hate and CRT learning. They have lost the Military, they have lost the true Christians (not a Joe Biden part-time Catholic), they have lost the educated blue-collar worker and now need to open the doors of our country to find a vote. They can only be elected by putting a foreign-born politician against America's racial past, which the Democrat party started. They do not want a better life from droughts, poverty, and drug cartels; they just want to take MY life. It is plagiarism, of my people. Barrack Obama and Joe Biden said while in office that "you did not create that; it was done before you." My country feels what they are saying now. We made the greatest country in the world. Now we are being bought out by foreign hate, foreign money, and foreign greed. Our land plagiarized, our jobs plagiarized, our schools plagiarized, and our way of life taken from us. Why? Because I Love My Country!

The PowerPoint is disgusting because instead of worrying about foreign people replacing Americans like an elected official of America would, it shows how and encourages it. She is now working on the US census of 2020, pushing the White House to keep all data from individuals and households confidential.[183] She is saying that the US Census of America is violating the rights of people; even non-Americans have rights in America. She calls it "differential privacy," kind of like when your medical records are taken and shared with another doctor. So, she says that we can still do a US Census, but the data results cannot be shown to anyone under a person's rights and privileges.

So, let us not even do it, or better yet, let us not even care. America is now a free place to live, do not pay taxes and steal from people as long as it is under one thousand dollars. Criminals are being let out to commit more crimes. The Wisconsin Christmas murderer,[184] the guy who stabbed the girl in LA, California![185] Now the latest incident involving a six-month-old baby, killed in a drive-by![186] The criminals I just showed you are the same criminals that are shipping Illegals over the border for money and drugs. I am doing justice for America by reporting her to the American people under the US Census Citizen's Awareness board. Become a member today!

Co-Presenter

Andrew Coppersmith THE THIRD WAY GROUP

Andrew Coppersmith is also involved with the Third Way. He spent all summer with Matthew Caulfield, finding out the "Business of Voting".[187] He sat as the Wharton School Public Policy Initiative header. Matthew Caulfield and Andrew Coppersmith contacted every voting machine procurement officer in the United States for each state. A procurement officer or procurement director is the person who purchases, buys, and stocks such places as hospitals, schools, and townships.

A county has a procurement officer, a University like Texas has about ten procurement officers. They were part of a team picked by the Zhang Jindong Professor of Operations, Information and Decisions at the University of Pennsylvania, Wharton School Lorin M. Hitt. He asked six students in 2016 to find out everything about voting machines used in America during Trump's victory. WHY? In the letter, they ask the voting machine procurement officers the costs of the devices, when they were purchased, the data that comes with machines, and if he could have any public records or contracts with your procurement purchase of the voting machines.

Now, remember he works with Matthew Masterson, the ex-Elections Assistance Commission director; Matthew certifies all the voting machines used in the country. He works with Third Way members anti-Trump activists and is a left-wing Democrat seeking information and, in some cases, legal action to get a response from counties in America. Why would the University of Pennsylvania need to know what voting machines the countries use? Primarily set up by a foreign teacher! To help, The Penn Biden Center for Diplomacy and Global Engagement at the University of Pennsylvania opened at The Wharton School on February 8, 2018.

In 2018, before Afghanistan, the border crisis, and even before the pandemic, The Biden Center had a Refugee relocation program. Yes, I am not lying. The Refugee Admissions Project is to help people that suffered over the last decade with persistent armed conflicts, pervasive violence, and the erosion of international norms. The protection of civilians has contributed to an enduring refugee crisis on nearly every continent. All the problems he started back up in his first year in office!

The Penn Biden Center for Diplomacy and Global Engagement and the National Conference on Citizenship has launched a joint project to strengthen US global leadership in refugee protection.[188] They planned for the chaos in Afghanistan; they helped get 13 US soldiers killed by making a made-up crisis. The border is open because of The Biden Center from the Wharton School of Pennsylvania. They feed disinformation, and Biden can hold courses on Global engagement.

The Biden Center works with Matthew Masterson and the EAC, so they know who not to certify, and then they will be forced to use Unisyn, Sequoia, or Dominion voting machines. Now, remember only a particular group of states use the EAC certification system. States that do not use it are California, New Mexico, Vermont, Massachusetts, Connecticut, Rhode Island, New Hampshire, almost all of Nevada and New York. So that means they do not need the US EAC to write off and certify their voting machines! That does not sound fair. All states should follow the same laws. If one state has to have verified voting machines, they all need to be certified.

This letter to all procurement officers was sent out in 2016, they asked county clerks, and people sent back information about the costs spent, contract dates, renewal dates, and whatever they needed. I thought Russia helped Trump win, remember Google, Facebook, Twitter, and Amazon told us. Oh yes, the three biggest Cooperate Sponsors for The Third Way in America are Facebook, Google, and Amazon.[189] They stepped up their secretive influence campaigning in 2019. Spending millions extra than usual to help sell the "Lie," the "Collusion Lie," the "Russia Hoax," The "Racist Encouragement," whatever they could do to manipulate and send disinformation out to the public. As media groups banned Trump but allowed ISIS to show beheadings.[190]

They handed over the findings to the Biden Center and the co-presenter of this conference, Matthew Masterson. Full Circle! He and co-author Matthew Caulfield fed the disinformation and propaganda research to the students of Penn. They just flipped the script on voting companies, changing the requirements, and closing the market down to a few certified voting machine companies. They were verified by Andrew Coppersmith's friends from the EAC and the Third Way. In the Politico article done 6/25/2021, Andrew Coppersmith also says they worked day and night for months getting to the bottom of the 2020 "big Lie"! Every letter that they sent out to procurement officers was for what? The Wharton School has its name on every letter sent out. The article and his friends are misleading you, or in America, we call it lying. Why because you are a dumb kid on his phone, head in the clouds, underlining unaware racist in hiding, and you are also anti-American.

In the Politico article, Matthew and Andrew could have crushed the "Big Lie"; they could have been the big Men on Campus. They could have been the Louis and Cark of our generation. Instead, they took the low road and followed the dirty path of Democrat disinformation. Do not tell me in an article in 2021 that you are looking into voting in America when in 2017 you were at a Voting Conference to change votes! Andrew Coppersmith is a Wharton School of Pennsylvania director. He was the Managing Director of the Wharton Public Policy Initiative until the program came to a halt, and he was let go by the University. The program would be phased out due to a lack of funding and support. So, where does he go from there? What did he do after the Wharton school let him go?

Co-Presenter

Matthew Masterson *was nominated by President Barack H. Obama and confirmed by unanimous consent of the United States Senate on Dec. 16, 2014, to serve on the US Election Assistance Commission (EAC). Before his appointment with EAC, Masterson served as Interim Chief of Staff for the Ohio Secretary of State, which he held since November 2014. He previously served as Deputy Chief of Staff and Chief Information Officer from 2013 to 2014 and Deputy Director of Elections from 2011 to 2013. In these roles, Mr. Masterson was responsible for voting system certification efforts by the Secretary of State's office, including being the liaison to the Ohio Board of Voting Machine Examiners. Additionally, Masterson was in charge of Ohio's effort to develop an online voter registration* *database and online ballot delivery for military and overseas voters. He is widely regarded as an expert on elections administration throughout Ohio and the country.*

Before joining the Ohio Secretary of State's Office,

Masterson held multiple roles at the Election Assistance Commission from 2006 to 2011. Masterson was admitted to

practice law in Ohio in November of 2006. Masterson graduated from The University of Dayton School

of Law in May 2006. Before law school, Masterson received BS and BA degrees from Miami University in Oxford, OH.

Andrew Coopersmith serves as Managing Director of the Penn Wharton Public Policy Initiative, a hub for research and education headquartered on the University of Pennsylvania campus that focuses on issues at the intersection of business, economics, and public policy. He earned his bachelor's degree in Economics from Georgetown University and his Ph.D. in History from Harvard University.

After leaving the EAC, he said on file, "that it will take years to undo the disinformation"! So, the fake Russian Hoax by Hillary, the phone taping from Barrack Obama, and the fake racial lies and hate from Joe Biden and the Democrat media will take years to get over. Guess again, we are over it. Remember the 2022 voting cycle? I do![191] All the fake hoaxes they have started about Trump are disinformation! Former House Speaker John Boehner, a fellow Ohioan, was the one to pick Masterson in 2013. Then Matthew was appointed by Barrack Obama in 2015 to head the US EAC. He worked with the Wharton School and worked with students from the University of Pennsylvania on new voting machine systems. Their devious work did not pay off. Their values were not bipartisan because the election of 2020 is still contested today.[192]

I have spent the last year digging up names, dates, files, cold calls to people I do not know, and traveled the country over the previous 18 months investigating a failing government. In Las Vegas, you can buy weed paraphernalia, vote in US elections, use the US Post Office, and buy soda and chips all in the same voting center.

The problem with our elections is not the voting part nor the outcome. Everybody loves Tom Brady, and you are ok with it when he loses fair and square. If Brady is cheated, you want Blood! We want a fair election. Appointed officials from a hate-driven political party would make anyone question the election. Like the Democrats questioned 2000, 2004, and now the 2016 election.[193] If computers are supposed to make our life easier, and every business in the world uses computers to streamline and perfect their business. The Democrat party of America has used technology as a crutch and an excuse. No other business in the world gets a computer and says this is hurting us.

This is the work of Barrack Obama and Joe Biden to ruin America and take foreign money to lower the standard of America. To knock us down a peg because we are Deplorables and Americans![194] When they lose the vote to redo election integrity in 2022. They will use a new Covid variant as their following reason to secure a win in 2022. The variants will not go away, more mandates, school closures, then we must vote by mail again.

Matthew worked for the Trump impeachment whistleblower, Christopher Krebs, the one that was feeding misinformation to the press. So, when Matthew Masterson goes in front of Congress and pleads it will take years to undo misinformation, maybe he and his former bosses should listen too. Everyone on Christopher Krebs Twitter account still bad-talks Trump to this day! Christopher Krebs was fired days before Trump left office; Trump was his former boss.[195] This is where the Russia collusion came from as well. The whistleblower was giving misinformation and was working with the Obama/Biden team to spy on Trump while in office. These are the actual pushers of disinformation.

The "Big Lie" made Donald Trump a crazy, red-faced Russian spy who won the election.[196] He is supposedly an Epstein Colleague, Lying Ukraine Calling President, Cheating Husband (Stormy Daniels), Tax

Dodging (pays Millions),[197] Anti-Female Hillary hater (Trump donated 10million dollars when she ran against Socialist Barrack Obama and Joe Biden).[198] Trump is an Anti-Immigrant Racist person (every time Trump builds a casino, and the state of New Jersey makes him build thousands of HUD homes for poor and homeless people of color, and Trump employs more people of color than any politician in America). Plus, who do you think works there?[199] They paint him as a phony who never made, built, or even had a good thought. I guess Donald Trump is just like his voters, deplorable people who are not that bright! But, bright enough to write this book!

Thursday, June 15, 2017

Election Security: The What States Can Do

MODERATOR:

Adam Ambrogi* *is the director of the Elections Program at the Democracy Fund, a bipartisan foundation working to ensure that our political system can withstand new challenges and deliver on its promise to the American people. Focusing on modern elections and the role of money in politics, Adam leads the Democracy Fund's mission to invest in organizations working to ensure that the views and votes of citizens come first in our Democracy. Adam previously worked as Chief Counsel for the US Senate Committee on Rules and Administration, addressing a wide range of issues related to election law, campaign finance, and legal matters facing the administration of the Senate. He received his law degree from the University of Texas-Austin, where he served as the Editor-in-Chief of the Texas Journal on Civil Liberties and Civil Rights. In addition, Adam received his Bachelor of Arts in Government with high distinction from the University of Virginia.*

He has served on the Washington Council of Lawyers board and has worked with other public services.

Adam previously worked as Chief Counsel for the US Senate Committee on Rules and Administration, addressing a wide range of issues related to election law, campaign finance, rules of the Senate, and legal/ethical matters facing the administration of the Senate.[200] Why, what was broken? Adam was the lead staffer for the Rules Committee on passage of the Military and Overseas Voter Empowerment Act, the DISCLOSE Act of 2012, [201] and led the committee's legal team in examining and making changes to the Senate Rules[202] related to the filibuster, back in 2010.[203] He served several different Senate Chairs and Ranking Members over his time on investigations and oversight, with committee hearings and public engagement around elections and voting. In 2010, Adam tried to end the filibuster during Barrack Obama and Joe Biden's term. Barrack Obama started the fight, then dips out! Why would the playbook of 2022 be any different?[204] Joe Biden has the most challenging Democrat president job ever! He must finally do what every single Democrat caucus wants. The Socialist, the Black Caucus, the Communist caucus, and even the far-left liberal caucus. Good Luck, Joe!

PRESENTERS:

Denise W. Merrill* *was elected to her second term as Connecticut's 73rd Secretary of the State on Nov. 4, 2014. As Connecticut's chief elections official and business registrar, Merrill has focused on modernizing Connecticut's elections and business services and improving access to public records. Merrill is concentrated in both civic engagement and fostering business enterprise. Since taking office, she has supported and expanded Democratic participation, ensuring that every citizen's rights and privileges are protected, and every vote is counted accurately. Merrill has extended voter participation through Election Day and online voter registration.*

She has also improved Connecticut's Democratic accountability and integrity with a series of rapid response processes to Election Day problems. She was elected president of the National Association

of Secretaries of State for the 2016-17 term and served on the Board of Advisors to the US Election Assistance Commission. Before she was elected Secretary of State, she served as State Representative from the 54th General Assembly District for 17 years, representing the towns of Mansfield and Chaplin. Merrill is a graduate of The University of Connecticut, licensed to practice law in California, and is a classically trained pianist. She lives in Hartford.

She works with the US EAC group; they are the ones who certify all the voting machines. Matthew Masterson's old co-workers! So, if Merrill is an upstanding and honorable person, she will sit down with any Newsgroup and tell them what happened at this meeting when this book comes out. Was any real government work even going on at all? It seems we have more suggestions of conspiracy, corruption, hacking over our elections every voting cycle.[205] If voting is causing so much pain, hate, and anger, what is this committee doing? Actions like January 6th will become routine if we cannot trust our election system! She had every right to write a letter on January 5, 2022, and tell her feelings on the anniversary of January 6th, 2021.[206] She sits on the Board of Advisors to LET AMERICA VOTE,[207] it was started under Barrack Obama in 2017 to stop the Trump administration from voter suppression. Every politician has questioned the legitimacy of our voting laws and system, even Barrack still today![208] Did Trump not get the second and third most votes in American history? Voter suppression is happening on both sides. Every time someone questions the election that is suppression. They will allow you to vote, but do they suppress your cast ballot? Does every state follow the same election laws set by the US EAC? Does Connecticut follow the strict election laws under the US EAC? Is the answer No?

Her family includes her husband, **Dr. Stephen Leach***, his two sons, her three grown children, and five grandchildren.*

Dr. Stephen Leach writes articles for left-wing media propaganda groups. Keep it all in the family.

Edgardo Cortés* *has worked in elections for over a decade, with experience in all facets of the electoral process: including campaigns, nonpartisan voter registration, federal and state election policy, and local and state election administration. As the first Virginia Commissioner of Elections, Cortés spearheaded the Commonwealth's modernization of voter registration and election administration. Cortés currently serves as the Chairman of the Board for the Electronic Registration Information Center (ERIC) and Chairman of the US Election Assistance Commission Standards Board. Cortés previously served as General Registrar in Fairfax County, VA, and Deputy Director for Policy and Grants Director at the US Election Assistance Commission. He also directed Congressional field campaigns, a national, nonpartisan voter registration program, and led efforts to implement automatic restoration of voting rights for individuals with prior felony convictions in Virginia. Cortés holds a bachelor's degree from Cornell University and a master's degree in political management from George Washington University. He lives in Springfield, Va., with his wife and son.*

Edgardo Cortés was the first Election Commissioner of Virginia.[209] As the first Virginia Commissioner of Elections, Cortés spearheaded voter registration and election administration modernization efforts in the Commonwealth. He is also another Barrack Obama appointee who holds conferences with the Elections Assistance Commission employees. He was fit to do this conference and the 2020 election, but in 2016 was replaced due to nonpartisan politics by a Democrat Governor![210] When let go, he was not upset; he even said," he is not sure yet what my next adventure will be." His next adventure was being an Advisor for Election Security with the

Brennan Center for Justice at NYU School of Law. The Brennan Center swore in 2016 that there was Russian Collusion in our elections. They even went as far as to propose legislation to fund much-needed updates to our election infrastructure. They offer to spend taxpayers' dollars, or we could just use an ID! Show your license and vote, no groups, think tanks, conspiracy, and legislation funding. He advises who, the uneducated and misled voter? When will these people be brought to justice? It is called the "anti-Stark Law," monopolizing the voting system in America. He verifies voting machines for his state, works with the voting machine companies, and is paid by taxpayers to secure them and uphold the Constitution.[211] Can someone just do their job, right!

Geoffrey Hale *is an Information Security Strategist at the Enterprise Performance and Management Office (EPMO) in the National Protection and Programs Directorate's (NPPD) Office of Cybersecurity & Communications (CS&C). Hale supports CS&C efforts in strategy and policy, legislative affairs, performance management, and international engagement in this role. Previously, Hale managed the One DHS Emergency Communications Committee. He promoted intradepartmental planning and strategy for the department's operational communications equities in this position. Before working with DHS, Hale served as an associate for Nahigian Strategies, LLC. In this capacity, he supported the planning and implementation of political and media campaigns. Hale graduated from the University of Virginia in 2007 and completed a master's degree in Systems Engineering from George Washington University in 2014.*

Geoffrey Hale worked for Nahigian Strategies, a full-service strategic communications and public relations firm located in the heart of Washington, DC.!

Since Barrack Obama's appointment, Geoffrey Hale has led the Cybersecurity and Infrastructure Security Agency (CISA). Hale has been a critical part of CISA's election security mission since it began in 2016.[212] Began in 2016? This is where Matthew Masterson ran before working with Stanford University. So, when you elect a politically immature politician to power, these are the people you get in charge of significant Government associations. Since he took over the CISA, the US government has been hacked and tampered with numerous times.[213] Since Biden took office, we have had multiple attacks on our country. From gas lines to now our elections, and now election computers are being hacked! How secure is a computer? The computer works on the binary system of counting ones and twos. It counts either one or two and goes from there, the basis of all computing.[214] An election for the president of the United States is between two people. You either pick one or two, and you count the results, and bam, we have a winner. So, you are telling me a computer that mines a bitcoin and uses more energy than a small city in Mexico to do so, but it cannot figure out a vote.[215] The computer that launches, separates, and lands two pieces of the Bezos Blue Origin cannot count one or two and be done by midnight that day. So, the computer that does surgery through robotic hands and sensors cannot add either a one or a two. I think a computer that controls the banking system, the internet, and monitors heart machines can count either one or two.

Barrack Obama set up the CISA to spy on Trump's campaign and interrupt and misinform the future of elections. The actions of people like the attendees to this conference show Americans that we need fewer election days. The president should be on a particular day and have a separate ballot. Then the vice president and Senate should be on a different day. Stop blaming a computer when you are the head of cyber something. I spent my whole life working with computers, going to school for networking, and using them in everyday life. It is always a "user error." The computer does not make mistakes; it just gets hacked or programmed to cheat. It is like a chef blaming his pans. It is like a barber blaming his scissors. It is like a parent blaming their kids. It is like a political party blaming a whole group of people.[216]

Ron Bandes* *is the cyber security member of the Pennsylvania Legislature's Committee on Voting System Technology. He participates in the National Institute of Standards and Technology's (NIST) Voluntary Voting System Guidelines (VVSG) Cybersecurity public working group. He is a member of several election integrity organizations, including the Election Verification Network. Bandes has contributed to the election-law review committee for the League of Women Voters and helped design a remote ballot-marking system for the National Federation of the Blind. He presents on election integrity and is a Judge of Elections in Allegheny County (home of Pittsburgh), Pennsylvania. Bandes makes a living as a network security analyst.*

Ron Bandes is 67 years old, lives in CT, and is a registered Democrat. He is still mad that Al Gore lost and made sure that Alleghany County would have new voting machines. He is from Connecticut, and Alleghany County is in Pennsylvania! That is a far commute. Do the people of Pennsylvania know an outsider decided their election machines? I guess no one cares in PA? He worked for Gore and Lieberman![217] Bandes testified that Alleghany needed new voting machines, and the cost to replace the voting machines was between $10 and $22 million. He was paid by Pennsylvania taxpayers, not people from Connecticut! Ron also testified that it would cost hundreds of thousands of dollars to maintain each year. His team of Democrat loyalists was so worried about cheating he was one of many who signed a letter to Congress after Trump's victory.[218] Asking them to secure the vote! The Alleghany Board of Elections had tens of thousands of registrations of deceased voters, people who moved away, or have not voted in several years, which voted in the 2020 election.[219] All the technology conferences, Wharton School of Business back-room meetings, cybersecurity, and spying on the future president, well, it worked. The Biden Center pushed their public policy initiative on every voter. Ron Bandes does not live in Pittsburgh, Alleghany County, or even Pennsylvania; he lives in Connecticut. Way to go, bipartisan think tanks; you made Steel County a Flimsy JOkE.

Using Elections Technology to Make Better Decisions

MODERATOR:

Rebecca Green* *is Professor of the Practice of Law and Co-Director of the Election Law Program, a joint project between the law school and the National Center for State Courts. In that role, Green oversees its annual symposia and speaker series and undertakes a series of projects designed to educate judges about election law topics. With generous funding from the Democracy Fund, Green has recently begun work on a series of state election law eBenchbooks. Green's research interests focus on the intersection of privacy law and elections, most recently on the topic of election transparency. She has also explored the use of alternative dispute resolution in election processes. Before law school, Green earned a master's degree in Chinese legal history from Harvard University and assisted with U.S.-China trade negotiations at the US Trade Representative in Washington, DC, during the Clinton Administration.*

Rebecca Green is a Professor of the Practice of Law.[220] Including producing a webinar series for judges in advance of the 2020 election. She set up the Election War Games, which offered state judicial conferences in Virginia, Colorado, and Wisconsin.[221] She also helped with the US and China trade talks during the Clinton era. So, while the United States and the world's children were damaged during a worldwide pandemic, the people on her webinar played "Election Games"! She focuses on the intersection of privacy law and elections, election transparency, candidate privacy, and redistricting transparency. She believes in using alternative resolutions to the election processes in the United States. Redistricting is the same as ballot harvesting, and both should be crimes.

PRESENTER:

Charles Stewart III* *is the Kenan Sahin Distinguished Professor of Political Science at MIT, where he has taught since 1985, and a Fellow of the American Academy of Arts and Sciences. His research and teaching areas include congressional politics, elections, and American political development. Since 2001, Stewart has been a Caltech/MIT Voting Technology Project member. This leading research effort applies scientific analysis to election technology, election administration, and election reform questions. He is currently the MIT director of the project. Working with the Pew Charitable Trusts, he helped develop Pew's Elections Performance Index. Stewart also provided advice to the Presidential Commission on Election Administration. He received his BA in Political Science from Emory University and SM and Ph.D. from Stanford University.*

Charles Stewart III is another super-smart man that lives and breathes America's freedom. An intelligent person could change the world in hunger, childhood cancer, pandemic virus research, and stopping drug addictions. He could help millions; instead, he worked with the Pew Trust group on changing American elections. He works in elections and election reform. Can someone please understand why there are so many Democrat election administrations, technology groups, and reform platforms? They must sell you on a politician from redistricting to canvasing your streets. What happened to the days of a great leader, a self-made person, a hero for the people, or a person with a vision? Today the Democrats sell hate, race, color, gender, and equity as a candidate. No one's lives are better not because of what is happening; it is all getting worse because of the unreachable promises. The promise is that Biden will bring America together by stealing an election. Executive decisions and vice president tie-breakers guarantee that Joe Biden is bipartisan? The contract that America is back, as we are losing at every challenge we face. The security of green energy and climate change. We have the highest gas prices ever, and all the green energy products will come from overseas, China.[222] The frozen wind turbines in Texas were natural! The promise that Trump lied and colluded with Russia to win the 2016 election is False! We will see how Biden used Russia and China to crush the world during their manufactured unleashed pandemic as we find out more. The unleashing of false narratives to sell a politician to ruin your lives. Charles Stewart III is an accomplice to misinformation, high gas prices, and another terror attack from Afghanistan. Another person is hiding in the disinformation Grassy Knowle as America is assassinated. Another is like a "Misinformation Kamikaze pilot" flying his plane into US Hospitals, attacking them while they try to fight Covid-19 deaths. We were told to "Follow the Science," people like him say it! Did we follow the science but the wrong scientist? He sure was on top of the 2020 elections and misinformation![223]

Trends and Trendsetters in Post-election Audits and Recounts

MODERATOR:

Barbara Cegavske *was elected to her first term as Nevada Secretary of State in 2014 and assumed office on Jan. 5, 2015. With over 35 years of combined public service and small business experience, Cegavske brings a unique blend of business acumen and legislative expertise to the Secretary of State's office. Cegavske entered public service in 1996 when she was elected to serve in the Nevada Assembly representing Clark County District 5 for three consecutive terms. In 2002, Cegavske ran for and successfully won a state Senate seat for Clark County District 8. She served three full terms before assuming the role of Secretary of State. Born and raised in Minnesota, Cegavske has been a proud Nevadan for the past 43 years. She has two sons, Adam and Bret, who graduated from the University of Nevada-Reno and University of Nevada-Las Vegas, respectively, and are raising their own families in Las Vegas. Cegavske and her husband are the proud grandparents of six grandchildren.*

Barbara Cegavske is from Clark County, NV, another district during the 2020 election that had fraud claims. The area holds Las Vegas, the most populated place in Nevada. Barbara is a Republican and the Secretary of State for Nevada. The State's secretary's responsibilities include serving as the State's Chief Elections Officer implementing electronic filing and internet disclosure of campaign and lobbyist financial information.[224] In April, Barbara was censored by her own Nevada GOP after the findings of ten of thousand examples of voter fraud from the 2020 election.[225] She denied any claims and blamed the State Republican GOP for blaming her for a failed presidential run by Trump. They cannot win yet because most of our country is still primarily an American population. That is why they will send millions of migrants to every state and county they lost in 2016 and 2020 to change the next election's outcome. Is this what politicians call a Pay to Play millionaire? She is getting ready to retire with her grandkids and ride off into the sunset with a big check!

PRESENTERS:

Dwight Shellman *is the County Support Manager for the Elections Division of the Colorado Secretary of State's office. He is primarily responsible for managing the division's externally focused resources to support Colorado's 64 county clerks and recorders in conducting elections, including the statewide voter registration database and support team, the voting systems certification program and support team, and the election official training and certification program. He received undergraduate and law degrees from the University of Colorado at Boulder and practiced law in Denver before starting a second career in elections administration by accident. That happened in 2010 when, after returning to his hometown of Aspen for family reasons, he applied for the Pitkin County elections manager position because it sounded like a fascinating 9-to-5 job. He was only half right and has been privileged to work in this field ever since. He is married and lives in Denver.*

Dwight Shellman oversaw the groundbreaking voting machines used in 2020 in Colorado.[226] He complained that the old machines that were ten years old needed to go. He oversees Colorado's 64 county voting clerks, ensuring they follow procedure and the voting laws. Does that mean that Dwight made sixty-four counts of state fraud in Colorado, and I think all sixty-four county clerks should be investigated too?[227] After the elections in Colorado, the fraud claims came piling in. After the election, Tina Peters was a county voting clerk in Mesa, Colorado, under investigation.[228] When the police looked for her, she was gone. Tina Peters later returned to Mesa County and was barred from the November 2021 elections. She is under investigation by the FBI and the Colorado Department of Justice for her involvement in the 2020 elections.

How could this be possible? People at a conference in 2017, set up and designed to stop voter fraud! It just so happens that Dwight Shellman and Tina Peters were at this conference and helped plan the misinformation. The worst part is that the American Taxpayers paid for these people to have a meeting to create this chaos. Because why? They knew the Democrat party was in trouble. Instead of doing remarkable things for Colorado and its people so they could stay in power and control, they would instead steal and cheat. They just took the low road and manipulated the voter, then blamed you for being a Racist Republican Deplorable. Insult to injury, a slap in the face, and another person who should hide in Colorado after this book is out.

Mark Halvorson* *is the founder, former director, and a current board member of Citizens for Election Integrity Minnesota. He has observed four statewide recounts six statewide audits and has recruited and trained many nonpartisan observers. In 2007 Mark helped to organize the first national Audit Summit. He created the audit and recount state laws searchable databases. He was an executive editor of "Principles and Best Practices of Post-Election Audits" as well as "Recount Principles and Best Practices." He served on the Brennan Center Audit Panel, the National League of Women Voters audit working group and the* *advisory board for the California risk-limiting audit pilot program. Mark received the Election Verification Network's 2017 John Gideon Memorial Award for his long-standing and highly effective advocacy for election integrity.*

Mark is the brainpower behind the Hillary Clinton recount and recalls against Trump.[229] Mark is a statistics guy; he tells people about close elections and the need for better systems than counting by hand. They all push the same narrative, a safer voting system with computers. Do you ever remember when a dead person voted in person and on paper, me neither? Did you ever see a person go to the same voting center and vote ten times after showing ID? No, me neither? These things only happen because of the computers and people in charge of them. Hillary Clinton is mad at the world, and Donald Trump is part of that world.[230] She has been ridiculed more by her husband than anyone else.[231] Hillary Clinton used to be a defense lawyer before her days in political life. She once defended two adult male rapists because Hillary could prove the ten-year-old fantasized about older men.[232] When I found the records in court, my mouth dropped.[233] The 41-year-old drifter served less than a year in prison; it sounds like 2022! Girls, women, half a nation, and even my daughter wanted her for president because of who she was. Well, they never knew that side of her. Mark Halvorson knows that side of her; he helped create it. Was he behind the creation of Trump's collusion with Russia? Did he spread misinformation so Trump and his Deplorables would look bad and lose their country? Your husband cheats on you and lies to the world, but you still hate me! We find out that Monica was not the only woman Bill cheated with. There was more and maybe even a young girl with Jefferey Epstein.[234] Epstein is found dead, and Trump is kicked out of the White House.[235] What about the person who did it all, Bill Clinton? Or did Monica suck her own!!!

Clean Voter Lists: A Gateway to Election Integrity

MODERATOR:

Amy Cohen* *is the Director of Government Outreach for Democracy Works. Previously, she spent four years with the Pew Charitable Trusts. She managed the Voting Information Project (VIP), guided national research projects, and forged relationships throughout the corporate and nonprofit sectors. Most recently, she co-founded and served as the Director of Operations for the Center for Election Innovation & Research (CEIR), which works to improve the security of elections and increase efficiencies in election administration for both administrators and voters.*

PRESENTERS:

Amy Cohen worked with all fifty states and the US commonwealth to help secure better voting machines? She is the state Election Director for all fifty states and voting areas overseas. She attended the Personal Democracy Forum 2018 as a guest speaker at the New York Law School between June 7-8, 2018. The 2018 THEME: HOW WE MAKE GOOD would make sure that tech acts as a force for good in the civic life of the citizens of a Democracy.[236] The new voting machine push could cause more hackers![237] She is another member of the PEW Research, which works with The Wharton School and the University of Pennsylvania. The Pew Trust wrote negative and false articles during Trump's term to sway their general podcast viewers. The reports can be found online, and you can judge yourself.[238] The Pew Research Center is the third-largest think tank in Washington, DC.! They believe that the US Supreme Court uses voter purging to eliminate eligible voters from voting.[239] How do we know who is eligible or even legal to vote? I got It! Voter ID, I will call Congress right now!

Shane Hamlin* *is the incoming executive director of ERIC. The new director brings a wealth of experience in elections administration and experience with ERIC to his new job. While serving as co-director of elections in Washington from 2010-2012, Hamlin served as the first chair of the ERIC Board of Directors. Hamlin's elections background also includes a year as Deputy Director of Elections, three years as Assistant Director of Elections, and three years as legislative liaison, all for the Washington Secretary of State. Since January 2014, he has served as a budget assistant to the Governor at the Washington Office of Financial Management.*

Shane Hamlin helps unregistered citizens register and vote. He is determined to get as many people to vote as possible. His group has twenty-one members nationwide. The group ERIC (Electric Registration Information Center) has done interviews shaming Trump and his supporters![240] In that article in 2017, when talking about voting reform and voting machines. Shane said, "There's no reason to re-invent the wheel when we're already here…and we do it very well." So why hold a Voting Technology Conference a day before the interview to help verify new voters and new voting technology! Some states that used Shane's company during the 2020 election are the same ones registered with the US EAC. So, the same thirty-two states that follow the voting rules set by the United States Election Assistance Commission are also voluntarily paying members of ERIC. What are the other eighteen states doing? Why are only some states' voting programs registered and verified? Mostly every State where his company has a representative, there was a fraud claim over the 2020 elections.[241] So, why does Shane's company not push for more rigid and stricter regulations when voting?

Picture ID or a recent tax form showing you are not a deadbeat citizen that should not even be allowed to vote. I suppose he does not want a dirty, fraud-claimed election with proper transparency. Then make the elections harder than putting a ballot in a mailbox. Shane tells people he helped find voters to vote; what does that mean? If a person does not want to vote, you pick them up and drive them, possibly bribing or coercing them to vote. The purpose of voting is not a popularity contest; it selects who will serve the best. Enough with think tanks, Pew Research on voting, technology voting conferences, and politicians doing stuff that does not pertain to get the hell back to work! And as my grandmother said, stop playing with your pudding! For America and its people, we want someone in politics to work for us. It was not me up on TV telling people how disgusting Trump was, how he lied in life and on his taxes. It was not me that cut a fake Donald Trump head off on TV.[242] Is it all because they hate half the population of Americans who voted for Trump, or because they hate Donald Trump? Whoever it is, it makes us all hate. Put that in your Think Tank and smoke it! What did you think would happen when you decided to go back to a Civil War mentality over politics during a pandemic! If they thought smart, they could have figured out ways to help Americans from dying during multiple waves of Covid!

Representative Keith Esau of Olathe*, *Kan., has served House District 14 since 2013. He serves as vice-chair of the elections committee. Representative Esau also serves as a member of NCSL's redistricting and elections standing committee. In addition, he is an independent software development consultant and a graduate of Tabor College with a BA in music.*

Keith Esau of Olathe, Kansas, got his retirement package at this conference. He ran on being a computer software developer when running for re-election. He is the hidden spoke in the wheel of disinformation on regular Americans. America is now aware of why a Republican would be invited to an Obama/Biden Voting conference.

On May 2, 2018, he voted YES to pass a bill that amends the requirements for gubernatorial candidacy.[243] The one part that was weird, in 2018 before the pandemic was section 5, which authorized the secretary of state authority to prescribe the general format of advance voting ballot envelopes. Why? Why mail-in ballots if fraud is the topic of the conference? Why mail-in ballots if we are at a Technology Conference on Voting? Do computers use envelopes? Enough America, Kansas, wake Up!

Senator Cheryl Kagan* *is the Vice-Chair of NCSL's redistricting and elections committee. She served in the Maryland House of Delegates from 1995 to 2003, representing District 17 (Rockville & Gaithersburg) in Montgomery County, and has served in the Maryland Senate since 2015.*

Cheryl Kagan is making Maryland voting even more accessible. After all the complaining she did in 2016 about Russian collusion and about everything President Trump said![244] After a year or two of Political fighting, voting fraud claims, and attacks on our Democracy! The State of Maryland made it easier to vote in 2021.[245] In the future, she will make it even more accessible while pushing for more mail-in ballots, offering voting through work incentives, and online registering. This is how we stop voting fraud? The State of Maryland has been in turmoil ever since the Democrats took over Annapolis.[246] The State bleeds money from taxpayers, allows corruption and crime, and is a big believer in foreign investors and handouts. The State is also the first to push to Defund ICE and the Police![247] READ: A List of Disturbing Crimes by Illegal Immigrants in Montgomery County!

Elections Tech Procurement and Funding from the State Perspective

Senator John Murante* is the co-chair of NCSL's redistricting and elections standing committee. Senator Murante was elected to the Nebraska legislature in 2012 and was re-elected in 2016. He is the chair of the Government, Military, and Veterans Affairs Committee, overseeing election issues in the State. He is a graduate of the University of Nebraska-Lincoln.

MODERATOR:

Amanda Buchanan*, *NCSL, National Conference of State Legislatures*

Amanda Buchanan is a primary pusher of the new voting Democrat-certified machines. The same voting machines were being used in the 2020 elections. She authors articles telling the state legislators what can be done to purchase new voting machines. She tells the same story of accessibility, voting accuracy, and integrity in American elections. Let me get this straight, the party of collusion whistleblowers is now calling for fairness, accuracy, and integrity. Folks, this has been the playbook for Obama, Clintons, and now the Biden's. First, Bill ran, then Hillary, Barrack, then Good Old Joe, next will be Michele Obama, then Biden's sister will give the presidency a chance. A fair bipartisan presidential committee did not set up this voting conference; Obama and Biden did. The states that want new voting machines are mostly the Blue States to use RCV voting.[248] The integrity and accessibility to voting is another smokescreen by Democrats to show division and hate by lying about America's election process. RCV is their way! The misinformation is out there; we cannot do anything right because we voted in the Trump. We betrayed America by voting in a pro-American president. That is the angle with which they are going. While Trump was a president for Americans first, Biden is a president for himself and everyone else but Americans first. Amanda is making sure of that.

PRESENTERS:

<u>**Nellie M. Gorbea**</u>, *Rhode Island Secretary of State Nellie M. Gorbea made history when she was sworn in on Jan. 6, 2015, becoming the first Hispanic elected to statewide office in New England. She has rapidly emerged on the national scene as a leader, taking on some of the most challenging issues and getting results, leading the way for other states across the country. Before she was elected Secretary of State, Gorbea headed a leading organization working to make housing affordable in Rhode Island, served as Deputy Secretary of State (2002 to 2006), and led the creation of the Rhode Island Latino Civic Fund. Originally from Puerto Rico, Gorbea is a graduate of Princeton University's Woodrow Wilson School for Public and International Affairs and holds a master's degree in public administration from Columbia University. She and her husband, Steve D'Hondt, and their three daughters live in North Kingstown.*

Nellie M. Gorbea is probably a nice person, so is the kid at Dunkin Donuts who messed up my medium Black coffee with 2 Splenda. I am saying that even a simple job can be a "Splenda tough" task to some. Working in a restaurant is not for everyone. People should not get a job because of their race, color, gender, or historical first. A person should be hired for what they can do on the job. A politician's job is to help all people, not just her race and color. If I hired Asian men and not Spanish men, that would be racist. If it happens to a White person, then it is ok because why? Every human race was an enslaver at one time; even Africans owned slaves!

Nellie is a Democrat politician who relies on misleading the people by disinformation. She boasts on her website for re-election time by saying Rhode Island started the most businesses this year than ever before. A study from University of Rhode Island professor Ed Mazze[249] has shown that almost 50% of all small businesses that started during the pandemic will fail in 2020. Rhode Island has over 90,000 small businesses registered in 2020, but only 32k have actual employees. Meaning they are either self-employed contractors with a W9 at the end of the year, illegally hired under-the-table employees, or an individual who files as a small business to get tax write-offs and free government handouts. Either way, the number is a fraud, it is not accurate, and the reason for all the business growth this year was free money. The Governor of Rhode Island passed a bill giving relief to all small businesses hit by the pandemic in early 2019. The process and costs to start a small business in Rhode Island are under 250 dollars, and only some companies require a license. So, people started filing for two years straight to receive free money. The reason is that 65% of the businesses have no employees.

Rhode Island is expensive, the working middle class is small and hurting. She is running for Governor; on what record? Is she qualified to run a state for all Americans or just those who think like her?

Elaine Manlove *has been employed by the State of Delaware as Election Commissioner since 2007 following eight years as* **Director of the Department of Elections for New Castle County.** *New Castle County Government formerly employed her as an executive assistant. In both elections' positions, she has seen many changes from both sides of the election process – local and State perspectives. As commissioner, she is responsible for the Help America Vote Act funds, the statewide voter registration system, campaign finance, and the Parent/Student Mock Election. Under Elaine, Delaware was the second state to join ERIC (Electronic Registration Information Center). She is currently ERIC treasurer. Elaine is a graduate of The Election Center's Certified Election Registration Administrator (CERA) program and is a member of NASED (National Association of State Election Directors). A native Delawarean, born and raised in Wilmington, graduated from St. Elizabeth's High School and Goldey-Beacom College. She lived in Hockessin for many years with her husband and three sons. Now that her sons are grown, Elaine and her husband reside at the Delaware beach.*

Elaine and her husband were killed in a CAR ACCIDENT right before the election.[250] She has spoken out against Trump and his claims for fraud in the election.[251] Elaine was worried about fraud and put in stricter policies for the 2020 elections on November 6. She was so concerned that she oversaw the purchase of 1,100 new machines the month before the election in 2018, two years before the election between Trump and Biden.[252] A $13 million-dollar purchase had to be made, and the machines had to be calibrated before the November election. She could not properly do so because she was killed just days before the machines went online. The tractor-trailer driver never stopped and hit them from behind while she and her husband were stopped at a red light. The tractor-trailer was going so fast that it ran the car straight into a tree, killing both Elaine and her husband, Wayne, on impact. She died three days before the elections in Delaware being hit by a tractor-trailer. The biggest accomplishment she felt she made to the voters of Delaware was new voting machines before she retired. These new machines could audit and have handheld printouts for recount decisions.

Ironically, a tractor-trailer killed Joe Biden's first wife. The truck driver that hit Elaine and Wayne was never charged; you cannot even find out who he was.[253] Articles say the tractor-trailer operator, a 41-year-old Pennsylvania man, was not injured in the crash. A ghost! Right after the elections in 2020, the Delaware House Administration committee tried to pass a bill allowing childcare reimbursement for candidates during a campaign run, automatic registration for any person in Delaware who uses his license or ID for a transaction, and multiple gun laws to stop gun purchases for felons and deadbeat dads.[254] The bill was dedicated to Elaine for her hard work. Her party killed her because she would have been in the way of the three-day cheating resurrection of the Democrats in Joe's backyard!

Brian Bean *is a policy analyst for the Utah State Legislature, where he has worked for the Office of Legislative Research and General Counsel for several years. His expertise is in election law, campaign finance, government ethics, and government administration. He has drafted legislation and conducted significant* *research for the Utah Legislature on funding for voting equipment. He graduated from the University of Utah with a Master of Public Administration and earned a bachelor's degree in Political Science from Brigham Young University.*

His LinkedIn account has this Statement on it. "I am a senior policy advisor for the Utah Senate. I help the Senate develop and work to achieve strategic policy objectives." Has Utah had any claims of fraud during the 2020 election? [255] Are all these specialists and tech pros even working? Mitt Romney is from Utah. We all know how he felt about Trump and his supporters!

Stanford Ward *has served as counsel to the Election Law Subcommittee of the Maryland House of Delegates since 2007. In that position, he is responsible for drafting bills, conducting research, and assisting the lawmaking process in election administration and campaign finance. In 2010, he oversaw an independent study of the cost of implementing an optical scan voting system in Maryland. In 2011 and 2012, he staffed the Commission to Study Campaign Finance Law, which resulted in a comprehensive revision of campaign finance law. Since 2006, he has been a policy analyst with the Maryland Department of Legislative Services, the General Assembly's nonpartisan staff agency.*

This is a Gold Mine. So even before the election, this committee in 2017 came to be, they started the ball rolling with election fraud.[256] He is a lawyer, and he was assigned the task to dispute all claims and allegations of fraud by all. He was there to study election law and put the "Lie Claim" to rest. He would also sew any Trump Supporters from trying to call foul. Underneath is an excerpt from a court case in Arizona, where The Government assigned Ward to defend the election and any fraud claims. They knew Americans were going to be upset and planned. They set up a law firm to debunk fraud claims on an election two years before the election. Do you pay a lawyer to defend a speeding ticket two years before you break the law?

There are numerous cases where Ward is involved. Ward works with Jaime Raskin, the impeachment manager, on the Trump trials.[257] You can google his name Stanford D. Ward, Maryland delegates, hit an image, and nothing! Then when I go on Rep. Jaime Raskin's webpage and hit search, type in Stanford Ward, nothing. Well, someone with Stanford in their name is posting the truth. There is a list of all the court filings by the GOP, Donald Trump, and Trump voters on fraud during the 2020 election. Stanford University has ongoing and closed cases about the election process.[258]

The sad part is that Rep. Jaime Raskin lost his son to mental illness, death by suicide on New Year's Eve 2020.[259] Writing the reference and seeing his son's face made me cry; I had to stop and clear my eyes. That is horrible, upsetting and I feel bad for the sisters. I feel awful, and I am so surprised after seeing that mental health was the cause of his suicide and that nothing has been done. The Mental Health of criminals, young adults, and children since Covid started is a pandemic in itself. Maryland will have an alarming mental health epidemic in 2022.[260] We already had a problem in America in teens and young adults with mental health issues before the pandemic and impeachments.[261] The crisis was here before the death of his son.

Well, I guess they can just let them out to commit crimes! So, is that the plan for America's youth. You had one Representative from Maryland lose their son to suicide. You have a President who has a son addicted to opioids![262] So, is that the plan? Our sons are gone, now let me kill yours? The Fentanyl pouring in from China and Mexico to the US is enough to kill us all![263] Is that the plan? With a father's love for his family and others, you would think he would crush the mental health issue forever. Instead, a fake impeachment was more important![264] The years before the 2020 election, Ward, Raskin, Pelosi, and the bunch pushed for an impeachment trial of Donald Trump over Russian collusion with Biden and Ukraine. Who would have thought! Do you believe Raskin could have those two years back, those long hours that amounted to nothing! If only his friends, two years before his son's horrible death, wanted to impeach mental health from

Maryland. Maybe they could have spent two years tackling mental health issues! I am sorry, sir, for your loss. May God Bless your family, your daughters who lost a best friend, and your wife who lost a part of her. We need better leaders to tackle the problems we all face. Even he faced! The hours wasted, millions of taxpayers' dollars wasted, the media coverage wasted, and we still have a mental health problem worse than ever in 2022! Let us get this country back on track for Thomas Bloom Raskin. May you rest in peace!

__Ward v. Jackson__, No. CV2020-015285 (Ariz. Super. Ct., Maricopa County.)

They planned for collusion claims by hiring a lawyer. They lawyered up!

Case Summary

Plaintiff, an Arizona voter, alleges that poll workers were not fit to verify absentee signatures and that observers were not present to replicate damaged ballots in violation of state law. The lawsuit requests an audit and requests the election results be annulled.

Filed

11/30/2020

State

Arizona

Election Tech Innovation

MODERATOR:

Monica Crane Childers *is a digital product design and project management background in election technology nerd. As Democracy Works' Director of Government Services, she champions collaborative design, partnering with state and local officials to build low-cost, open-source solutions for election administration. Since getting her start in the Massachusetts legislature, she has worked primarily in digital media, both on campaigns and political technology firms. Monica held a bachelor's in Communication Studies from the University of Kansas. She was named the 2008 Rose Scholar in Communication Management at Emerson College, where she earned a master's degree in 2010.*

This is her LinkedIn account bio, "Over the past decade, she has designed online voter engagement platforms, vote-by-mail ballot tracking systems, text/email election reminders, and a national trouble-ticket system for reporting problems with election mail. Having served as the project manager for Colorado's post-election audit software for the past year, she is currently working with election officials implementing risk-limiting audits and helping shepherd the development of nationwide RLA software." She has been involved in elections to help with Bipartisan elections and nonprofit elections.

Monica Bell Crane's Connecticut Voter Registration
Is Democrat, not bipartisan at all.

PRESENTERS:

Amber McReynolds* *is the Director of Elections for the City and County of Denver, Colorado.*

In February 2021, Joe Biden paid his friend for all her hard work. Bi-partisan hard work that did not go unnoticed. Joe Biden, on February 24, 2021, appointed her to a vacant seat on the Board of Governors in the US Postal Service.[265] Sworn in by Susan Rice, McReynolds will be the first to serve on the US Postal Board of Governors who worked in elections and voting. She claims no party affiliation but is a registered Democrat, and Joe Biden appointed her. She is also the CEO of National Vote at Home Institute to advocate for universal mail-in voting.[266] So, let us be clear, she started a movement for more mail-in ballots, which was the big concern and argument from the Right; she claims to be bipartisan and believes in voting rights for all.[267] Then, with so much controversy, why not for a sign of good faith elect a person who created so much anger to the US Postal Service Board, another slap in the face. Insult on top of injury. The voting by mail was the problem, there was a date set to have it mailed in, and it still took days to count votes that should have been in already.[268] So, elect her to a power where mail is involved. Amtrak and the US POSTAL service made billions under the Biden presidency.[269]

Dean Logan *is the Registrar-Recorder/County Clerk for Los Angeles County, Calif. - the nation's largest, most diverse, and complex local election jurisdiction, serving more than 5.2 million registered voters. Logan serves as president of the California Association of Clerks and Election Officials (CACEO). He is an active participant in the future of California Elections collaborative: an initiative sponsored and funded by the James T. Irvine Foundation and serves on the Board of Directors for the National Elections Center. Additionally, he teaches Organizational Leadership, Public Sector Management and Intergovernmental Relations courses in the MPA program at California State University, Northridge. Mr. Logan holds a degree in Organizational Leadership from Azusa Pacific University and earned an Executive Master of Public Administration degree through the Evans School of Public Policy and Governance at the The University of Washington.*

Dean Logan is a registered Democrat, and he was elected to help keep California Blue at all costs during the election and the Governor's Recall.[270] His department is responsible for registering voters, voters' files, and administering federal, state, local, and special elections. He oversees the verification of all recall petitions. He also maintains the voter's files, deleting deceased, illegal, or unregistered voters. The more population we have, the more we can manipulate the vote. Or just take care of it for them. There are multiple lawsuits and claims against California's voting system.[271] They do not follow the recommendations or protocols by the US EAC. They are not registered or a member of ERIC. He could have registered California's voting machines while at this conference. All of those groups were represented at the meeting he attended. Did he not register California's voting equipment with the United States Election Assistance Commission?

Noah Praetz* *has been the Director of Elections for Cook County, Ill., since 2013. Praetz, formerly the Deputy Director of Elections, began working for the Clerk's office in 2000 as a temporary employee entering voter registration cards before that presidential election. Praetz is active in several election organizations, including the International Association of Clerks, Recorders, Election Officials, and Treasurers. He is a graduate of Bradley University and DePaul College of Law. He lives in Indian Head Park with his wife, Megan O'Connell, and their three children.*

He was brought in to oversee the overseas military votes and all US territory voters. He is from Cook County, Illinois. He works for a group called HAVA. HAVA or Help America Vote Act, passed in the wake of the 2000 election debacle, authorized money for states to upgrade their voter registration databases and voting equipment. He was elected to run up the group HAVA to bring in a new era of technology voting.[272] Noah is the person who pushed the narrative that we need fair elections, and we cannot be bullied at the voter's blocks.[273] He from day one pushed the "Lie" about the George Bush Jr. voting scandal in Florida. He had never stopped the Boy who Cried Wolf blame game about election fraud during the Al Gore Lose, The Hillary Clinton Lose, and now in a speech in June 2021, he still pushed the threat that Domestic Terrorists are still a significant threat to voting. Only if we had more money?[274] Meaning let us just stay home because the rioters, the drug dealers, the hate groups are scary and mean, but a White Republican voter will kill you. He was the originator of the Trump Lie, and he pushed for the recount for Hillary. He worked for Clinton and helped Gore's election.[275] Do you think his name will come up in the new trial against Clinton's lawyer who pushed the Russia voting hoax? Maybe he was behind it too, behind the Russia voting collusion, the Phone call to Ukraine, perhaps he was the whistleblower, or he helped take the wrapper off the cigar for Monica?

Vendor Session

MODERATOR:

Doug Chapin* *is the Program for Excellence in Election Administration director. Chapin came to the Humphrey School after ten years at The Pew Charitable Trusts, where he served as director of Election Initiatives for the Pew Center on the States. Under his leadership, Pew's elections team successfully lobbied to enact military and overseas voting reform in Congress and state legislatures; enlisted dozens of states and technology partners like Google, Microsoft, and Facebook provided official voting information online and via mobile technology. They worked with election officials, academics, and technical experts to design and implement efforts to upgrade the nation's voter registration systems. Before serving at Pew, Chapin was an attorney in private practice specializing in election and ethics law. He served as elections counsel to the Democrats on the US Senate Rules Committee from 1997 to 2000. He focused on federal election legislation and reviewed the disputed 1996 Senate election in Louisiana. He holds a law degree from Georgetown University, a Master of Public Administration degree from*

Harvard's John F. Kennedy School of Government, and a BA in politics from Princeton University.

Friday, June 16, 2017

Under his leadership, his team successfully lobbied to enact military and overseas voting reform in Congress and the state legislature. Wait, I thought that is what Noah Praetz did? Then he enlisted dozens of states and technology partners like Google, Microsoft, and Facebook to provide official voting information online and via mobile technology.[276] By putting Millions of Americans' information out in the open, could that cause voting fraud? Can any single voter vote in any state by giving out voter identification? Then he did not stop there; he went and worked with election officials, academics, Colleges, and technical experts. Technical experts like who? So, they could design and implement efforts to upgrade the nation's voter registration systems. They use examples of other countries and compare them to the US voting system. What and who controls the US Voting Registry?[277] He was around when Al Gore lost, which did not sit well with him either. See, his group started the US EAC to monitor state elections, well, only the registered 32 Republican states.

The Election Assistance Commission is an independent agency of the United States government created by the Help America Vote Act of 2002. The HAVA created the US EAC, another Government Agency paid by American's. Friends create groups and hire more friends. One agency was made by another agency that was made by a think tank to monitor you and me; why? This is a program they can cut and fast.

The Commission serves as a national clearinghouse and resource of information regarding election administration. After losing an election, all these people got together for what? Not to lose an election again. These people are the original January 6th rioters, and they never stopped being angry either! They attacked the will of the voter. They climbed the walls of freedom and broke the windows of Justice. They broke the law too. Devising a plan and taking action, these elected officials changed the landscape of politics in America. Instead of storming the Capital where their friends work, they went through your computer and attacked you where you live and work. These are the ones who cannot let the election go! From 2000 to 2020, they set in motion ways to take back the election. Joe Biden knew how and did what it took to secure the victory. He knows if people register, someone will pull the lever for them on election day, maybe not them but someone, just register, so I have a name. The President made an executive order to push for voter reform and proclaimed September 28, 2021, as National Voter Registration Day.[278]

Election Modernization is Great! But Can Your Tech Keep Up?

MODERATOR:

Senator **Daniel Ivey-Soto****is a life-long public servant. Currently serving as Executive Director for County Clerks, Daniel is a former state elections director, prosecutor, and teacher. He is also a successful entrepreneur, having started and grown two small businesses focused on helping others and improving our community; Daniel will take a uniquely broad base of experience in the public/private sector to the Roundhouse. Over the past few years, Daniel has written over a dozen bills that the Legislature has passed. All legislative work has been based on a philosophy of good government and accountability. In addition, he is co-chair of NCSL's redistricting and elections standing committee.*

Mr. Ivey-Soto is the best spin man of them all. He started the Vote Smart initiative to inform voters, young and old, on the truths about the candidates running for office. Funny because I did not see any mention of Forever Chemicals under Joe Biden when I researched. He is the person to help the young voters truly understand a politician who has been around for 50 years and has never changed. He has a website that shows all of the candidates' contributions, voting tactics, and backgrounds that should be known. Who bought the art from Hunter? Who worked in Ukraine with Hunter, and how much Chinese money did the Biden's receive?[279] You left something out, Senator Daniel Ivey-Soto, in 2020!

So, this is where the big Tech companies come into play; instead of the big three media online giants taking criticism, Trump was the bad guy. They will ban Trump and any voting questions and concerns, making it seem to be bipartisan.[280] Then, the only choice left for information is from a Democrat politician's website from New Mexico.[281] The website also has voter registration information, voter mail-in ballot information, and a section for a voters' defense. Self Defense like someone is stealing your votes and holding them hostage. They are not only stealing your votes; they are stealing your tax dollars to waste on Un-American policies and fraud. Self Defense voters can go to a section called "The Political Courage Test," a section on the website where they rate and rank all politicians serving the American people today.[282] Yes, bold and wise, but fewer and fewer do it!

Instead of worrying about politicians from another state, worry about your people. Senator Ivey-Soto voted on where in March of 2019 he voted YES to authorize the States investment in Renewable Energies.[283] Yes, with your tax dollars. Then the following year, he refused to vote for an Electrical Vehicle Credit for consumers. So YES, spend your tax dollars on the State's Electric investment in a healthier America. While not voting to pass an incentive to save Americans' money by paying less for a better tomorrow[284]. That is a politician, all smiles but no action. The state can invest your money in green projects, but you will not be as lucky. Well, I searched and searched on your website and found no collusion. Good job, guys; America owes you a debt of gratitude and taxes.

New Mexico is a pure example of a politician working for others instead of the people. Honestly, why would the Senator of New Mexico care or even worry about a politician's people in Ohio? Do they just want the hate for Republicans to grow nationwide? A Senator in Ohio should only affect the people of Ohio. It is harmful when a red state like Ohio gets influenced by a blue state like Virginia or New Mexico. The people of Ohio have different goals and dreams than those from other states. This is a great idea, but the problem is these people knew what to do before the" Lie and Misinformation Campaign" started. They were the creators of it. They knew the outcome; they knew the blame game, and they knew the reaction the United States of America would take. Frustration, the same frustration they all felt in 2008.

Hillary felt the same frustration when she was promised behind closed doors that an old White man would not embarrass her again. They lied to her, and she lost by underestimating the power of the "VOTE." Hillary Clinton made sure the power of the "Lie" would prevail ever after. She was crying fraud and foul, only years before Trump's victory, not ready to concede with Obama.[285] The sad part about the whole thing is that Trump supported Hillary in every one of her elections. He donated money because he, too, had a mother who had a harsh life.[286] He never supported Bill but loved and financially supported Hillary. They pinned them against each other, and she got beat up again, looking like a fool while the man won. Trump was the second "husband" that paid for all the first husbands' faults and mistakes. They turned on her and used Hillary, and now she might be in trouble for the Russia hoax? Trust me, she is! They knew that would be the last time an election would be out of their hands. They knew she was on her last breath, and just like the mob, they axed her out of the plan, the club, and now they will start damage control to avoid being involved in the Russia hoax.

In 2019 when he squashed a tax on Renewable Energies, he voted Yes on a bill to have same-day registration on voting.[287] So, a bus can drive around a state dropping off loads of people, no ID required, same-day register and vote. It is too late when the voters are verified and the election is over. If the vote and ballot cannot be verified, what is the use? The vote already counted! No renewable energies, but New Mexico and Washington DC share voter rights. I traveled the country for one hundred days driving from one coast to another, TWICE, while drafting this book. I know, and the people of New Mexico know, they have nothing in common with people from other states. I stopped at a gas station owned by the Native Tribe off Rt. 66, where the roadrunner hangs by the busy intersection, you know the one. They were open during the pandemic, but you could only come in and not touch, walk around with only two people in the store besides employees. They were polite, stirred my coffee, and let my son use the restroom. At the same time, Washington DC was a ghost town, dark, scary, and the thing by the busy intersection was trash. I would not compare both places. Both in the USA, but oh so different. He also, in 2019, voted Yes to decriminalize abortion. The Outcome: It Failed, Thank God!

I am trying to say that I know Rep. Jaime Raskin would give his life for his son back! So how can he vote along party lines with a person who votes yes on killing an unborn baby? The abortion of a baby with a heartbeat is criminal. The death penalty is inhuman and wrong in New Mexico and Maryland. The willing killing of a baby is not. When someone commits murder, are you there to help, your tax dollars buy the bullets, or maybe a doctor you know was involved? Multiple people are helping you through the process of an abortion. Your taxes pay some! Killing a convicted murderer is wrong, but killing a living heart beating baby is accepted? America, wake up, and please stop the cycle of Democrat conflicts on our children!

PRESENTERS:

Representative Mike Fortner *has been a member of the Illinois House of Representatives since 2007. Representative Fortner is a former mayor of West Chicago and a retired physics professor from Northern Illinois University. Among* *his legislative assignments this term, he is serving as the Republican spokesperson on the Elections & Campaign Finance Committee and the Cybersecurity, Data Analytics & IT Committee. He was the chief co-sponsor of automatic voter registration this year and the amendment sponsor that led to the unanimous passage of AVR in Illinois.*

This is tough because he is a Republican, but is he a Democrat in disguise? A RINO, Republican in name only. Send a Democrat in disguise to run as a Republican, then do not put up a candidate. Then when voting comes around, both Democrats and Republicans vote for the wrong person. His record on votes cast is available.[288]

The votes he voted "YES" on would be: Increasing Taxes to fund State Budget, Authorize Drug Crime Violations across State Lines, Downgrade Marijuana charges to non-criminal Civil Violations, Limit Community Colleges Severance packages, Establish Immunity for Underage Drinking if Medical Response is needed, Prohibit Requiring a Criminal Record before a Job Interview, Authorizing 17 year old to vote in Primary Elections, Repeal the position of the Lieutenant Governor, voted Yes to authorize Licenses to Undocumented Immigrants, Authorize Individuals to RECORD LAW ENFORCEMENT WORKERS ON THE JOB, voted yes to Allow citizens to buy Ammunition from In-State Companies, limiting Health Care Benefits for Retired State Employees, Firearm Waiting Period Exemptions, Limit Free Mass Transit for Seniors, Impeachment of Rod Blagojevich, voted Yes for Recall Elections and Audits, voted Yes on Limiting Medicaid Funding and voted yes on Recycling of Plastic Bags law, just to name a few. All over the place and not a real Republican agenda.

He did vote "NO" like a Democrat. Here are some of the bills and laws he voted "NO" on: Prohibiting the use of a HANDHELD CELL PHONE while driving, (GOOD) Establish Cost Of Living Adjustments in Pensions, Requires Increase in Teacher Salaries,[289] Expand Sex Education in Public Schools, Abortion Notification Bill,

Wrongful Death Damages, voted NO for Agreement Among the States to Elect the President by Popular Vote, voted No on a Property Tax Exemption for Disabled Vets hurt in action, No on Extended Parental Health Insurance for Unmarried Dependents or Single Mothers, allowing Teachers to Conduct Silent Reflections in the classroom, voted No on Homeowners Emergency Assistance Plan, voted No on Limiting Campaign Contributions, Voted No on a Ban of Cell Phone Use while Driving near a School or Construction Zone, Voted No on Expanding Red-Light Traffic Camera Enforcement, the Limits of Artificial Trans Fat Usage, No to Abolish the Death Penalty, Voted No on the Local Food, Farm and Jobs Act, requiring Schools to Enact Bullying Policies[290] and Punishments, No for Nursing Home Infection Control and also Voted No to Paying Regional Superintendents.

That is a short record of his political career; one vote makes sense, whereas the others make you scratch your head. Take a look for yourselves, Illinois! This is a big match that helped start the fire burning the great city of Chicago.

Kyle Bailey *has over a decade of experience in management and fundraising for candidate campaigns, ballot measure campaigns, and nonprofits. In 2016, Kyle led the statewide ballot measure campaign that won ranked-choice voting by the second-largest referendum vote of the people in Maine's history, making Maine the first state to adopt this voting reform for the election of state and federal officeholders. Kyle is the owner and president of Peachtree Strategies LLC and lives in Gorham with his husband,* **Representative Andrew McLean*.**

So first off, a guy who works as a campaign fundraiser for a company changing how voting is done in America is married to a politician. His husband was a House State Representative from Maine, but he lost to his husband, Kyle Bailey.[291] Andrew McLean was a state representative but submitted a resignation letter to the Maine House in 2020. He did not lose the seat, though. His husband, a Campaign Manager from the (RCV) voting system, Kyle Bailey took the job over.²⁹² Kyle Bailey took over the State Representative job from his husband. He easily beat the other candidate that ran against him in the primary election. His husband Andrew McLean only lost due to term limits reached; he was in office too long. The term limits were created so one party or person would not monopolize elections and power over people. They found a way around it by electing family members. Kyle beat the Republican candidate too, and ironically 100% of the votes were counted. So, the beauty of the (RCV) voting system is that it works; it works maybe too well!

Kyle Bailey was the campaign manager for ranked-choice voting (RCV).²⁹³ So, a Non-partisan voting reform group has a campaign manager to sell the reform.²⁹⁴ Dick Woodbury was the first to introduce RCV voting to Maine in 2014. Woodbury began a statewide citizen's initiative to replace Maine's voting system, but the people did not want this type of voting system! They were able to push their non-partisan agenda on the state of Maine's presidential and statewide elections anyway.

At first, they were denied; year after year, the politicians saw no reason for Voting Reform. Until, this committee held their meetings, filled lawsuits, numerous phone calls, and a couple of back door meetings (The Democrat Way)! Then unexpectedly and surprisingly to half of the state of Maine voters, RCV voting was implemented on election day in 2018. ²⁹⁵

Thanks to Kyle Bailey and the extraordinary individuals from (RCV), Maine will officially be the first state to use (RCV) in the presidential general elections. Other states that allow (RCV) voting in only Local Voting Elections are New York, Oregon, California, Michigan, Minnesota, Colorado, Utah, New Mexico, Vermont, Massachusetts, Maryland, and Delaware. Tennessee and Florida only use (RCV) voting in Memphis and Sarasota counties. Some states use (RCV) voting platform for Military and Overseas Runoff Elections. Illinois, Arkansas, Louisiana, Alabama, Georgia, and South Carolina.

The following TWO states only use (RCV) platform for party Nominations. Virginia uses the platform for Republican and Democrat party nominations. Texas is the only other state that uses the RCV voting platform for Democrat Senate district voting. Maine uses (RCV) for all its state elections voting. From Presidential to electing School Board members. ALASKA uses (RCV) for State and Federal elections and the state's Democratic Party Presidential Primaries. The following states use this platform for only the State Democratic Party Presidential Primaries. Those states are Wyoming and Kansas, and the first year they used it was the 2020 election.

Every state on the list changed and used (RCV) voting platform for the 2020 elections. The last state is the Great State of Nevada. This state changed and used (RCV) for only the Early Voters in the Democratic caucus in the 2020 election cycle. All these states plus a couple more will now use (RCV) for every election from now on out. Did you know about RCV voting in your elections? Did you know that our election system was changed by the state of Maine and its voters? Did you know that every election will be changed from now on, for what?

So, what is (RCV) and what is wrong with it? Well, to show you an example, the RCV system is used by the Academy of Motion Pictures to pick the winners of each category each year. Other non-political voting platforms use it too, like the New Jersey Library Association, the Memphis Farmers Union, and even the Colleges and Universities for student government. So, the voting platform is an electoral system where voters rank candidates by preference on their ballots in four tiers. There is a first, a second, a third, and a fourth spot to place a vote on the ballot. WTF? Only two candidates are running for president, right!

Ballotpedia.com is as follows [296]…

"A ranked-choice voting system (RCV) is an electoral system in which voters rank candidates by preference on their ballots. If a candidate wins a majority of first-preference votes, they are declared the winner. If no candidate wins a majority of first-preference votes, the candidate with the fewest first-preference votes is eliminated. First-preference votes cast for the failed candidate are eliminated, lifting the second-preference choices indicated on those ballots. A new tally is conducted to determine whether any candidate has won most of the adjusted votes. The process is repeated until a candidate wins an outright majority."

Ranked Choice Voting (sometimes referred to as Instant Runoff Voting) is a voting method. Instead of voting for a single candidate, the voter ranks candidates on the ballot in order of preference – first, second, third, and fourth; a four-tier voting system counts a four-tier ballot. Voters can cast their vote for the candidate they honestly prefer. If no candidate gets a majority, then a series of virtual runoffs commences (virtual because voting takes place in the computer program, and "runoffs" occur in the tallying process). In each runoff round, the last-place finisher is eliminated from contention. All ballots on which that candidate was ranked first are now repurposed and given to the second-choice candidate. That process continues until a candidate wins with the majority of the votes.

So now you know why misinformation is so essential. Why does voting take weeks after every election now? This is what is in the Constitution about voting? When you hire a politician, the first thing they change is how we vote? Unreal that this is allowed, well, only allowed in Democratic-controlled areas. Colleges, MLB, school boards, and even the Oscars vote like this. Why do the Oscars and Internet Video gaming Awards use this system?[297]

Well, how can a committee narrow down 40 MLB players to just one MVP award? The only problem is the 2020 Presidential election was between two people, with no second place, and just winner takes all. What countries vote like this, what countries use an (RCV) voting platform, NONE, only corrupt politicians in America. This is one of the two people behind the 2020 election conspiracy fraud! Will we allow Kyle Bailey and RCV voting to be a part of every other election from now on? These people, Kyle Bailey and Amber McReynolds made the American vote a toss-up.

The process can count cast votes by monitoring ballots from redistricted areas. Like counting cards at the casino, illegal! So, if a candidate is winning, or the wrong candidate is winning. Then they feed the machine the ballots harvested from illegal voters, redistricted areas of blue voters, overseas voters, and military votes now will be counted. Remember, no ID is required, which means anyone anywhere can vote in our elections. The ballots can never be verified; an ID is not required. A robot can vote online; he has no ID.

That is why the 2020 election had the most votes ever, now that number of voters is the new standard. If we do not control our elections with proper ID, voter turnout will grow every year. The process can now be swayed for fraud. An overseas ballot comes from where, are from who, and with what verification if no ID is required? Once the verification process is removed from voting, like proper identification, School ID, or anything else we do, we do not know who is voting, do we?

So, when the night of the vote comes, and the candidates watch the TV for updates, as one person receives the majority, they have to make the 2nd, 3rd, and 4th choice nominations count.[298] On the night of the election, they know where the Democrats come from, where the Republican votes come from, so they choose to add accordingly. Keeping the vote score close, remember 48% for Biden and 49% for Trump all night?[299]

Mail-in ballots are a group of votes, overseas ballots, same-day registered, mailbox drop centers, and wherever they allow voting now. When people vote, they pick one candidate and leave the other slots empty. The vote only counts first, and the vice president is elected with the winner. Then if 2nd, 3rd, and 4th place selections are not picked, just like the SAT exam, the computer fills in the blank space, that is RCV Voting.[300]

So, when a person votes in a two-person election (Trump vs. Biden) because no one else was running, they pick someone for their first choice. The game of politics starts here; when the voting machine sees only the first choice marked, it automatically picks the voter's 2nd, 3rd, and 4th choice before processing the ballot. RCV voting allows all votes to count![301] The computer knows your pick, so it picks different candidates for the 2nd, 3rd, and 4th vote. When only two people run for office, the only choice would be the one you did not pick. So, when the computer tallies the votes, Trump might have received 80% of the first vote, but Joe Biden got 100% of the second vote, 100% of the third vote, and 100% of the fourth vote. Add 2nd, 3rd, and 4th votes with the percentage of first votes Biden received legitimately, and then there is your winner. Military and overseas voters and every voter not aware of this system would not fill out 2nd, 3rd, and 4th choices.

The people who had their voting system changed three days before the election did not know either! Who knew RCV voting was being used?[302] Do not worry, the computer did. This all makes sense; the year of the pandemic and people dying and sick, quarantined, we had the most votes ever cast.[303] People were afraid to come out, wearing gloves, masks, and sanitizing everything, but the most ever voted! The pandemic year showed some districts, counties, and states had 100% of voters voted; all votes came in.[304]. A 100% voter turnout in some areas during a worldwide pandemic?

The 2020 election was when winning first place did not matter, or is it the majority of all four votes that count? Did you know that you had to vote four times? Did you live in one of these states and see a ballot like that? This only helps corrupt officials and lying politicians. Your vote does not count, your say did not get cast, and America, this is a damn shame that now the greatest country in the world votes like the Heisman trophy Award votes.[305]

Do you know why they use (RCV) system for voting the best athlete in college sports each year because there are thousands of college players from four different levels of competition? The NCAA would have to make it fair to write in and add up the votes. Now you know why this system is terrible for voting in politics in America. Only two candidates are running for office. Not four, not second best, not maybe fourth choice if everyone dies of Covid. The primaries are there to narrow down the field; if they lose in the primaries, then that is life!

Why change voting now? Why change after Barrack Obama and Joe Biden won by landslides. Systemic racism voting elected Barrack Obama and Ilhan Omar? Major League Baseball votes like this too, Bonds out, but Ortiz is in! This is the great fall of America, taking the vote from the voters. This is why America is where they are because two people today have changed voting in America forever. They changed it and added a few more choices and levels of deception. You know why because the guy behind this (Kyle Bailey) was just elected to the House of Representatives. How many others won this way?

How many Americans are unaware of this voting system in our politics? Politicians are sealing the deal with misinformed voters. Democrats are using disinformed voters' ballots against them. So, did you know you had to vote that way?

Kyle Bailey is from Florida and moved to Maine after attending College. Kyle is already working at that 2022 vote, his first two bills for the State of Maine, secure Ballot Boxes for Absentee voters, and access to early voting for Absentee voters.[306] Now, who were the Deplorables that changed America's voting system? Now you know! Please go in the bathroom and scream with a vent on and simultaneously flushing the toilet. God Bless America and free speech. Busted! He has already resigned from office; what is next? (**307**) This Book is Toxic to traitors.

Amber McReynolds* *is the Director of Elections for the City and County of Denver, Colorado. Amber has administered elections in Denver for 12 years and has worked in public policy and administration for over 16 years. Amber is nationally recognized as a strategic planner, creative thinker, and problem-solver; she is valued, praised, and relied upon for her leadership, innovative thinking, project management expertise, and fiscal responsibility. In Denver, Amber is focused on continual process improvement, which includes implementing innovative solutions* *to improve the voter's experience. Under her leadership, the Denver Elections Division has earned national awards from the election Center and the National Association of Counties for Ballot TRACE (a first-in-the-nation ballot tracking, reporting, and communication engine), iAPP (iPad Accessibility Pilot Project), and eSign (a first-in-the-nation Digital Petition and Voter Registration Drive Application). Amber currently serves on the Council of State Government's Overseas Voting Initiative's Technology Committee, Advisory Committee of the MIT Election and Data Science Lab, and various statewide and national committees and working groups. She has also served as an election expert witness assisted with legislative and policy development. She has been invited to participate with various national and state professional organizations to identify and implement best practices in election administration. Amber enjoys spending time with her family and loves to ski, read, golf, play music; and especially enjoys her role as a mother to her young children.*

Amber McReynolds is the second key to controlling the votes. Mail-in voters grew because now we can make up fake voters. After all, no Identification or verification is needed, and then who is filling out the ballots. Ballots that vote like (RCV) system, ballots that would give votes to whoever they choose, 1st, 2nd, 3rd, or 4th. This is the person Biden elected to run the US POSTAL Board of Governors in 2021 after he was elected, to say "Thank You."[308]. Is this why the voting system failed the American people? Is this Biden's new thing? He likes Forever Chemicals; maybe this is the new Forever Voting system? The Forever Vote that is not yours. You pick the first choice and will decide the rest! Does your state or town, or even business use this system for any kind of voting? Not first place winner, but the majority of all four votes now count. Ridiculous. She knows the number of votes that had to be created to win! So that number will match up with the states that are seeing a rise in illegal immigrants, you will see.

The whole reason Biden needs those bills passed. So, she can register all those people as legal voters and control where those free votes will go. So, if New Jersey is short 20k votes for a Democrat candidate, then she pulls 20K illegal's documents, registers them to New Jersey, and their vote counts. She has an unlimited amount of foreign illegal's information, and we do not know the state in which they were placed. There is no record of where 12k Haitians went, but when they need a couple of thousand votes to win an election, trust me, those Haitians will be there. The absolute biggest JOkE is they know they cannot win an election from here on out without stacking up illegal voters that are slave voters—taking the most significant gift that separates America from the rest, free elections. The Haitian President was killed because he would not allow the foreign politicians to steal his people.[309] So, with help from US Democrat officials, they used Columbia and other Triangle countries to start the mass illegal immigration crisis we have now. For what, for votes and power! Why, Because Joe Biden started the Refugee Relocation Program.[310]

Lester Bird *is a senior associate for the Election Initiatives team for The Pew Charitable Trusts. He focuses on the Voting Information Project (VIP), where he helps voters find their voting locations and ballot information. He works directly with state election officials and experts from across the country to provide data to VIP, in addition to managing the technical relationships between Pew and its VIP partners. Before Pew, Bird worked various aspects of election administration for the Washington, DC Board of Elections and the Martin County Supervisor of Elections in Stuart, Fla. While working in DC, he co-founded the Knight Prototype Award-winning program, Erase the Line, which helped election officials develop strategies to alleviate lines on Election Day. Bird received his undergraduate degree from The University of Florida.*

Lester Bird works on projects called "How Artificial Intelligence Can Improve Access to Legal Documents," this is just one example of what Lester Bird does with Pew Charitable Trusts. Lester Bird is a principal associate with The Pew Charitable Trusts' civil legal system modernization initiative. Can the Pew Charitable Trusts guarantee election integrity in America? When he does an article about Voting and Voting rights, he is a senior associate for election initiatives at The Pew Charitable Trusts. When he holds an LSC INNOVATIVE in Technology Conference [311], his guest speaker makes statements about American politics like this: you tend to understand his views!

By: Ismar Volić | September 9, 2020 (312)

Example of RCV voting in American politics.

"To the skeptics of ranked-choice voting: Look no further than last week's Fourth District Democratic primary elections, where Jake Auchincloss won the primary with 22.4% of the votes. Jesse Mermell was a close second, with 21.1% of the votes, and seven other candidates won between 1.6% and 18.1%. The fact that a candidate who was the first choice for less than a quarter of those who voted will represent all of them should give us pause. Until Nov. 3, that is, when we should go to the polls and vote "yes" on Question 2 to bring ranked-choice voting to Massachusetts.

Since Auchincloss won fewer than half the votes, how do we know he accurately represents the electorate's choice? Perhaps those who did not vote for him or Mermell would prefer her over him if they knew their candidate had no chance of winning and had a way to express this preference. Or they might support Auchincloss, thereby solidifying his win with an absolute majority. They might even coalesce around a third candidate, giving them more than 50% of the votes, with the way elections in our state — and most others — are conducted."

These are the people changing voting by holding Technology Conferences in June 2019. While a second impeachment trial was blinding the world, the previous administration held voting technology conferences. During a second trial where president Donald Trump was being charged with working with Russia to secure the elections of 2016, this group was securing the elections of 2020! Lester Bird works with people like Jack Haycock; he attended the Technology

Conference that Lester Bird held in June. Jack Haycock works for Pine Tree Legal Services.

This Nonprofit Law firm specializes in Housing Law, Consumer Protection, Poverty Law, Social Justice, Economic Justice, Education Law, Victim's Rights in Family Law, Low Income Taxpayer Clinic, Farmworker Rights, and Native American Rights. I searched and searched and found this one-time lobster boat deck hand-turned internet content controller from the Obama/Biden fan club. Jack Haycock does a lot for Pine Tree Legal. At the same time, working at Pine Tree Legal of Maine, Jack drafts and publishes explicit language client education content of all types. Administers PTLA's three Drupal websites, leads client-facing technology projects, heads social media efforts and schemes, dabbles, and innovates in everything from AI-driven chatbots to unconventional education and outreach efforts. What do the Pine Tree Legal Assistance's three Drupal websites do? What is a Drupal website?[313]

A Drupal is a global content management software in many of the websites and applications you use every day, and you do not even know it! A Drupal website platform is the #1 rated and used platform for web content. The creator is Belgium, brilliant, even from his couch![314] Drupal websites are used by NGOs, universities, governments, and businesses. The government is learning how to make Web Content control, and they are becoming the new Google. The larger the site, the more the traffic and users, the better the Drupal platform works. The venue is the same as Facebook; when you Google glasses, Facebook posts the same glasses on your page, it works like that. The Drupal website uses the same concept to change what content, ads, and stories you see.

Why would Barrack Obama and Joe Biden worry about controlling what the internet puts out in 2020 during an election! Worrying back in 2017 about what I would see in 2020! He was editing the news and actual stories by creating their platform. Why would they need to monitor and baby feed the content people see on major giant web platforms? This was to cover up the Hunter Biden Stories, to make Trump look like a crazy liar, to make it seem like Joe cares about America!

Since the Civil War, the Democrats have been hiding something to keep the lie secret. They do not care about doing things for the country's good; they just worry about themselves. To put hundreds of IT professionals together to find a way to make the Democrat party as big as Google, Facebook, and Twitter. How can they hide the truth and control the election stories? The Taliban is on Twitter, but Donald Trump is not. The January sixth rioters are criminals and held in jail still to this day, but illegal immigrants get free US-funded legal care on the taxpayer's dime.

Pine Tree Legal Assistance Mission Statement: *"To achieve our mission, we provide free civil legal assistance in cases where it can make a difference in one's ability to meet one's basic human needs or in enforcing one's fundamental human rights, including access to housing, food, income, safety, education, and healthcare."*

Government-controlled media, internet, propaganda, and internet content control! Where do I live? Pine Tree Legal Assistance's mission statement seems to be more than just free legal services.[315] It is an advanced NGO that works with the Democrat party and Democrat politicians to help place the people Biden is letting in our country. Also pushing back against Donald Trump![316] How does an advanced NGO / Law Firm for Hire help non-Americans? Simple, their mission statement says one thing; their goal is another. They provide free civil legal assistance in cases where it can make a difference. The argument that we hear today on the news, the cops arrest them, but they get let out free on no bail. Free legal representation to stop Law & Order in America.

In one's ability to meet one's basic human needs or enforce one's fundamental human rights, including access to housing, food, income, safety, education, and healthcare. Including accommodation, food, income safety from deportation, education for free, and of course, free accessible healthcare. Now, stop and ask yourself whether we would need half the government programs we had today if every Law Firm paid for your traffic case, paid for your tickets, gave you the flu shot, and paid for community College also. WTF, if any Law Firm would do this just for one community alone, we would have less poverty overnight.

America, if you read this and do not run screaming for the hills, then check for a pulse, people. A government-funded Firm, fighting courts in America for non-citizens, for free. They are fighting the criminal system to get paid by defending criminals and illegal foreign immigrants during the worse pandemic in 200 years! Paying for a client's healthcare is not free; it is taxpayers' money. This is what they do for non-citizens! The law firm shows the Illegals how to lie, hide and evade the police. They start the process of lying to your American government. This is what the people coming over the border see first-hand, some Americans are good, and others are bad. Lie to some, and others will pay your way and defend you. Creating soldiers for a Civil War, the enslaved people had to choose too during the Civil War in 1861. What side to fight for, what side was good, and what side were liars.

Nobody helps Americans; we pay for all of our problems, bills, food, and healthcare ourselves. A Law Firm associated with Biden/Obama set up a safety net for when they knew they would open the borders. They cannot get deported or have problems at court because their Democrat Government-funded Law Firm is their Sugar Daddy. An NGO is more powerful than the American people who support the NGO. Our tax dollars will keep the police, the courts, and the system working for the wrong people. Imagine having a Law Firm funded by taxpayer's money supporting Illegal immigration.

Democrats put a plan in place in 2017, during Trump's impeachment, to do just that. The Democrats were plotting a way to change the American population. While you could go in a store without a mask, they tell your kids in school to mask up and get vaccinated or go home for two years. When you lose your job if you do not get the vaccine, these people walk in unvaccinated and unmasked. They take the government's payout and do the dirty work for the Democrats.

This is why NGOs are helping Illegals over the border.[317] Why private companies are flying terrorists out of Afghanistan. Biden is paying the NGO and the Catholic church to help the people over the border and into your neighborhoods. They set these people free, giving them a court date to return to court and check in. This is where Jack Haycock and Pine Tree Legal Assistance come in. They set up the court date and defend the immigrant, showing working papers, income, any false document needed to stay in the country.

The NGOs and Private Companies get them to states like Maine, and then Maine receives funding from the US Government to house, feed, and educate these people. Then when their court case comes up, people like Jack Haycock's co-workers keep them safe from our laws. The laws that keep us Americans safe are jeopardized for a foreign person in America! The state of Maine General State Funding gives millions of taxpayer dollars as grants every year to Pine Tree Legal Assistance.[318] When you look at their PowerPoint 2020 Annual Report, slide 15/16 shows expenses. Enjoy watching the breakdown of your tax dollars to help who!

Plus, they receive donations and surprise grants from friends of the Democratic Party. They use taxpayers' money to support Pine Tree Legal Assistance Services. The state of Maine defends the rights of illegal immigrants with American taxpayer's money. The scary part is that a Pine Tree Legal Assistance is in every state helping hide and fund unlawful immigration only if all those companies took their money and helped out American taxpayers. How one person like Jack Haycock, who once was an angler, now runs the IT department of Democrat Funded Law Firm that helps fund, house, and help secure criminals against America?

Defending criminals is one thing; protecting illegal immigrants to secure votes for the Democratic party is criminal. They know they are breaking the laws and undermining America, so why care about you and your freedom? They are letting a refugee become a political football during elections. Pine Tree Legal Assistance takes Amber McReynolds, the Postmaster of the White House, secures the names. They find no crime in defending Illegals in court on the taxpayer's dollar and controlling your internet, defending criminals to be corrupt, and censoring your thoughts.

Hello, what has become of the Democrat party? They are the slave owners all over again. Controlling what we see and believe. The crime is actual, life does not need WIFI, and you cannot shade crime, poverty, and lies with rainbow-colored sprinkles. Steal my country, and no one knows. World, say hello to Jack Haycock, an Obama/Biden operative trained to control your thoughts and government. Why Jack, why?

Where the Rubber Meets the Road: State Statutes & the Certification Process

MODERATOR:

Senator Dee Brown* *has served four terms in the Montana House of Representatives and has one more to go in the Montana Senate. In the Senate, she chaired the State Administration committee and the State Administration/ Veterans' Affairs Interim Committees. She also served on the Transportation, Business, and Labor Committee. Senator Brown was an elementary school teacher for 26 years and owned an RV park outside of Glacier National Park. She has been married to her husband, Steve, for 46 years, and they have two children and five grandchildren.*

This was the most significant find when drafting this book. Yes, the long-term Republican Montana Senator was the find of the century. She was in the House until 2011, right alongside Nancy Pelosi. This explains so many leads I have been following, stories from news articles, and articles that just had weird dead ends. Like why are two guys, two multi-billionaire old White men buying up everything? Buying hotels, land, farms, federal buildings, and of all things, RV parks in Montana. The same town Dee Brown is from. The same RV park that Dee Brown owned for decades!

When looking up information on a Senator that has been in office for almost 20-years, I figured it would lead to pages and websites of information. I found nothing, and it was hard even to find out statistics, voting records, any bill she supported, or even pictures of herself. I found three photographs and maybe five sentences on a website. How can a US politician for almost 20 years have no information or photos on the internet? She is part of the committee on US Federal Telecommunications[319]; this makes sense, nothing on her or her husband, two kids, nothing, Drupal Control. What happened to her in 2020? She could not run for re-election in 2020 because she had reached her term limits.

Senator Brown decided that her last year as a public servant, I should attend a conference on how to change elections in America forever? While the people of Montana needed a strong voice in government, she was out securing her retirement package. Her retirement package involved selling her family RV Park to a self-proclaimed "anti-Trumper."

This was the weirdest and most challenging part. I traveled the country searching places to write this book. The campground was closed down, with 15-foot walls with barb wire surrounding the campground. I read some posts online from patrons, asking what happened? So, that only makes me hungry for more! I called the RV camp next door to find out, and she sold me everything. I used my NC southern charm, and the beans spilled all over my phone. I had called the other RV park, and we gossiped about Dee selling her place to Xanterra![320] Xanterra Parks & Resorts is an authorized concessioner of the National Park Service. The lady's husband screamed in the background as soon as she said, "Old Dee," "Hang it Up!" Before I hung up, I asked her how far Wyoming to Montana is; she said she had never been there!

Why would a Senator own an RV Campground her whole time in office and sell it even before being elected? As soon as she retires from the public office, she sells it to Xanterra! This is where the shit hits the fan. This is where the wealthy elite influence leaks through the cracks, and thy true self will cast a shadow. During Trump's presidency, the bottom half of the population saw their wealth grow; in 2021, the ten richest men almost doubled their total wealth! Under Trump, the average taxi driver made an extra $4,400.00 in his paycheck each year to understand better. Jeff Bezos's, for example, went from $117 billion to $211 billion by 2022.[321] Xanterra is owned by one of the 50 richest men in the world, Phil Anschutz.

Who is Phil Anschutz, you might ask?[322] So, this is where you start reading, and if you listen closely, you can hear the Civil War cannons in the background. Wealthy billionaires have bought up everything since the beginning of 2019. Think Tank supporters and landowners?[323] Including Bill Gates, the largest landowner in America today.[324] Phil has bought up land, railroads, sports franchises, and even an RV Campground owned by ex-Republican Senator Dee Brown.

Phil has been friends with the same companies that destroyed Delaware. Phil owns Pacific Railroad, and Joe Biden wants a bill passed that would give billions to a dying form of transportation called a railroad.[325] Pacific Railroad, you know the name, the train station in California with all the packages everywhere. The pictures of consumers' packages, medicine, Christmas gifts, and covid test lined the tracks as the Pacific Railroad let it happen.

So, the Democrats and Joe Biden are mad at Trump! We know that, so I lost my country because other Rich guys are jealous of Donald Trump and what he did for Americans? No offense, but I would rather have secure borders than 2-day shipping on overseas dollar store crap. No offense, but I would rather have fresh vegetables, chickens farm-raised, and responsibly sourced meat instead of Bill

Gates being the largest landowner in America and buying up farms and closing them down? No food on the shelves of grocery stores? This is getting good!

The second-biggest landowner in the United States behind Bill Gates is Phil Anschutz. They invited a self-proclaimed Republican Senator to gobble up her land in RED STATE MONTANA, where her RV Camp was. Phil and his Democrat donors bought her campground, and it is now a haven for Illegals, foreign refugees that Biden bought from Afghanistan, and whomever else they can find. They are using Lackland Air Force Base in Texas too! Fort Dix in New Jersey houses Illegals too! The RV Camp is not far from where many people in 2020 have been murdered and disappeared.

Dee Brown got her farewell retirement package on the day she spoke at a conference set up two years before the refugee problem. Did she talk about how to cheat your fellow Americans and steal their country under their feet? Montana is a prominent Republican stronghold, and all she did was sell her RV campground to an Anti-Trumper, as a cover-up for the Democrat Party.[326] He is buying up old hotels as housing for the refugees! It is hilarious.

The Democrat political party uses Hollywood and the Media Mogul to change, control, and steal our country. Hello, anyone remembers the Civil War, when the Democrats, rich dudes (Slave Owners, aka Democrats) and Hollywood, aka John Wilkes-Booth, tried to change America for their interest?[327] Not the best situation for us all. Did I just lose my country because a greedy politician hated Trump and sold her land and support and my freedom so a rich guy could hurt another rich guy? Phil Anschutz owns the LA Kings, part of the LA/China Lakers; he owns AEG, a multi-billion media and entertainment corporation.[328]

He also owns Xanterra, the billion-dollar vacation company that bought Dee Brown's RV Campground. He also owns newspapers, International Soccer teams, movies, theaters they play in, stadiums his teams play in, railroads (Pacific Union) just like the one Biden is giving billions of tax dollars to, and he owns oil.[329] Liquid Gold that is, he made his fortunes by drilling for oil on the sacred Utah-Wyoming border. Over nine million acres were purchased, and a billion barrels were drilled and sucked out of the United States.[330]

He made his money from oil, then bought almost every MLS soccer team; he is the league's co-founder.[331] So let me get this straight he hates Trump, he is the owner of Coachella Music Festival but then sells his oil fortune land to Mobil corporation for $500 million. From all the Oil his family dug out of this country through the years, creating massive environmental and health hazards for us all, they managed to buy the news up.

Phil Anschutz learned that if you control the mind, spirit, and heart, you can change their way of life. By hiding lies and shocking news regarding his friends. The Democrats, by adding advertisements about Socialism and hate for the right during every movie played on his 7,000 international screens, Phil Anschutz could change the world. He owns the Washington Examiner, the Denver-based media group Clarity Media, the Oklahoman Newspaper, the Baltimore Examiner, the Gazette of Colorado, and the San Francisco Examiner.[332]

He also buys Right-wing newspapers and keeps them separate from other media groups. He supports them for a while then closes up shop in the middle of the night.[333] Phil Anschutz has been criticized for supporting both sides of the playing field. He used up all of his oil rigs, the world is having climate control problems, and a guy like him gets off the hook. He has pledged to open up a $6 billion-dollar wind farm that is half paid for by the Biden administration, aka taxpayers' money.[334] He has been Pay to Play with every politician who can help his goal. Senator Dee Brown was another person he bought out, another person on the payroll to turn their back on us Americans. Is he like Donald Trump? Does he know the system they created?

In the 1980s, the famous Forbes wealthiest people in the world list came out for the first time. Only one person was on that list that is still on the list today, you guessed it, Phil Anschutz, not Donald

Trump. You cannot blame him or any businessperson that pays to play. The politician is the civil servant, not him! He is doing what is best for his company!

He has also confused people over the years with his double-sided donations. He supports groups like the PBS-funded adequate shows for children and groups like the Alliance Defending Freedom council.[335] This group was designated by the Southern Poverty Law Center as an Anti-LGBTQ hate organization. Double-sided donations. Phil Anschutz supports Christian Values and gives money to anti-gay groups that oppose Gay Marriage, Transition Therapy, and transgender lifestyle.[336] So, the self-proclaimed glass house group Southern Poverty Law designates Alliance Defending Freedom a hate group, but Phil Anschutz supports them financially. Southern Poverty Law monitors hate groups in America, but not the people that fund them?

So, when I am being told about hate in the Republican party, Joe Biden and his Choo-Choo friend Phil Anschutz take the cake! He supports both sides of the fence and sits back as Americans fight. Phil Anschutz also supports Southern Poverty Law Center with significant financial donations.[337]

This is the same game since the Civil War. Now the Slaves are just illegal immigrants and refugees. He also gives money to support the Republican party each year, fund Trump's campaign, and support groups fighting against the Equal Rights Act. He donates to ultra-Right Christian conservative groups to defend the pro-life movement and anti-gay marriage rights and freedoms. Then in the same year, he gives to Elton John's Aids research for gay men of England. He has been in the public eye for years, but you will find maybe a handful of media interviews and some public and court records can be found. This is the person that liberal news should be doing stories on.[338] Pro-Life billionaire that supports anti-LBGTQ lifestyles.

Every newsgroup should have this guy on and be asking financial and ethical questions. He should be running for president of the

Republican party! He is their type of person. Big Oil, prominent Conservative, Capitalist lifestyle, and pro-Christian supporter. This is the guy for the Republican party. If Biden were going to Tax the Rich, would this guy be helping out the Democrats? He could liquidate all of his assets, and the country would be on easy street! Is he one of the people JOkE Biden has in his closet of lies? Whose life matters to him? This is one of many wealthy people working with the media, the Democrat elites, the rich Hollywood actors, the kneeling athlete, and the foreign money interest.

Rich people, a corrupt Government, foreign interest, and financial support make people of the same country fight a battle they created. Is this the Civil War all over again or what? The Democrats are separating our country again; only the Slaves are all of us this time! Why would a self-proclaimed Republican Senator attend a voting technology conference set up by the former Democrat party in the last few years of her political career?

After attending, Dee sells her family's business! Sold it to an anti-Trump, anti-gay marriage, pro-life supporter, pro-LGBTQ, pro-AIDS research, and pro-gay marriage rights?[339] Dee Brown sold out to the who. Did she sell her soul too? Or just America's?

Are Phil Anschutz and Dee Brown for defunding the police in your town? They vote to defund the police in your neighborhood, but not in theirs! Sound familiar? Hate on Trump all you want; people like Biden and Obama are just public servants, like a police officer, a trash collector, a post office worker, and even a school crosswalk officer is a public servant. The only difference between the public servants you see every day and those in the Democrat White House pay to play. No one works for a company for eight years and gets a 33million dollar house or bonus, except Barrack Obama! A trash man, a teacher, and a police officer do not work for only eight years and get a 33million dollar mansion in Hawaii when they retire.[340]

The people like JOkE Biden, Barrack Obama, Phil Anschutz, Bill Clinton, Dee Brown, Kamala Harris, and John Kerry are only showing you what you need to see. If you knew the games and tricks they played, you would storm the Capital and fight through walls to get your country back every day. Fight for our freedom! Just like they are fighting for their power and wealth. We know JOkE Biden has stepped and crushed on anyone in his way. Phil Anschutz is probably a fierce businessperson, and he has every right to be that powerful.[341] He lives in the greatest country in the World, America. They have every right to fight and claw their way up the corporate wall to success.

Real Freedom-loving Americans fought and clawed their way up a wall for their countries defense; they are now called Domestic Terrorists! Why would Joe Biden cut big Oil production and hurt Phil Anschutz? Gas is how much a gallon now? Because he allowed him to buy up half of America and falling resorts during the pandemic due to lockdowns put in place by the Democrats. When they cannot keep the lights on, Phil buys them up.

What is he doing with all this unusable real estate during a pandemic? He is leasing resort properties to the US government to house and support all foreign Illegals Biden has shipped into America this year. This is where they hideout until they can be placed without being seen. Some Illegals live on-site with their families and work at the resorts. While tourism closed down for over a year, the most prominent resorts and property owners got even more prosperous due to the Politicians in office. All Illegals shipped out on planes in the middle of the night; where are they staying? At luxury resorts throughout America, on your taxpayer dime? This is what is going on all over Florida, Colorado, Montana, Texas, and every other area they are buying up. The rich guy hurting America was never Donald Trump, it was JOkE BIDEN and his RICH FRIENDS lying to you as you buy their goods, support their business, and fall for their lies.

The only guy that started on Forbes 5o richest men in the '80s that is still on it today made his fortunes on OIL and Fossil Fuels. One of the reasons we have climate change and struggle to make alternative energy sources. So, what will America do after the pipeline shut down and the Left-Wing Democrats cry for green energy?[342] Do not worry for Phil Anschutz. He has been fine since 2017. He has been lobbying politicians for the largest, most expensive Solar Farm to fuel Nevada, California, and other states in need.[343] So, just like in Delaware in the '80s and 90's when Biden's friends, the DuPont's, poisoned the state with Forever Chemicals and never paid the price! Never held responsible, just opened up cancer research hospitals throughout the state. DuPont still made their billions; Biden covered it up and took the side of the rich guy, not the people of his state.

The same thing is happening now; drilling in almost every state making billions on fossil fuels was OK back then. Then Trump became president, and the entire world cried for our planet.[344]. Trump became 'big Oil, and the world's children blamed him for Climate change, land leasing, and the pipeline. Because Trump made us Energy Independent, he now was an Oil King.

In his first year, Joe Biden has issued more permits for drilling than Trump did![345] The same fossil fuels that are harming our planet and making climate change worse are the ones they sourced. Phil Anschutz is not being punished; he is not being held in Congress; he is getting a trillion-dollar government hand out to build Wind Farms. He bought up all of his needed properties, including Republican Senator Dee Brown's campground. Then when Biden passes his Build Back Better and Infrastructure deal, who will get their wind farm?[346] Another Paycheck from the taxes collected from Americans? He could build his own Wind Farm with his own money made from big Oil. Is he being punished for helping create a problem like climate change? Is he being rewarded for harming the planet? Let me guess, Biden has no idea; Biden never meets his Old Friend Phil Anschutz!

This is Biden paying back his friends. The money from the Infrastructure Bill will go to Wind Farms, Phil Anschutz's wind Farm. America, again the back door politics with rich wealthy donors is the playbook the Democrat party is using. Wind Farms are probably the least effective means of Green Energy to tackle Climate change.[347] It is a place to put tax dollars into, hire foreign employees, and waste time and money on a nonproven energy source. Wind Farms use blades the size of Airplane wings to create energy by spinning in an open field. Imagine being a bird or a bat flying through swinging 300ft swords. The waste from Wind Farms outweighs the gains made by the energy produced.[348]

The whole reason Phil Anschutz is not paying for his billion-dollar wind farm to be built. He would never make the same fortune as he did when he took oil from our earth. The return on investment is not equal; the startup is more expensive than the reward. We cannot blame Phil; he is a businessperson and has seen an opportunity! He is free to work with anyone! Will Phil Anschutz use China products to make his Wind Farms? Will Joe Biden give Phil Anschutz billions of tax dollars to build his wind farms? Will then Phil Anschutz purchase billions of Wind Farm products from China? Then China will give him a kickback; they both own the Lakers![349]

Whoever voted Democrat in 2020 owns this, the inflation, the taxes going up, and our country being sold to foreign powers. Before the Civil War, the Democrats went to England, Scotland, and whoever else wanted to end America![350] The Civil War that divided America has begun again, just as it did on the hands of Democrats; their hands are in the cookie jar of American prosperity once more. The cycle continues with wealthy Democrats using people and their emotions as slaves again.

Phil Anschutz does go to church regularly as Joe Biden does. God Bless America. God Bless You, Joe Biden. You have pimped out Americans to support the super-rich during a pandemic. He is making them more prosperous and more powerful than before the pandemic.[351] JOkE Biden and his friends can do whatever it takes to be rich, powerful, win elections and avoid being accountable in front of the TV. When an average American fights for his freedom, he becomes labeled a criminal and a terrorist! Marked by his own country that he fights for and loves. Wake Up America!

PRESENTERS:

Brian J. Hancock * has served on the US Election Assistance Commission (EAC) staff since its establishment under the Help America Vote Act (HAVA) in 2003. As director of the Testing and Certification Division, Hancock's programmatic areas of responsibility include overseeing the EAC's efforts in testing and certifying voting systems working with the NIST National Voluntary Laboratory Accreditation Program (NVLAP) to accredit independent testing laboratories and develop and maintain the EAC's Voluntary Voting System Guidelines. From 1984 to 2003, Mr. Hancock served on the Federal Election Commission (FEC) staff as an Elections Research Specialist in the FEC's Office of Election Administration. A native of Pittsburgh, PA, Hancock received his undergraduate degree in Political Science from Thiel College in Greenville, PA. He earned his master's degree in American Government at the University of Virginia in Charlottesville, VA.

Brian Hancock has served the US Government for many years. He started at the FEC Federal Election Commission in 1984 till 2003.[352] He also was aware of numerous complaints throughout the years on elections. Numerous states alerted the FEC that WYLE/Huntsville & SEQUOIA voting machines showed four problems.[353] The same four problems from other machines! When Barrack Obama made history in 2008, they said he could have won even more votes! Like when Joe Biden beat his vote tally in 2020, even with Russian collusion. Sound familiar, folks? The Democrats win an upset, then complain about voter fraud! When he was elected by Barrack Obama and Joe Biden, of course, Brian Hancock fixed all the problems, and election integrity was upheld. Super Brian!!!

The states that had problems sent letters about freezes and ballot skews, ballot insertion problems that led to uncounted ballots, unlogged errors, logged-in system errors, TDP, the Technical Data

Package (was overheating processing chips that would cause the system to shut down or freeze) errors, and other problems with the voting machines.[354] The TDP or the brain of the voting machine would freeze the machine counting and tallying ability but still accept ballots like usual but never counted. 2010 was a big year for Republicans if you can recall. The Republican Party swept the elections and won control of the Senate, and won a majority of governorships and state legislatures from the Democrat Party.

This was when the Democrats realized they were going down a dark road, either accept their defeats and let voting Americans reject ideas like Socialism, Wokeism, and Communism? Or do the unthinkable, set up the voting machines to show numerous problems in 2010, pretend to fix, somehow get re-elected in 2012 by being the worse elected anti-American president and anti-American vice president in history! Nothing changed from 2010 to 2012 politically from the Democrats.

Brian Hancock is no stranger to walking, swimming, or even bathing in the Washington swamp; he helped create it. When I looked up our dear Democrat friend who has been on the US Government's Administratively Determined pay scale, he was registered as an AD-00 pay scale member.[355] That means he could make between the ranges of $80k to $175,000k a year working for the US Attorney's Office. When you work for that US office, you can make, on average to start $80k a year. After working for a few years or a decade, you get pay raises, and you can top off at or around $175k a year. Brian Hancock was AD-00 every year he worked for the US Attorney's Office. His occupation descriptions for every year he worked are Miscellaneous Administration and Program, that is it.[356] So, I dug deeper, and before working for the US Attorney's Office in 2004, he was like a ghost until we contacted an old friend, the whistleblower.

We all have a whistleblower; even Hunter is a blower of art; we all know somebody that just blows at life. The whistleblower was CSPAN. Yes, cable news networks used to be legit and have a conscience.

Through the years, four videos show how Mr. Hancock has pushed for Voting Systems Certifications for a long time.[357] Since 2004, he has been saying and pleading the same efforts from one president to the next. He did a total of thirteen CSPAN interviews up to 2019, his retirement year. Brian Hancock is the winner of the retirement plan sell-out award.

Brian worked and served as the first director of the US Election Assistance Commission since 2003. After working 35 years in supporting campaigns like Help America Vote and Rock the Vote, before he decides to attend a conference on Technology voting, you know the one! He lays out the framework on how past elections and other countries try to steal elections, cheat in elections, and scam the vote. He would know he has been behind it for 35 years.

He retired and left public office when the country needed him the most. When asked why he is retiring after 35 years, he said the commute was starting to get on his nerves.[358] So, for 35 years driving back and forth from Silver Springs, Maryland to Washington, DC (only ten miles), he had enough traffic during a pandemic when people were not commuting to work anymore. We all stayed home, and the commute was killing you! So obviously, he is untrue. The ten-mile drive to work every day was too much, so he went and worked for another company that is two thousand miles from his home in Silver Springs, MD.

He now works for Unisyn Voting Systems, located in California.[359] The commute must be a lot smoother with how easy it is to travel from California to Silver Springs. He was replaced just in time for the 2020 election. Benjamin Hovland replaced Brian Hancock in January 2019.[360] Brian worked for the US Elections Assistance Commission and then went into the private sector and worked with the US Government on election security protocols. This should be a conflict of interest and should not be allowed. Brian Hancock, Benjamin Hovland, Karen Brinson Bell, and Kentucky Secretary of State Michael Adams held a cyber security summit in October of 2020 before the US

Presidential Elections.[361] The Cyber Security summit was on Voting During Covid.

As elections got close to happening, the plan was already set in place by the IT conference and the Cybersecurity summit. Both meetings were attended by people like Senator Dee Brown, Amber McReynolds, and Brian Hancock; you know these people! Then the US Elections Assistance Commission (US EAC) retires Brian Hancock to attend the IT conference on regulating elections by being a keynote speaker at his conference. Then was a guest speaker in October of 2020 at a cybersecurity summit with his old job, the US EAC, on voting during Covid. So, the IT conference that was in June 2017, that he was a guest speaker at had nothing to do with the cybersecurity summit?

The framework for voting for the 2020 elections was revamped by the cybersecurity summit held by the US EAC. The US EAC and the Cybersecurity & Infrastructure Security Agency (CISA) used the recommendations from an IT conference set up by the previous administration as their blueprints and playbook for the 2020 elections! Is this not misinforming the American people? This is how and why JOkE Biden is in office. This is how and why The Greatest country in the world cannot count votes on the day of the election as it has done for generations.

Brian Hancock and his friends in the United States taxpayer-funded EAC & CISA use RCV voting to control the elections. The conferences are all the same: growing problems, extreme examples, and a simple solution. RCV voting laws will be put in place, and all for the same reason, VOTING SYSTEMS CERTIFICATION!

A voting system certification is only as secure as the group creating the system. If we cannot trust or even know who makes the system, what good is a certification? When they talk about securing the integrity of the vote, then holding IT voting conferences, it seems a bit hypocritical. A voting system is only as secure as the people who create it. If the people in charge are biased and holding meetings in June 2017 on the importance of mail-in ballots, even before Covid started, then who do we trust! The credibility of their work for securing elections means nothing to them. The guy in charge of verification in 2019, Brian Hancock, now works for the voting machine companies in 2022!

The US EAC and CISA are taking advice from outside groups on security for US elections. From one cybersecurity summit to the last elections, Brian Hancock used his friends from his old job, the EAC, and pushed their agenda from the IT conference held a year before on Covid voting. Before the elections, the Democrat party put Covid Election Protocols in place; before the Covid virus pandemic was fully known, the Democrat party and private IT companies knew the future. Covid was the gift from China to cover up the success of Donald Trump!

The plan from there was simple, control the flow of votes and push RCV voting as much as possible. Brian Hancock is now working for a Voting Machine company that owns the US Elections. His company is trying to sell its machines to every state and overseas.

He works for Unisyn Voting Solutions out of California. Unisyn was one of the first voting systems accredited by Brain Hancock's old EAC job.[362] The "about us" part on the Unisyn Voting Solutions website is a good laugh. They have partners in every swing state that had problems with elections in 2020.[363] The credibility of our countries elections comes from lies and dishonest people. The election process was altered, and companies like Unisyn should be under FBI watch and Congressional hearings. Unisyn Voting Solutions uses an address in California but is registered in Virginia. The business address in California is above a martial arts studio. I was there; it is above a martial arts studio. Travel the country and see for yourself. Or call them, good luck!

Unisyn Voting Solutions is registered under people other than Brain Hancock. Brian Hancock was used by the Democrat party, paid to play retirement, and worked for a Chinese-based election voting machine company that only needs one thing to change US elections. Accreditation from the US EAC the US Elections Assistance

Commission. Brain Hancock worked for years and was a guest speaker at their cyber summit in 2020 before the elections. Matthew Masterson worked there, Christy McCormick worked there, and Thomas Hicks. You know Thomas Hicks, he was on CSPAN in March of 2016 and said, "we distributed $3.2 BILLION to the states to reform the election process. So, that the things that happened in Florida do not happen again."[364]. Then in December 2016, he claims they were hacked! When you read this next part, look at the Business partners of Unisyn.

Business Information of Unisyn: *(*365*)*

Who is Chun Keat Ching, Kyong Davis, Lee Meng Oii, KENNY SIAW PENG LOW, and Jefferey Johnson? They run Unisyn Voting Solutions; when writing back to Senators and addressing the US Congress, Brian Hancock is nowhere to be found. Unisyn Voting is owned by a company from China called International Lottery and Totalizator Systems Inc.! A Chinese gambling machine company is the maker of US voting machines used in California and other Democrat lead states. The California Governor Recall election was decided before it even started. Do you think Eric Swalwell and his Chinese spy girlfriend are very familiar with this company?[366]

Business Overview

Entity Name
UNISYN VOTING SOLUTIONS, INC.

Principal Address
2310 Cousteau Ct Vista, California 92081

Office Effective Date
2016-06-16

Entity Status
ACTIVE

Status Reason
Active and In Good Standing

Status Date
2016-06-16

Incorporate Date
2016-06-16

Duration
9999-12-31

Incorporate State
CA

Stock Indicator
S

Total Shares
1000

Assessment
NON-ASSESSED-MUST FILE ANNUAL REPORT AND RA

Stock Shares
Class A

Registered Agent
Registered Agent Name
Registered Agents Inc.

Agent Address
4445 Corporation Ln Ste 264 Virginia Beach, Virginia 23462

Business Officer
Officer Title
Officer Name
Chun Keat Ching

Chief Financial
Kyong Davis

President
JEFFREY M JOHNSON

LEE MENG OOI

Secretary
KENNY SIAW PENG LOW

This is the company behind our new voting systems. This was set in motion before the 2020 election even took place. The same company making our election machines also makes gambling, horse betting, and gas station lottery poker machines. We are gambling with our future, thanks to using unauthorized election machines. Trust Joe Biden and Barrack Obama, trust the betting gambling world with the US elections? Can Joe Biden, Barrack Obama, and the whole Democrat party be an ally of the CCP government?[367]

This same company also worked with many US states and Democrat leaders to use these machines before the 2020 elections. This is all you need to see, foreign powers interfering in our elections, years of lies about Trump, and Russian collusion. Now the Clintons are in trouble because they were contacting Russia. Did Joe Biden and

Barrack Obama use the CCP government to win their elections? What's next? Will Iran use their interest and win nuclear enrichment?

This is the biggest threat to our national security: outside foreign powers and foreign leaders holding political offices in America. You cannot allow this to happen in your hometown. We can stop all of this. Let them know that you had enough. Biden used foreign influence and crime to change our country's elections, votes, and confidence.

Katy Owens Hubler *is a consultant specializing in election administration policy, especially issues related to election technology. She is a former member of the elections team at the National Conference of State Legislatures (NCSL), where she conducted research and convened meetings to support the work of state legislatures nationwide. Before joining NCSL, she worked for the Denver Elections Division and the Carter Center's Democracy Program. Owens Hubler's recent consulting projects include a continuation of work with NCSL; supporting the Voting Equipment Selection Committee (VESC) on behalf of the Utah Lieutenant Governor's Office; the development of an online election observation training course for The Carter Center and the League of Women Voters; and assisting with the continued growth of standard data format for election systems. Owens Hubler has a bachelor's degree in International Affairs from Lewis and Clark College and a master's in Political Science from the University of Colorado-Denver. She authored a thesis on election management bodies in transitioning democracies.*

Katy Owens Hubler ran for office in 2020 and lost. She worked with groups like the Get Out and Vote campaign and defended voting for democracies. She attended a political event held by Barrack Obama, Joe Biden, and people who spread disinformation. So, while she is authoring article after article about voting security, is she writing about herself? As she promotes her education, background, and arduous work for the American election system, is she working to undermine her purpose in life? She has said repeatedly in articles that we must be aware of Politicians, liars, and ultra-rich powerful politicians.[368] Does she author an article about low profile under-the-radar politicians like ones that go to conferences about voting technology and voting propaganda? She wrote about Teddy Roosevelt, not understanding who he was. But she authors an article about a past Republican loudmouth politician during the Trump years to compare loudmouth rich White guys. Comparing Teddy to Trump is a win-win for the Republican party. Teddy Roosevelt was the first green president; he created the National Parks we love today.[369] This is why CRT is not suitable for America's youth. People like Katy can put out an article about hate. Teddy was a great American and a great President. He is ranked as one of the top five presidents in American history. If we teach what they want, not the truth, Teddy was a loudmouth jerk! Not a bad comparison for Trump either. She writes about voting integrity, but she undermines our elections by attending such a convention.

Irwin James Narum (Jim) Silrum *has served the people of North Dakota as Deputy Secretary of State since 2003. After taking office, he immediately began establishing critical partnerships between the legislature, local election officials, and voter interest groups to implement the Help America Vote Act (HAVA) of 2002. He also provided oversight for all other duties of the office of the Secretary of State. Silrum work in state elections has allowed him to procure and deploy a statewide HAVA-compliant voting system and build a comprehensive election management system called ND VOICES, which all elected officials in the state use as a project management tool for the administration of elections. Silrum is currently pursuing the procurement of the next statewide voting system. Nationally, Silrum has been a member of the Standards Board of the United States Election Assistance Commission since its formation. He served as vice-chair and chair of that 110-member board from 2009 through 2011 and has served on many committees to develop the Voluntary Voting System Guidelines. The pilot projects enhance access to voting for US citizens living outside the country and serving in the military overseas.*

Irwin James Narum (Jim) Silrum is another ghost online. I dug and made a lot of phone calls until something slipped up. The 2020

Voting machines salesperson of the year award went to you know who, Jim. His current job is the procurement of voting systems for the whole state of North Dakota.[370] He is responsible for Election Integrity in North Dakota. They were securing voting systems for members outside the country. Who else is voting outside of the US? When did this become such a problem for people that voting from overseas has become a new talking point for the Democrats?

When we leave military bases empty throughout the world, do we still have military personnel unable to vote? If the Biden Administration moved all those Afghan Refugees to US military bases, are they overseas voters? This is the new lie, game, and racial, political smear tactic that Obama and Biden have cooked up. Start a lie, use the media to do an article, and the lie is now the truth be told. The Democrat smoke screen media tactic that Obama perfected. The truth is, voting has been fine for generations; the results are the problem. Americans are voting, just not the way they like it.

Increasing Access for Military and Overseas Voters

MODERATOR:

Tammy Patrick *recently joined the Democracy Fund as a Senior Advisor. In this new role, she will help lead the Democracy Fund's efforts to foster a voter-centric elections system and provide election officials across the country with the tools and knowledge they need to serve their voters best. Formerly with the Bipartisan Policy Center, she focused on furthering the recommendations of the Presidential Commission on Election Administration (PCEA), to which she was appointed as a Commissioner by President Barack Obama. Former Federal Compliance Officer for Maricopa County Elections Department for 11 years, Ms. Patrick served more than 1.9 million registered voters in the greater Phoenix Valley. She collaborates with community and political organizations to create a productive working relationship with voter participation. Ms. Patrick has a bachelor's degree in American Studies from Purdue University has attained accreditation as a Certified*

Election Voter Registration Administrator from the Election Center and Auburn University.

Where have we heard of Maricopa County before? Oh, wait, I know in the 2020 election cycle. So, this was the plan of Obama/Biden, find the counties in America that the Democrats could never win at and push hard. Find a person, find a contact from the inside and change the outcome of voters in that county. Tammy Patrick![371] When I came upon this, I almost threw something; I am not a superstitious person but come on, America![372] The one county in America that has been a target for The Elias Law Firm of the Democrat party has a representative at America's Obama/Biden Voting takeover.[373] How bad did Donald Trump scare these people? They must have feared the American comeback again. They had a plan to change the election results, and Maricopa County was on their list of objectives.[374] Obama lost Maricopa County twice in both presidential campaigns. He knew what counties needed to be changed to keep a Socialist Democrat Party in power.[375] Was Barrack Obama the first president for the Black Community, or was he a Socialist Marxist Democrat hater of America?

While he acted like he was helping America, he was only securing the downfall of America. Was he not saving the legacy of Slaves and the struggles of Black Americans? He was making us all slaves! People like Tammy Patrick, who went along with the destruction of voting integrity in Maricopa County and all across the country, are Barrack Obama and Joe Biden's appointee. The Help America Vote Act and A Hate Driven Campaign is the way they can call fraud racism and take control of the ballots.[376]

The program was to secure America's elections is the same playbook they used to call foul and create problems. Problems were never seen before until technology and voting combined. We never had week-long or even two-day results to determine the winner of an election until computers came in. The same product gets hacked, hit with a virus, and where personal information is stolen every day. The same product that cannot stop credit card fraud and porno website viruses is now how we trust our elections! Now anyone can hack an election? Is it wrong to be all digital and have no ID required simultaneously?[377]

Kamanzi Kalisa *directs the Council of State Government's Overseas Voting Initiative in collaboration with the US. Department of Defense's Federal Voting Assistance Program. The Council of State Government's Overseas Voting Initiative convenes and supports working advisory groups promoting best practices and facilitating data standardization policy solutions to improve the voting process for over 5 million US military and civilian overseas citizens eligible to vote in US elections. Kalisa previously directed a Help America Vote Act program targeting 159 Georgia counties for the Georgia Office of Secretary of State. He holds a bachelor's degree in political science from Tufts University. Also, a master's degree in public administration from the Andrew Young School of Policy Studies at Georgia*

State University.

Create a problem, have the media confirm the situation by airing it, and now the problem exists. They are creating the narrative at every art show in DC that people of color cannot vote. They can only go to art museums and buy Hunter's $500 thousand worth of art. Are people of color not allowed to vote in the United States? Enough with the misinformation about voting. They are pushing a lie on uneducated people! The US military has a challenging time getting ballots out to their soldiers? Are they behind on payments to bills too? Do they have a problem controlling their soldiers? Does the US military have a problem securing the votes of the military that serve for them? They cannot secure votes and handle collecting votes, but we just heard how great a logistical evacuation we did in Afghanistan. We can evacuate thousands of Afghans, fly them across the globe, and house them in American Military bases in a week. Still, they cannot get an envelope to our military personnel serving there in 45 days to mail back before an election. They can have a weapon of death, but an envelope and ballot are above their pay grade. Did you ever see a sign outside a business hiring "VETS"! Now a VET is untrustworthy and undependable!

The US government can control what a soldier eats, internet searches, payroll, vaccination requirements, and housing. The super grueling task of collecting a page with votes is the biggest obstacle to the US military. So big of a barrier that we need to hire an Art Director to run the Department of Defense Federal Voting program. Now we know why Hunter Biden's artwork is worth millions. Because of the Joe Biden Payback, you help Hunter sell art, and I will make you in charge of all the votes from overseas. This guy will push Hunter's art as something more than what it is, and in return, you will receive a job that can control the votes of over five million people. I would love to see the voting results of what soldiers overseas voted in 2020. Is he qualified to do such a job? Such a job that four armed forces HR departments cannot handle supposedly. Managing an Art district in a small urban city is compared to collecting and being responsible for millions of votes into our election.

Did the FBI and CIA verify him to hold such a job? His job title on his website says nothing about voting; it evaluates and initiates action on matters relating to the arts and humanities and encourages the development of programs that promote progress in the arts and humanities. It has nothing about handling and being responsible for US soldiers' votes and their families' votes. Is an Art director from the DC area qualified to handle such a task?

When you look up his name online, it differs from search engine to search engine. It was another person flying under the radar under YAHOO, but under GOOGLE, I found a little more information. This also explains why people pay half a million dollars for Hunter's art. This guy looks like a genius having his artwork in any DC museum for sale. This is clearly how the Democrats run their politics, backroom deals, and misinformation.

There are even more problems with voting after reading this. The country runs itself on tax dollars. So only a person that contributes to taxes legally should be allowed to vote. Being a contributor to taxes and wanting to know how and what my taxes are spent on is not racist; it is my responsibility. Are these voting controls more illegal than showing an ID to vote? Voting suppression and fraud are happening, just not how you think. He served on the DC Art Council, Overseas Voting Initiative, Council of State Governments, and ex-Georgia Secretary of State.

David Beirne* *currently serves as acting director of the Federal Voting Assistance Program (FVAP). He administers the federal responsibilities of the Uniformed and Overseas Citizens Absentee Voting Act (UOCAVA) for the Secretary of Defense. With an extensive background in election administration and voter education, Beirne works with FVAP to ensure that UOCAVA citizens are aware of their right to vote and have the tools to do so – from anywhere in the world successfully. Beirne joined FVAP in 2010 and served in various capacities spanning the organization, including Director of Voting Assistance and Deputy Director of Technology Programs. Beirne holds a Master of Public Administration degree from Florida Atlantic University and a Bachelor of Science degree in political science from Appalachian State University. In 2014, he completed the Leadership for a Democratic Society through the Federal Executive Institute. In 2007, Beirne received accreditation as a Certified Elections/Registration Administrator through The Election Center and Auburn University.*

David Beirne is the next person to see how the works of Bill & Hillary Clinton, Joe Biden, Barrack Obama, and the foreign influences they support. They do the same in other countries; they work to control and share the same about their voters, sheep to be slaughtered! The Democrat party is tired of campaigning, answering questions, and doing town halls. You saw it firsthand in the 2020 election; they showed the same respect as Putin does to his defensive media. They used a virus or an outbreak like China does to shut down areas, cause mass chaos, make laws and mandates, and control the fear and minds of their people.

The Democrat party holds less respect for the American voters by using foreign influence to lobby away our country. A lobbying group appointed this person in 2007 after the Information Technology Association of America merged in December 2008 with the American Electronics Association. They would lobby as one as the new Technology Association of America. The original group was started by the founder of Hewlett Packard, David Packard.[378] They showed their hate for Trump during the 2016 campaign run.[379] This went so far that the CEO of Hewlett Packard Meg Whitman in June of 2016 held a close door event in Utah with three hundred or so billionaire Republicans and Senator Mitt Romney to decide Trump's presidency.[380] They attacked him and never excepted the election result from the voice of the Americans. They all have foreign influences. China told the technology world of America to "decide what team you are on." Team America, where America is first, or Team China, who will make you rich if you make China first.

The CEO of Hewlett Packard and the Technology Association of America did not lobby Americans for their vote. They got the machines from their foreign friends and took the election. This is where big rich money changes America for their vindictive behavior.

Tying it all together: Your Questions, Answered

MODERATORS:

Merle King* *is the Executive Director of the Center for Election Systems at Kennesaw State University. He serves on the faculty at KSU Computer Science and Information Systems Department. In addition, King frequently supports the* *work of NCSL's elections team, presenting on elections technology procurement considerations to select states beginning the process.*

Brian J. Hancock* *has served on the US Election Assistance Commission (EAC) staff since its establishment under the Help America Vote Act (HAVA) in 2003.*

Another appointed group by Barrack Obama and Joe Biden would change elections in America, change the values in America, and plant misinformation as they tell you they will fix it. Another problem will arise after the election, but do not worry; anything a few billion dollars of taxpayers' money cannot heal. Barrack Obama and Joe Biden worked for and with Russia and China before, and they did it again.

The Obama Administration held an election conference weeks after being sworn in. Irony has a four-letter word behind it, JAIL!

US Election Assistance Commission

Voting System Testing & Certification Division

Unified Testing Initiative and Cost of Testing Meeting

(January 29-30, 2008)

Final List of Attendees (revised 2/3/2009)

Organization Name

The people whose names are **underlined and bold** because they were at both conferences. This one was held to see who was on board with change America, then once they found the people who would help Biden cheat, they went ahead and held the next conference in 2017. The same people from both meetings whose names are highlighted all have something online or in the media about being Anti-Trump or Anti-America. Fair and Honest elections from people holding a grudge or having an issue with what? Freedom, American Pride, or just being #1 in the world. They have a problem with American greatness.

The people at this conference are all Voting machine company spokespersons; this is voting integrity at its best. Elected officials from the Democrat party meet with voting machine CEOs about purchasing billions of dollars of voting machines for a fair election. The conference had Unisyn Voting Machines there, the spokesperson **Chris Ortiz** [381] can get any certification he wants. The new director of the US Election Assistance Commission is a former boss and coworker appointed by Barrack Obama. The US Election Assistance Commissions Director that Barrack Obama and Joe Biden appointed is Brian Hancock, the same guy who works with the Chinese-based election machine company called Unisyn.

The election fraud and corruption allegations were not a crazy Right-wing hoax.[382] It was a planned takeover of our society, country, and people. We cannot have a fair and honest election when every name on this list has a post, a tweet, an article, or an interview where they are documented saying we want fair elections and that then Donald Trump is not fit for the job! They said it, not me.

They did not concede the 2016 election, nor did they accept it, so then they will make right the 2020 election.[383] Their words, not mine! This whole conference was to plan for that when the Covid attack on the world hit, election fraud and changing the votes are the plan for the cyber election of 2020. Secure elections with computers? Laughable! Seems like a setup. What GOP and Democrat officials were on the list and knew the plan of attack for 2020? Who was going ahead with the virus, lockdowns, and mandates that held America still for two years as China and Russia gained superiority in the world?

This is why people charged on January 6th! This is why neither Hunter nor Joe Biden will do an actual interview. This is why Barrack

Obama only talks to HBO, and with Lebron James, they cannot be questioned because they will break. The people at the conference in 2008, weeks after Barrack/Biden took office, need to be examined. It is a sure sign of corruption and greed of the Democrat party and its members. When you live in a town with floods, flash fires, a high crime rate, poverty, lack of government support on even simple day-to-day activities, they are busy planning an election result 11 years away.[384] They are not governing for the people and the country. They govern to secure a job, financial freedom, and make sure their party is a one-party rule in this country, Autocracy.[385]

It is like a little league coach poisoned the other team weeks before the championship by lacing the hotdogs at the concession stand. Yes, everyone will eat the hotdogs, and yes, everyone who eats the hotdog will get sick. It is all worth it as long as his team stays away from hotdogs and the other team eats away. So innocent people will get hurt, but the result is, bad news bears America!

Welcome to the 2020 elections held for ransom by the Democrats and their friends, the Covid pushers! Barrack set this up, a voting fraud plan, in the first weeks of being in office. He had to be a two-term president. Corruption takes time! Do you think no Black Republican Americans were hurt over the last two years with Covid or deaths in the family? Do you believe no Black American person had crime done to them during the previous two years of Covid lockdowns and mandates? Do you think any American, Black or White or any color, deserves this hate? Was it hate to fight a Covid war as others planned our elections?

We are all slaves when our government picks and chooses winners in an election. After buying out its founders, China owns Unisyn Voting Systems and Dominion Voting Systems. Russia was able to hack an un-hackable voting system by working with China. Russia hacked an un-hackable system set up by China; they could hack it because China showed them how. This is where Hunter and people like Phil Anschutz come in. They have already bowed to the foreign power and money. They just needed to hand over the elections and put America in lockdown for years so China could eventually surpass America as the supreme power in the world. Thanks to Barrack Obama, Joe Biden, The Democrat Party, and rich, angry people, it was a success. All of this as childhood cancer is on the rise this year. All this as children and young adults commit suicide at staggering rates. All this while we just surpassed a million deaths in America due to Covid. The war has begun; it started with a virus and ended with a book!

Final List of Attendees

Organization Name: Representative attending

Allen County Board of Elections…Keith Cunningham

American Samoa Elections Division…John Faumuina

Avante International Technology, Inc.…David Alampi

California SOS Office…Lowell Finley

Center for Election Systems…***Merle King***

CIBER…Ann Griffiths

Colorado Division of Elections…***Stephanie Cegielski***

Colorado Division of Elections…***Wayne Munster***

Comisión Estatal de Elecciones de Puerto Rico…Maria D. Santiago Rodriguez

Comisión Estatal de Elecciones de Puerto Rico…Nestor Colon

Delaware State Elections Commission…***Elaine Manlove***

District of Columbia Board of Elections and Ethics…Mohammed Maeruf

District of Columbia Board of Elections and Ethics…Sylvia Goldsberry-Adams

Dominion Voting System Corporation...***James Hoover***

Dominion Voting System Corporation...***John G. Poulos***

Election Systems & Software...John Groh

Election Systems & Software...Steven Pearson

Election Technology Council...***David Beirne***

Florida Division of Election...David Drury

Florida Secretary of State...Hon. Secretary Kurt Browning

Freeman, Craft, McGregor Group, Inc...Kathleen A. McGregor

Freeman, Craft, McGregor Group, Inc...Paul Craft

Georgia Elections Division...Wes Tailor

Hart InterCivic, Inc...Andy Rodgers

iBeta LLC...Carolyn Coggins

Illinois State Board of Elections...Diane Felts

Indiana Election Division...Brad King

Iowa Secretary of State...Michael Mauro

Kansas Election Division...Brad Bryant

Maryland State Board of Elections...Paul Aumayr

Michigan Bureau of Elections...Christopher Thomas

Miami-Dade Supervisor of Elections...Hon. Lester Sola

Miami-Dade Supervisor of Elections...Michael Johnson

MicroVote General Corporation...***Bernie Hirsch***

Minnesota SOS Office...Gary Poser

Montana Elections Division Justus Wendland

N.V. NEDAP...Jacques Hulshof

National Institute of Standards and Technology...Gordon Gillerman

National Institute of Standards and Technology...John Wack

National Institute of Standards and Technology...Lynne Rosenthal

Nevada SOS Office...Ryan High

New Mexico SOS Office...Anita Baca

New York State Board of Elections...Douglas Kellner

North Carolina State Board of Elections...Keith Long

North Dakota SOS Office...***Jim (Irwin) Silrum***

Ohio SOS Office...Eleanor Speelman

Ohio SOS Office...Erick Gale

Ohio SOS Office...Kirk Walter

Ohio SOS Office...Terry Dick

Oregon SOS Office...Dave Franks

Pennsylvania SOS Office...David Burgess

Precise Voting LLC...James Kapsis

Premier Election Solutions, Inc...Ian Piper

Premier Election Solutions, Inc...Kathy Rogers

Premier Election Solutions, Inc...Talbot Iredale

Rhode Island State Board of Elections...Robert Rapoza

Sequoia Voting Systems...Edwin Smith

Sequoia Voting Systems...Michelle Shafer

South Dakota SOS...Jennifer Headlee

SystTest Labs...Traci Mapps

SystTest Labs...Mark Phillips

Texas Elections Division...Juanita Woods

TruVote International, Inc...Larry Holmstrom

U.S. House of Representatives (Committee on House Administration)...Jennifer Daehn

U.S. House of Representatives (Committee on House Administration)...Peter Schalestock

U.S. House of Representatives (Committee on House Administration)...***Thomas Hicks***

Unisyn Voting Solutions...***Chris Ortiz***

The University of Iowa...Doug Jones

Verified Voting Foundation...Pamela Smith

Vermont SOS Office...Kathy DeWolfe

Virginia State Board of Elections...Alfred Giles

Washington SOS Office...Nick Handy

Wisconsin Government Accountability Board- Election Division...Ross Hein

Wyle Laboratories, Inc...Frank Padilla

Wyle Laboratories, Inc...Jack Cobb

Wyle Laboratories, Inc...R. Bruce Bateman

Wyoming SOS Office...Peggy Nighswonger

Chapter 8

The Curse of Joe Biden's America

When I was a kid, there was the curse of William Penn. It had to do with the sports teams of Philadelphia and the William Penn statue on top of City Hall.[386] When the William Penn Statue was placed on top of City Hall in Philadelphia, it symbolized that Philly will always win if its founding father watches over us. When politicians came to City Hall, father figure and pure Quaker William Penn watched down to ensure we held to what he believed. The curse was invented when a "gentleman's" agreement for decades was broken.[387]

A true sign of True America, a "gentleman's" agreement and a handshake, no contracts, lawyers, court, media, depositions, just a "gentleman's" agreement. Never build any structure in Philadelphia higher than William Penn atop City Hall. The curse was to symbolize failing and losing sports teams in Pennsylvania. In Pittsburgh, the Penguins, Steelers, and Pirates won tons of championships from 1987 to 2008 until the curse was lifted. William Penn was the founder of Pennsylvania, Delaware, and South Jersey. The curse had nothing to do with bad trades or horrible owners like Leonard Toes[388], a missed call, or even a lousy stadium built in Philadelphia. The curse put on America and Americans for breaking a Gentleman's Agreement.

The bound that means so much to real Americans, your word is everything but means nothing if your actions do not back it up. I can build you a sturdy home and tell you that, or I can show you. Actions speak louder than words. Breaking deals and agreements are the first stages of failure.[389] The statue was replicated and replaced on Liberty One to end the curse officially in 2008. The Liberty One building was now the tallest structure in Philadelphia; the building symbolized Philadelphia and the Tri-State Area as the next New York business skyline in America on the East coast. The curse was lifted from Philadelphia sports but not our country.

The agreement that kept William Penn towering over Philly was a symbol, not just a gesture of goodwill. William Penn was raised in England. His father served the Crown for years as an Admiral in the Royal Navy. After his father spent decades serving in the King's Navy, Penn wanted to follow in many others' footsteps and be a Puritan in the Americas. After years of service, his father fell ill; the British rule and Crown eventually let them go. His father's regret was for all the cruel acts done under the name of the King of England.

England was losing control over religious freedom, which was still not allowed. The New World allowed people to practice religious freedom and still pay and honor the Crown. Even though William Penn's father served the Monarchy, he went to the King and demanded release for religious reasons. William Penn spoke disrespectfully towards the church and crown. William Penn called the Catholic Church of England the "Whores of Babylon," talk like this got Penn and his family in trouble.[390] The people of England stood up for and saved William Penn and his family. The people reminded the Crown of the Great Service his family had done for the Monarchy and the church. People like William Penn only hurt the Crown with talk of disdain. His family was free to live in America, and William Penn was ready for a taste of freedom!

Penn came to America for a fresh start. People like Penn knew how the British and The Crown thought of and treated British

Americans. He saw how they used his own family and was not going to live in a country without individual freedom, a fair and just system, and a place where God-loving people could live in peace from each other, other armies, and The Crown!

Everything Penn stood for and accomplished is now in jeopardy because some politicians use his namesake as a cover-up. Are you tearing down statues tonight? William Penn owned slaves, and he used them to make money.[391]

If you ask some people, William Penn was a traitor to England; he was anti-Catholic and anti-cities. He did not want a city, row homes, and dirty, crowded streets when he designed Philadelphia.[392] Philadelphia homes had yards and trees; he wanted spaces to walk and be free so people could think and pray. The modern Philadelphia, Delaware, and Maryland are total opposites of what William Penn dreamed of for the new Americans.

William Penn named the streets of Philadelphia after trees, so people could feel different when walking through "Penn Woods." He never wanted giant cooperation skyscrapers, subways, congested roads, homeless people, and trash lining the streets of freedom, religion, and peace. He never wanted center city Philadelphia, looking at the crime rate, either do most!

The Quaker religion is founded on the principle that all men are created equal. Wait, where have I heard that before. Yes, they believe all men are created equal, and even a King gets his power from the Divine God in heaven. He was never swearing allegiance to a King, only to God and Country. Is he a Marine or what? William Penn believed that God spoke to each individual, not at a congregation, not through a crown or King, and not through a donation or offering. William Penn wrote the framework for an ethical society to begin the New Americas.[393]

He laid out the blueprints for our Constitution; his ethical society would not follow the laws of the Monarchy and Elites any more. His radical laws consisted of no swearing, gambling, and bearbaiting; some may be too extreme but very Puritan indeed. His directions were to create a society where people could rule themselves and live-in mutual respect. The pains of big money, big Politics, and Elites' rule in England eventually wore him down and killed his spirit. He was always scared that the Crown or, even worse, an Autocracy would take over his land and his arduous work for a peaceful society before he died. He never heard of the Democrat Party then, or that would have been his biggest nightmare, not the Crown. His namesake and a university betrayed the true founding father of America, and they have stolen his image and put a shadow over it.[394]

The irony of the Pennsylvania University of Wharton Biden Center is that they have crushed the spirits, hearts, and minds of America's future. Quite the opposite from William Penn and his friend George Fox the founder of the Quakers, they valued the youth and their future. They are the ones that started pushing away from a tyrant controlling ruler and made the framework to what we know as Democracies. They started the "rights of an individual" under a crown. They laid the framework for the Revolutionary War, and they were the inventors of a Patriot, a Colonial, a Militia, and a Riot.

William Penn stood up to a corrupt, lying, tyrannic ruler for his own beliefs. People like him made America, the Revolution, and now they use his name and legacy to tear it all down. Who wants to tell Penn that a school named after him trains traitors to tear down what he started, his country, religious freedoms, and his beloved Philadelphia?

When William Penn founded America, he limited his powers to keep a genuine, accessible, and fair Democracy. It was William Penn who made two houses of government.[395] He made sure the rights of the people were upheld, with no unfair taxes. He wanted a fair trial for criminals with a jury to decide their fate. Most of all, he wanted free enterprise so a man could make what his God-given talent would allow. He was the first freedom thinker, and he was the anti-mandate kind of person we judge today! He would have gotten vaccinated because he studied medicine early in life, but he would have gone against a King Charles vaccine mandate. He left over not being allowed to worship freely. William Penn is America.

He founded Pennsylvania, the birthplace of Philadelphia. The birthplace of our nation, the place where they signed documents that made an idea called a constitution, and an idea made a reality. A reality called a Country. He created a country by breaking from British rule, starting fresh in America, and letting the people rule, not a crown or an autocracy.

Would he be a traitor to his people if William Penn were alive today? Would he vote to end police, end security, vote for high gas prices, foreign dependence, and be a part of the Lying Government Elite class? No, Penn left that all behind. He left that all behind and created a new home and eventually a new country. He was the birth of freedom, liberty, and revolution. Penn made it possible to sit, revolt, sign, and create a new one. Our founding father fought British rule and left for a better life in the new world, eventually the United States of America. Someday, people would sit in Independence Hall and sign the Declaration of Independence and the Constitution of the United States! That same place today, generations later, people would sell them out? Just like a traitor, they would hide in their basements!

They play dumb and laugh at questions against them! While sitting back collecting billions from foreign donors at his University of Pennsylvania Biden Center for Diplomacy and Global Engagement. Yes, it started in 2018 with a massive grant from China.[396]

Joe Biden never went to Penn, but his Third Way boys appointed from Barrack Obama did.[397] Why would the University of Pennsylvania and Joe Biden collaborate? Why would this be his launching ground? Why Here? Because of Wharton University, Delaware University and Washington DC Elite would be the only ones to take foreign money to turn their backs on their country. China stole intellectual property during the Obama/Biden era like crazy. Maybe they returned it?[398] There is a shortage of paper products, dispensing containers, batteries, and plastics. Perhaps if you look up at Liberty One in Philadelphia, you can see William Penn taking a knee. Joe Biden showed other countries after 40 years in office how Politics in America works. You Have to Pay to Play. In 2017-2018 Joe Biden went around the world to see who wanted to Play with America and their Politics and put his hand out to see who will Pay?[399]

From 2018 to 2019, Joe Biden made the University of Pennsylvania and the University of Delaware Biden Center his office. He planned every day with the head of the Biden Center, Secretary of State Anthony Blinken. Yes, Anthony Blinken started the Biden Center with him.[400] He helped pick out chairs, tables for the offices, phones, computers, and what bank to put the over one hundred million dollars China donated in the first two years. Tons of foreign "Pay to Play" countries and politicians knew where the hand was.[401]

The University of Pennsylvania and the Biden Center became a second White house. His guests range from Susan Rice, the Ex-President of Mexico, Eric Holder, Loretta Lynch, John Kerry, and anyone else who was in on the "Big Lie." The Barrack Obama team now will use the same racially dividing playbook on another helpless young impressionable generation during the 2020 election. The Biden Center, which started in 2018, has multiple links to articles on its web page from 2017 through 2020. In every article, Joe Biden talks about everything he can do for our country. The lies led to Trump's impeachment trials because of all the seeds grown by the Biden Center.

They were working behind the scenes with Susan Rice to tell the Clinton's on the tarmac to stay out of it.[402] Working with Third Way and the University Wharton Boys to get control of all voting machines in America and getting China and foreign interest on board by collecting massive donations and then keeping the inner circle of Barrack Obama close, the corrupt Anti-American cabinet at it once again.

The Biden Center collected donations before he told anyone he was running! Maybe because it would have been illegal? They collaborated with foreign teachers, leaders, and activists on exploiting our border. Remember the Biden shirts when they first started coming across the border? Not a coincidence. The Biden Center has been working since 2017 to put America down a peg.

The "Big Lie" is that years before the election started, the dismantling of our country started so a 77-year-old can have one more shot at greatness, accountability, greed, wealth, and corruption. The Biden Center is at the University of Delaware and Pennsylvania. His sister runs the Delaware chapter, and the original center out of Penn University is now relocated in Washington, DC. His fake White House office that holds Zoom calls for the Biden Center.

Two former Obama secretaries run it. Pay to Play and keep it all in the family. America, the "Big Lie" is that you believed that Trump collaborated with foreign leaders for financial gain; no, that is the Bidens. The "Big Lie" is that you thought Trump used election collusion and could not live with the election results, no that was the Democrats still angry from 2000, 2004, and 2016.

The Democrats and the Biden Center used their conferences with their University of Pennsylvania crew to corrupt and secure the voting machines. They hire the companies that make the machines, appoint directors of the companies that verify the devices, and accept huge donations and payouts from the makers of the voting machines. Is this corruption Impeachment worthy, or a firing squad. The whole Biden family has been in on the "big Lie" laughing at Americans since 1972. Was he securing American Democracy when he started the Biden Center? Or has he been dismantling our way of life?

While writing this book, I realized the war in America might be the same war going on since the beginning. First, William Penn broke away from Big Government and Elite Rulers. The Monarchies are the same today, the Clintons, the Obamas, and now the Bidens. The scary part is the quiet politicians that we do not see. The power of money and greed can buy anyone. In the Revolutionary War, we fought the English to be free from high taxes and Rich English lawmakers. It was not until the Stamp Act Tax and the Tea Tax took place then our Revolution took shape.[403]

The civil war was not about freeing people who were slaves. It was about paying every worker in America a fair share for a day's hard work in the new expanded America. It explains why men from other countries volunteered for both sides; whoever won did not go home to their families. The Democrats in the south were more prosperous than the Republican north; they paid no taxes, no employees, and kept living and working conditions so low that no one could save up and move on for a better life. During the Civil War, the Democrats from the south invented the term paycheck to paycheck. Just enough to get by but not enough to get gone.

The Civil war was fought over people making money on free labor, the Slaves could have been green in color, and the war would still happen. The battle was about money, one group made money by having their way, and another made their money their way. They could not decide which way was better for the new America out West, so they had a war. Money created yesterday's conflicts, and money is starting today's wars. We have rich people in America and overseas creating Proxy wars, no weapons of mass destruction because no computers are needed.

China, Iran, and Russia can make high-tech missiles, nukes, and bombs to scare many nations. The problem with big bombs like Nukes is the anti-defense systems. The anti-defense systems will launch counterattacks within seconds! Within an hour, the world will be under nuclear attack, and so will the atmosphere, environment, and all living things will no longer survive under the atomic fallout! That is, if they have not already perished from the attacks. China knows if they launch, it is over. Russia already played chicken and realized we are too far ahead of ourselves. Ukraine is the next pigeon chest Olympics!

The four most significant importers of Ukrainian goods are Russia, then China, then Germany, and Belarus. Germany gave Ukraine helmets to fight Russia back, Belarus is letting Russia place weapons in their country towards Ukraine, and China wants the metals in the ground for car batteries and cell phones. It is about the money. Ukraine has something, and someone doesn't want to pay anymore!

If any country launches a NUKE, they will be hit so fast with counter strikes that their country, which fired first, will still not last. So how does a country win a war anymore? The truth is that if we ever decided to go to a real war against another nuclear power, the world would end! The truth is that nobody wants that. Our biggest threat is on Biden's watch! Our biggest threat is an unmarked Air Force bomber from Afghanistan, flying over America or anywhere. They have a nuclear warhead from Iran, open the cargo bay, and drop like WW2. The firing of a warhead is what sets off counterstrikes and anti-defense systems. The warhead can fit in a bus, a motorhome, or a plane.

So, the wars today are fought differently than in WW2. By manipulating, controlling, creating chaos, and never moving forward. The politicians who fight in battles now fight in media propaganda towards their people. In their right mind, what kind of American thinks giving terrorists weapons to harm more people is all right? The thought alone makes people sick; well, maybe that is the whole plan. Not actually doing it but just telling it to you and making you watch it for days in the media, so now you believe.

See with your own eyes and get sick from the thought of what your country is doing. The idea then plants a seed of hate, anger, mistrust, and conspiracy towards my own country and people. The thought makes a person question the future, their country, and the economy every day and ask themselves why they work so hard if tomorrow will never come. This creates a less stable UNION and then starts division from within. I think less of my fellow Americans when something so crazy is being done to my country, and no one around me is upset or angered like I am.

The war that was supposed to between the USA and them is now between the USA and the USA. A Civil War was started by politicians, who were once Civilians like us. That one day you are a bartender, then you are a politician. Does that make you qualified to make laws that affect the whole country?[404] This proxy war that the Democrats and Republicans fight is not about their hate for each other, but the hate they have for us! If January 6th showed you one thing, that every politician that day was threatened by Patriotic Americans who had enough. If they were really on the sides they portray, then doors would have been open, people would have been able to do real damage. Every politician that day feared for their life. Why? Because it is all a fake war.

The struggles every day that we face are the fights they create. An actual Democrat political move, create a disaster and then be the shining knight riding in to fix it. The oil pipeline was canceled as soon as he won office in 2020. Gas is almost $5 a gallon. Then he opens up the reserves and saves the day, literally a day worth of fuel. The fake, made-up problems are caused by politicians who "Play with Their Pudding." They never want to solve real problems, only create new ones, so we fight over them like fools.

This last fight between the Democrats and Republicans nearly put the country into another Civil War, a war that never should have happened. Another War between the rich, the wealthy, and the greedy politicians in this country. We are supposed to believe that all of our latest problems result from a two-year pandemic and a one-term president. The high crime is due to the pandemic? People are being stabbed and mugged because of staying six feet apart. How long of arms do these criminals have. The mask mandates let criminals hide their faces and identity from security cameras. No ID seems to be the mantra.

Our gas shortage and price hikes result from being "NON-Energy Independent," under Trump, we became Energy Independent for the first time in American history. Now we bow down to the oil gods of the Middle East, and we buy toxic water-downed gas from European countries. Russia and Putin are now the biggest suppliers of liquid energy today, as it just hit $90 a barrel! Russia is the world's biggest fuel supplier now. Joe did That! Fuel shipped overseas and refined in a foreign country under foreign regulations. Dirty Gas?

Are the shopping crime spree and the "Smash n Grabs" due to people starving or people being unpoliced? When you watch Law & Order, imagine a show where the police officers catch all the criminals then nothing, no jail time, no court case, just let out on parole. It would only be a half-hour show. No criminal paying for the crime; arrest them and then let them free to do more crime. Look what the Democrat's "let criminals be free system" does to America.

We have a shortage of food, toilet paper, milk, bacon, cream cheese, and prescriptions. The one thing we do not have a lack of is hate and crime. Why have we not seen smash n grabs at a 24-hour store, like a Walmart or a Publix? There you can steal useful things like prescriptions, alcohol, clothes, food, bacon, money, pocketbooks, wallets filled with Holiday cash, safes in the back, employee's jewelry, and Hot Pockets in Aisle 10. Can you not wipe your ass with Jordan's? The people that steal pocketbooks sell them to buy food? High-end clothing that only the rich buy. High-end shoes that only elite athletes flaunt. Are we stealing necessities out of a pandemic, or are we stealing luxuries from a failed government?

The crime in California is in Nancy Pelosi's district (her term is up in 2023, but she is running in 2022) and Vice President Kamala Harris's old stomping grounds.[405] They both served San Francisco; Nancy still does; Kamal was the District Attorney of California and a Senator. The crimes could be stopped. They choose not to. Why not now while a Democrat is President? Why at this point does Kamala let San Francisco and America cry over senseless crimes? Because it does not affect them. The Elite class of America is above the pandemic, above the shortages, and above the mandates, which is for us fools to fight over.

During 2017-2018 before the Covid lockdowns, Joe and Jill Biden traveled the world with John Kerry telling people that same Blame America game Barrack Obama did.[406] Spewing hate from Guatemala to Haiti, telling countries that no Americans think and act like Trump and his supporters. The Donald Trump supporters are racist, and when I am elected, our country will be open. Remember the "Biden Let Us In" t-shirts when he entered office? In America, we faced crime waves, race riots, and impeachments. Americans did not react as the politicians hoped. We did not fall for the diversion, so what was left?

Unleash the China Covid-19 virus on the world. Then what did America's Elite do? Buy it all up. Bill Gates, Jeff Bezos, and Phil Anschutz did the same thing to America that China did to the world. Buy them up and out when they are sick and dying.[407] They bought up farms, dairies, chicken productions farms, vegetable farms, poultry farms, and slaughterhouses, all before the pandemic as soon as Trump entered office. They tried so hard for three years to crush him and the American spirit; they unleashed Hell on the World when all else failed!

Just like the Democrat playbook, make a disaster then be the ones to clean it up, only this time the pandemic was too messy. People were going to die, and people would feel this for years to come! Worse than the Great Depression, the 9/11 attacks, and even Pearl Harbor. If we do not change from being used as tools, we will continue on the same path as today if we listen to Hollywood or trust the media. Every day will be the same, and every day you will take a knee at a funeral for America. Then we will have to listen and change. Will it be too late?

Bill Gates, in 2019 became the largest landowner in America while divorcing his wife, rekindling an old college fling, and starting the destabilization of the American farm life as we know it. Once his wife found out and read his emails, she divorced him. Good choice, do not be around when the house falls. Bill bought up every failing farm before and after the pandemic started. He just closed them up; he never reinvested in dairy calves, never bought more hens, never replanted seeds in the fields, just let them dry up. He slaughtered everything over the summer. We had the chicken Fast Food wars, and we had burgers for the 4th of July! Then the holidays came around, and the 6 to 8week replenishment period of livestock, produce, and poultry products never grew back. If you do not replant, then you will not regrow a harvest.

A farm is a real job, not a place where we can Build Back Better after failure. Real Life only gives you so many shortcomings to mulligan! Real-life or real farm life makes you **BUILD** every day, so tomorrow is **BETTER,** so you never have to look **BACK**! We all felt the shortages during the Holidays; Americans feel even worse under the Biden/Harris administration. What happened to all the chicken sandwiches? Who wants to eat thighs? For years people in every walk of life described the pig as dirty and unclean. There are religions against it! Bacon is at its highest price ever. Who is not following their strict religious diets? We just had a shortage of food for the Holidays. Why? Because if you do not change, we will make you change. If you do not get the vaccine, then you will pay. If you fight the US school system, then gas will go up!

Bill Gates has stock in the largest meat protein substitute company globally, with no shortages.[408] Bill Gates alone has invested $50 million in Impossible Foods and actively finances Beyond Meat. KFC just launched fake chicken nuggets! The Colonel would flip his shit![409] Do not believe me? Look at the freezer section, full of fake meat. The election of 2020 was not won by the will and the votes of the American people. It was a pay-to-play money grab of the wealthiest country in the world. If the people of America will not change, then we will make you change.

If Americans do not want to recognize climate change, we will make you change. If America wants to vote a guy like that into office, then Biden, Obama, Hollywood, Left-Wing Media will make you change. Trump was not a fluke, not a Russian Hoax; it was a fair election where the people had their voice and votes heard.[410] Our debate of hate between the Left and the Right was never between the people but the greedy politicians. Why is the filibuster a big deal? Because the grown adults, called politicians, cannot trust each other!

Do you know why we need forty-plus election security groups paid with taxpayers' money? Not because I can cheat, it is because the politicians can cheat. If I cheat, I go to jail. If a politician cheats, he becomes president! The strict laws and rules on voting are because of the people we are voting for! When you take a drug test, does somebody watch you? YES! Because people cheat! We have all these regulations because of dirty politics, so why not have ID requirements?

It is like both sides of the table agree on one thing, keeping us down and fighting! Five people voted in the 2020 election. They might tell you about how more people voted than ever before.[411] They will tell you Biden got the most votes in history, but only five votes counted in 2020. The wealthiest Americans were pressured by foreign influence to control the vote, or they would stop the paychecks coming from overseas. America is not ready for the truth, but America has been had.

The same Democrat party who went for help overseas during the Civil War has again reached out their wallets for foreign interference.[412] Interference this time could not only come at election time but put the world on its knees. The wealthiest people in the world with foreign powers started today's World War 3 in their own countries. The only way to conceal and hide is to cause chaos. They were assassinating a President, creating a refugee crisis, opening up a border to allow crime and drugs to flow across America.

All this unrest is causing inflation and prices to rise. Riots, race riots, police shootings, protests, and the icing on the cake January 6th. The virus was strong enough to kill a few million, so the world, especially Americans, found its place in the new world order. Set by the Democrats and the foreign powers they use as allies. In his first months in office, the Biden presidency faced an oil hack from Russia and a Sloppy withdrawal from a War Zone. The policies snowballed into lousy economic growth. Giving out free money to eligible healthy workers only created more inflation. He goes to Dover and hides, as we face a food and household item shortage worldwide from MADE IN CHINA GOODS.

The only foreign powers that have benefited from Biden's victory now seem to be the only ones not affected by the Covid virus outbreak. They are likely marching into Ukraine as you read! Of all the countries affected by the various Covid strains, what three countries suffered the least financially, had the lowest death rate, and had a quick economic recovery time from such a devasting worldwide pandemic? The friends of China, of course!

Because Russia and Iran/Iraq never sent soldiers to the World Military games on October 18, 2019. Guess where they were held, please guess! Wuhan, China! On October 18, 2019, I swear to God that the World Military games started in Wuhan, China![413] The soldiers from over 150 countries complained of being sick, almost with Flu-like symptoms. This is where China could find a healthy host that can carry a virus home to every country. Nobody ever questions how a virus spreads so fast around the globe! After a 2-3week incubation period, they used healthy soldiers to carry the virus home, home for the holidays. October 18 was the first day, it lasted ten days, and then the soldiers took the virus home to every country they called home. They sent them home on the 10th day, right before the two-week incubation period, still healthy enough to go home.

Soldiers worldwide, especially in America, celebrated the holidays with their loved ones, 2-3 weeks after the games. This is how the elderly in America dropped first during the pandemic, from the healthy host so rightfully proud of his medal and duty, coming home for the holidays. It explains why the active military is against the vaccine mandates. They know the truth! They have talked to fellow soldiers who went to Wuhan, China, for the games.

At the same time and day in America, a think tank held a health pandemic crisis conference. On that same day in October 2019. The same day in New York, The World Health Organization (WHO) and some familiar famous faces from the pandemic held a convention.[414] That same day, the Bill Gates Foundation, Johns Hopkins University (the death count pros when Trump was in office, now they stopped counting dead Americans) held a medical pandemic convention or a think tank. The World Economic Forum (the G20 summit group that did not like Trump's America First Policy)[415] all were there. They called it a high-level pandemic exercise. On October 18, 2019, it was held in New York, NY. Humans manufactured the virus, and the vaccine research showed us that.

When they put the Covid Delta strain through the splicer, it revealed human-made protein elements. The whole reason we could do "Warp Speed" is because we could use reverse science on the virus! Who would sell their country to foreign powers to destroy their own home? What kind of person would jeopardize so much without being afraid of the unknown outcome of a pandemic? How could they put our lives on hold for two years while they knew it would be all right? When you see politicians not wearing masks at concerts, do they know something you do not? Traitors?

Once again, the greedy wealth of the country is about to jeopardize the most extraordinary Union in the world. When the world faces another shortage of computer chips in 2022, who has the answer? China and Hunter Biden. Ukraine! Trump kept America running energy independent. Now Russia is the biggest and is marching into Ukraine to refuel! I am tired of the Biden Redemption Catholic Boy Routine. Just like the DuPont's in the Tri-State Area in the '70s and '80s. The DuPont's made Trillions by causing harm with Forever Chemicals. So, what do the DuPont's do? They donate hospitals to child cancer research that they helped cause. On taxpayers' money, Phil Anschutz will look like a Pioneer in the Solar Clean Energy world, but uneducated voters will forget about fossil fuels and who caused Climate change, big Oil! He is big Oil!

If a race of White people is to blame for slavery over one hundred years ago, then maybe the man who made trillions on fossil fuels should be answering a few questions? If the company that sold prescription drugs to doctors that the FDA approved are to blame for the Fentanyl epidemic in America! Then a person who made money on oil should be responsible for the harmful effects of fossil fuels being dug from our earth. When you see that Native American Indian in the Wyoming canyons crying looking at Oil refineries, that is big Oil! When you see an oil spill on the California coast ruining the ocean, that is big Oil! It is about time we realize that a handful of people and their greed have changed America and its Politics forever. Forever Chemicals! It is a pattern!

The people in this book and The Democrat Party worked with foreign governments to set up a sure-fire way to win the 2020 election, bring the world to their knees, eradicate portions of populations and secure dominance over the world by military and financial gain. Hello, Ukraine is not being invaded over Covid vaccines or KN95 masks. People protest big Oil and the pipeline because it is the trendy thing to do. They must realize a war is being fought over metals that make batteries for cellphones, electric vehicles, and computers—stuff we all use constantly. The USA fought a war in the Middle East over oil, but we became energy independent at home to leave that warzone. The war in Ukraine is about Russia taking the land; they always wanted it back. China has the machines and resources financially to mine all the minerals they desire. Germany and Belarus are like the chubby twins who watch their backs. No NATO, no UN, just a country being taken over to make electronics! RadioShack is looking good right now.

They set up conferences on Technology and Voting during their terms, to be held during Trump's term. They planned the perfect place to unleash a deadly virus on thousands of healthy hosts and spread the most lethal virus in over 220 years.[416] In February of 2022, they can reinfect all over again! During the Olympics in China. Nobody is out rioting, trashing up, burning, and disrespected anything over China's human violations. After Biden left office in 2016, he went right to campaign, slander, downgrade, and trash-talked Trump from day one.[417] He went right to the University of Delaware and Pennsylvania and set himself up as a professor, a celebrity, a savior, and a good father. Of what I have no idea, but the youth of America ate it up.

He campaigned to the uneducated College students who had just started growing up and never voted before. Well, do not worry. The Biden Center will teach you about horrible politicians. Politicians like the kid who let companies dump illegal chemicals that caused cancer and maybe killed your grandmother. Do you know a bad guy like that? If you are a student who goes to the University of Delaware or Pennsylvania and you know someone who died of cancer, and you voted for Joe Biden, who is to blame? If you voted for Joe Biden, you would put your family member through soul chemotherapy in heaven.

Within months, he opened both centers, the Joe Biden Center Institute at the University of Pennsylvania and Delaware University. The Biden School of Public Policy & Administration vowed to attack apathy and inspire a culture of civic engagement through voter registration drives, facilitated discourse, and educational programming to create life-long ambassadors to Democratic involvement. Turbovote is an online service developed to fulfill this simple proposition by allowing students to register to vote, change their registration address, request an absentee ballot, or simply receive reminders about upcoming elections. Valerie Biden, his sister, was vice-chair at the Biden Center at Delaware University[418]. Anthony Blinken is the director of the Penn Biden Center. Anthony Blinken got 33.1million dollars from China and another $10 million from European governments to start one center. So, in 2017 when Joe Biden said he was not running for president, was he lying? He received money from foreign donors for what, retirement? To do what, apologize for horrible America as Barrack Obama did![419]

Was it to end America's rule and to hand over the greatest gift in the world to tyrants? True Freedom and Democracy is not given away or taken; it is earned! The guest that attended and spoke at the Biden's Centers range from celebrities, Hollywood producers, Ex-Government officials, athletes, actors, Directors of the NIH, Foreign Politicians, and anyone else who wants to get paid by the Biden Center for a public speaking check. They will say what the Biden Center is trying to push, a new Socialist public policy in America. Are you able to just go to any University for free? The student is fighting the thought of Capitalism but engaging in Academic Capitalism to thrive.

The Republicans had nothing to fear! Seventy-five million of us are still standing, waiting to vote again! They do not want to teach the truth, and they do not want you to learn the truth, ironic!!! The freedom to speak, self-express, and be politicly free at a public University stopped because a teacher cannot relate to his students? Why because he is not the same color or just a shitty teacher? All those freedoms they are trying to push on America are the same freedoms slaves died for. The same liberties that over 620 thousand Americans died for during the Civil War.[420]

The sad part is the children are the ones hurt the most! Math does not have a color. English is and will always be a, e, i, o, u, and maybe y kind of race. History is history. It is over, and we can do nothing about it but LEARN FROM IT. So, when they fail to teach children, they fall on every level.

The supporters and presenters for the Biden Center get to the uneducated youth before they learn about paying bills, taxes, student loans back, student debt, car insurance, PPI interest tax on a mortgage, should I go on. So, they get to the youth, and they misinform the child and ruin it for your kid; why? Manipulation and power! Are they all just influencers? The Biden Center paid a lot of people to lousy talk and trash Americans; you know, the "Deplorables." They paid influencers to influence your children at a college where they should be learning life lessons.

I guess they all learned the hard way; thanks, Joe! The College student is fed what they want them to believe and eventually control the vote. If Trump = hate, then Biden =? If a person has a negative opinion over Donald Trump because he acted like a disabled reporter [421], well, Joe Biden released Forever Chemicals into the grounds that lead to childbirth defects and disabled people being born.[422] If Trump is a scum ball because he slept with a Porno Star that sleeps with people for money as a career, then Joe Biden's son Beau should be dug up and re-killed for letting a wealthy elite donator rape his three-year-old daughter and get away with it.[423] If Trump is a bad guy because his dad gave him two million dollars to start his business, then Biden is the worse father for letting Hunter make money over foreign donations and ruin his dead brother's family and legacy.[424] If Donald Trump is a bad guy over a never-proven Russian Hoax, now confirmed as a lie, then Joe Biden is a disgusting person for Afghanistan, Ukraine border crisis, and the China Red Sea take over [425].

Children of America, this is your wake-up call, enough of being sheep. If you love your country, you are not a racist, then wake up. If you love your family and country, you are not a voter of Joe Biden. If you just want peace for yourself and especially your children, we all believe the same things. When someone is getting paid to speak to you, pay attention because the shit is getting deep, as deep as their pockets!!!

The same CRT learning they are trying to push on innocent young children who have never even had a racist thought is taught at every college, every Biden Center talk, lecture, meeting, and still at the White House today. If you tell an innocent child that everyone is a racist, then they believe it! They are innocent kids! They are brainwashing our children and have already ruined the millennials—the generation that hates a police officer or authority. The age is ashamed of being American because our grandfathers won a war or two. That will not stop here, and now they will go to our elementary public schools, fill them with non-English speaking foreign children, and tell you that you are a racist because your parents do not want to pay for more school taxes. They will have to teach slower so everyone can catch up, hurting the more advanced students and regular students even more. We have put education on hold for two years.

How much longer do our children suffer?[426] They have tried everything, and the parents of America have had enough. The parents of America are not allowing the Biden Administration to brainwash a generation of Americans.[427] We do not want our sons to be like Hunter. I am sorry, but I have that right. Is Joe Biden a good father? Did Joe

Biden know that Hunter had an affair with his dead brother's wife? Are Jill and Joe Biden good grandparents by allowing that? Is Joe Biden an excellent Catholic because he will not sign the abortion bill from Texas? Is his faith in God genuine? A True Catholic that is not pro-life after they hear a heartbeat. What kind of father is Joe Biden? A grandfather's most important day is when his son calls and says, "Dad, we are pregnant"! You live your life to make your children's lives better. Why am I a bad parent? Because Joe and Jill Biden said I was? Joe Biden is the worst President this country will ever have, mark my words. America, are you Woke yet? Here is the list of people who supported him before the "Big Lie" of 2020!

The Biden Center crew are the masterminds to Biden winning. They pushed Defund the Police, and now crime waves are in good neighborhoods! They made Refuge Relocation, and now we have a crisis at the border! The get out of jail card program that is ruining cities in America, are they behind that too? They mocked Trump for attending and graduating from The Wharton School of Business, one of the most prestigious universities in the world. I know Trump had to get at least a 2.0GPA or better during his years there. Do not worry if you cannot get into that great school; you can simply be fine and transfer.

Transfer into a Biden School Major at the University of Delaware. If you are a UD undergraduate student who wants to transfer into a Biden School major, please know that we accept and review applications throughout the year. To get started, click on UDSIS from the University of Delaware homepage. You must have a minimum GPA of 2.0 to change your major to energy and environmental policy, organizational and community leadership, or public policy.

This is the Transform form from the website of the Biden Center at The University of Delaware.[428] That is who Joe Biden primes to become a public servant and run our cities, towns, and country. So, when they blast the Trump and Deplorables in general, the standards to get into the Prestigious Biden Graduate program is not even close to the GPA to get into the Wharton School of Business.[429] With a 2.0 GPA, you cannot even get into the most common universities. The lowest-ranked GPA College in the US is at 2.2 at Concordia University in Ann Arbor, Michigan.[430]

The Biden Center has lowered the GPA to parmesan sniffing cheese levels. Wouldn't we want the best minds to become doctors, teachers, and especially political leaders and lawmakers to have a good grasp on education and intelligence? Why does the Biden School Major require C students barely? It makes Joe's career GPA of 1.9 seem better?[431] The University of Delaware is lowering its standards to allow people like Hunter and Joe Biden to flourish on campus and in life. Parmesan sniffers and plagiarism students all across campus. The University of Delaware lowered its standard and went down a peg just like Barrack Obama and Joe Biden have been telling us for years. They preach around the world, bending the knee and bowing down, asking for forgiveness that does not belong to them. Because we won a war or two, we should apologize.

They attacked Pearl Harbor twice![432] Did the Japanese people apologize twice? In 1917 the country of Mexico was asked by Germany to invade America and declare war on us. The Germans tried to get us into a battle; they promised Mexico land and power.[433] They promised Texas, New Mexico, and Arizona to the president of Mexico at the time. The letter was intercepted and was given to US president Woodrow Wilson.[434] The message was in code, so there are a lot of lies when people tell the story. The story of how the Mexican President denounced the letter and swore off the alliance with Germany is to save face; Mexico wanted war! The Mexican President only swore after the letter was intercepted! The letter was in code, code that only Mexico and Germany knew.[435]

If I were going to send you a letter in code, would I not think that maybe you need to know the code to decipher it. Or was Mexico going to figure out a German coded letter sent to them? How would they know what to do if they did not know the code! So, the lie that Mexico was harmless and unaware is another lie in history. So, if Barrack Obama, Joe Biden, CNN, and the left Democrats want to bring up history, please be right. Why did Barrack Obama and Joe Biden bow down and pledge to other countries that America is back and ready to work with their allies!

Only a student that gets a 2.0GPA would believe the rubbish, the lies, the fake history, and a narrative of being woke! It is the same country that people are dying to come to, crossing borders and leaving their homes for, a horrible place! The country people separate from their families for years to work in is such an awful place! Then why do refugees from over 60 countries come to our Southern border? I know because we are a hateful, ugly country! The Democrats sell America as the land of opportunity to the rest of the world but tell us how bad day-to-day life is on the TV every day. We live in the most fabulous place on earth, which is why they are trying to take it from your children!

The Biden Center is failing American students, just like he fails America! Free tuition, free health care, free childcare, free money, the only thing not free, is attending the Biden Center. According to former Vice President Joe Biden's recent financial disclosures, a report shows that the University of Pennsylvania has paid Biden $775,000 to be the University's Benjamin Franklin Presidential Practice Professor over two years.[436] So, for two years in time, the worst president ever taught a class on how to be the worst president ever! Would you trust Joe Biden with teaching your kids? Would you trust Joe Biden to keep your son off of drugs?

Here is a list of Paid Biden Center Speakers before the 2020 election. Many people talked about Russian collusion, not accepting that Trump won without cheating.[437] The Biden Center and all who worked there never accepted the election of 2016. They worked in the White House for eight years, and they did such a lousy job that Trump crushed Hillary fair and square. They could never get those votes as he did, so what did they do? They planned a government takeover. After two failed attempts to boot an American president, a hostile regime let out a virus. They never accepted the loss, and Americans attacked their government officials. They attacked the politicians, the leaders, the rioters attacked cops, buildings, businesses, and homes.

The American people have an internal will always to be the best! That scared them, and they hated Trump for doing as the people wanted. Secure streets, secure borders, secure energy, and low prices and low taxes.[438] Everything that Biden has changed or helped ruin with the help of his guest speakers and paid to disinform College students so the Democrat party can stay in power. These people are as low as the slave-owning Democrats of the civil war. They are the John Wilkes Booth and Lee Harvey Oswald of today. These are the traitors of America. Hillary cannot control her husband but wants to control you and call you a "Deplorable."[439].

Obama and the Left still talk bad on GOP supporters anytime they can.[440] The finger-pointing and name-calling go both ways, but when you deliberately and systematically design a plan to crush America with foreign money and influence, you must pay. The people on this list are the traitors of 2020, the crime causers of 2019, the CRT inventors of 2018, and the actual haters of American freedom. To them, America is obnoxious and overpowering. So, they decided to push lies and be offensive and cheat. So, they can overpower us and crush our spirits. They started at colleges with hate, division, and degrading speeches. Those speeches are the reason so many kids stood up and rioted during the last months of Trump's presidency. Those people are the soldiers doing the dirty work for the Elites.?

Then read this list of Joe Biden Center Speakers that got paid to sell the "BIG LIE"! That got paid to misinform and spread hate on half of America! The age of slave owners were Democrats!! They were the haters then, now, and trust me, and they will still be hating in the future. The Democrats live off the pain, hate, division, anger, and lies.

The world is tough enough without your government making it more challenging. The Democrats used everyone and anyone to disinform America about Donald Trump! They smear his family, his career, his past career, his years in business, personal love life, phone calls, investments, bank accounts, and anything else that stuck to the CNN media wall.[441]

The media is also in on it, we all know now. The Senate and the Chinese government were in on it; they gave Covid to the world. The big Tech social media was in on it; they blocked Trump Tweets but not ISIS beheadings. The only people not in on it were the taxpaying Americans. The people that fought in a world war and came out champions were not in on it. The greatest generation that ever lived took the most considerable death toll during Covid, and they were not in on it.[442] The seventy-five million people who voted Republican were not in on it. Thanks to this book, secret meetings made years before they were held, Hunter's addiction to everything, The Biden Center donations, RCV voting, UNISYN, and fixed machines companies are now brought to your attention. Now you are in on it.

Does this country even have a chance? The world, the Democrats, the Illegals breaking our laws, the purse snatchers, and the police haters', time is running thin. They have taken the Republican's kindness for weakness, and now it is time to show the world America is back and strong! The people who are hurting everyday Americans and the world are the Democrats. Wake up, America, and stop being used.

These people got paid before the 2020 election by the Biden Center to give speeches they did not write to undermine America! They trashed President Trump, undermined the Republican party for supporting their president, and gave speeches to undermine law and order of our country. These people got paid by foreign donations to lie to Americans so that America could fall!!

The Biden Center was started on foreign donations after he left office.[443] All of these Speakers were paid by the Biden Center with dirty money, and the speeches were all written by the Ex-New Kids on the Block tour manager. She was just nominated in April of 2021 by Joe Biden to work in his Administration! Catherine McLaughlin was appointed to the Board of Directors of the Corporation for National and Community Service[444].

The link www.bidenschool.udel.edu/bideninstitute. All the talks, speeches, pictures, and dates of their speaking engagements are available. All guest speakers talked about what was wrong during Trump's term. What could be better if we just had someone else as president, someone with experience. Setting up the punch is what they call it in boxing. Jab, jab, cross, jab then the haymaker, KO of a whole generation! Caught off guard, thinking people are speaking to me because they care, nope—a clear knockout of a society of un-woke, uneducated in life; generation lost in limbo and disinformation. As they are speaking, their plan is the front stage, and your opinion means nothing. It is a living purgatory, never making anything new, never advancing past decade-old problems, and constantly pushing the blame. May God help us!!

The List of Some Speakers at the Biden Center

Sally Yates: Spoke on being the second most powerful person in the Department of Justice. Yates was fired from the Trump administration because when he issued the travel ban in January during the Covid outbreak in America, she refused to hold up his order that saved millions of lives[445]. Sally now supports Biden's travel ban and is behind it [446]. She would have caused millions of deaths because she refused to let her personal beliefs interfere with her job of protecting Americans. She did not follow orders from her boss. Usually, that means you get fired. Sally was praised for standing up to Trump but now defends the same travel ban from the Biden administration. Why? Pay to Play.

Biden Policy Dinner with Sally Yates
Tuesday, November 19, 2019, 5:30 PM to 7:30 PM
Biden Institute - 44 Kent Way, Newark, DE 19716

Donna Brazile: Spoke on Race, Gender, and Politics, the conversations at every dinner table in America. She wrote a book starting the Trump Collusion Lie [447]. A former Fox News contributor is now back at her old job with CNN and ABC. A Career Democrat was the chair of the Democratic National Committee in 2007, 2016, and 2017. She still to this day questions Trump's election victory. Called the Hillary campaign an actual failure, frail and with an odor of failure from the beginning[448]. Donna Brazile, a veteran Democratic political strategist, is an adjunct professor at Georgetown University. Author, television political commentator, and former interim chair of the Democratic Party. The author of Cooking with Grease and the New York Times bestseller Hacks. She was appointed as the 2018-2019 Gwendolyn S. and Colbert I. King Endowed Chair in Public Policy at Howard University. Brazile developed and hosted a five-part lecture series to engage the Howard community on several subjects, including politics, voting, criminal justice reform, and civility.

Tuesday, October 23, 2018, 4:00 PM to 5:30 PM
Mitchell Hall 134 The Green, Newark, DE 19716
Four groundbreaking political strategists joined Biden Institute Vice-Chair Valerie Biden Owens for a conversation on race, gender, and politics.

Governor John Carney of Delaware: Spoke on Delaware Opportunity Zones, areas in Delaware where they can spur economic development in distressed communities. The plan is to have enormous incentives for the investor, have Tax cuts for the Rich, Investment opportunities for the super-wealth, show Investors how to defer taxes on investments, wait they don't pay taxes! Are they all Trumps investing gurus, not just Pay to Play Carney selling out his state and lowering the price of homes, businesses, and families in general?[449] If you live in Delaware, you may want to look up Opportunity Zones in Delaware. As an American, you should be eligible first. Under Trump's America first policy, you would have been![450] The Governor of Delaware took office in 2017; he has been in Delaware politics for many years. He once was asked about former Delaware Gov. Pete DuPont; John Carney described him as a "real leader."

UDiscuss: A student town hall with Governor John Carney
Wednesday, October 23, 2019, 3:00 PM to 4:00 PM
Trabant Room 209 / 211 Trabant University Center

Julie Mapes Wilgen: Spoke on Human Sexuality and Gender Studies. She gives $1,000 to any trans-gender student at Delaware University for achievement above others[451]. She pushes for transgender sports too. At the Biden Center conference, she said that "teaching sexual education at schools should be integrated into math, economics, and computer science classes." Parents participating with teachers and students in working groups should plan sex-ed programs in public schools?"[452] She is helping change Collegiate Sports, starting with UPENN girls swimming!

The Julie Mapes Wilgen Award is an annual award to honor Dr. Julie Mapes Wilgen's lifelong work and dedication to the field of sexuality education and family studies by providing a student with a $1,000 stipend.
Award Criteria
Applicants must meet the following criteria:
* *Undergraduate or graduate student in any major*
* *Has attended UD for at least one year*
* *Minimum GPA of 3.4 (1,4% higher than the Biden Center)*
* *Demonstrated appreciation for diversity and the betterment of society*
* *Demonstrated commitment to study or engage in the field of human sexuality and gender studies*

Tamika Montgomery-Reeves: Spoke on Women of Power and Purpose Celebration. She was sworn in as a Justice of the Supreme Court of Delaware on December 5, 2019.[453] She is a member of the Prisoner's Rights Project and one of twelve justices that President Biden is trying to elevate to the US Supreme Court [454] The Pay to Play nominee for the Biden Administration. She is the 2022 nomination for the Supreme Court; Biden says it must be a WOMAN OF COLOR. I feel like a kid at Easter that saw the bunny hide the eggs, but everyone else is sleeping! This is his pick for the Supreme Court, the world now knows Joe's pick, and she is an excellent civil servant only if she stopped hanging around people like the Biden's.

Women of Power and Purpose Celebration featuring Tamika Montgomery-Reeves
Virtual Zoom Event
Tuesday, October 6, 2020

Ann Navarro: Works for CNN and spoke about Latin X, on demographic voting trends in the United States, and how the minority vote in the United States will continue to grow in numbers and influence.[455] Ann is a CNN Paid Reporter, a Chris Cuomo Supporter, an anti-Trump Florida Supporter, and a Latinos Against Trump member! Oddly, the Latino community does not like the term "Latin X"; she still uses it.[456] Some people talk, talk and talk. They never listen to what someone has to say.

Biden Institute Special Event featuring Ana Navarro
Thursday, October 1, 2020, 7:00 PM to 9:00 PM
online - Zoom

Tom Manatos: Spoke about a career on Capitol hill, how to Find Your Dream Job in DC. George Washington, Bob Dole, and George Bush Sr. fought in wars to win our freedom. They gave us a country, let alone a capitol hill, and a job on capitol hill should be earned. A real public service job should be a term limit and no more questions asked. Working hard for the people and the government should not mean fame and fortune. It should not be considered a dream job; all that hard work and politics to do good for children and the future should be exhausting. Hiring just anyone to run Washington DC is not a good idea for the taxpayer. A Washington DC job placement guru for political, government, and most rewarding lobbying jobs, should not be handed out. Hunter Biden's emails have his name in them; he is the next Hunter Biden casualty[457] that had to Pay to Play with the Biden's.

Biden Policy Dinner with Tom Manatos
Tuesday, October 22, 2019, 5:30 PM to 7:30 PM
Biden Institute - 44 Kent Way, Newark, DE

General Ban Ki-Moon: Spoke on Climate change, Women's Rights and Humanitarian issues. Former UN secretary under Obama and Biden pushed Biden to rejoin the Paris Climate Accord.[458] He is an anti-Bush and Anti-Trump supporter. Ban almost ran for president of his home country, South Korea, after resigning as UN secretary under Obama.[459] Do our left politicians do things to piss off our enemies on purpose.

Biden Institute Conversation featuring the Eighth UN Secretary-General Ban Ki-moon
Tuesday, September 15, 2020, 6:00 PM to 7:00 PM

Bob Inglis: Spoke on Policy Change and how Abortion and Socialism should not turn Christian Conservatives against Biden.[460] Former Republican Congressman from South Carolina. Bob is for the Pro-Abortion Bill. Bob is also an anti-Trumper from day one.[461] Pay to Play politician for life.

A Different Approach to Solving Climate change
by Congressman Bob Inglis, Executive Director of the Energy and Enterprise Initiative Republican
Biden Policy Dinner Guest Blog by Congressman Bob Inglis
Biden Institute
44 Kent Way
University of Delaware
Newark, DE 19716, USA

Aneesh Raman: Spoke on Tech and Facebook. He runs Facebook's Economic and Social Impact department. Aneesh is a Facebook employee and a Senior Advisor to California Gov. Gavin Newsome during his career. He was Obama's ex-speech writer.[462] Now we see the pattern when Barrack warned us America about Joe Biden.[463] All ex-Obama employees are continuing the work that he started. Biden was never Socialist. He is a capitalist. [464] Another Facebook employee ruined children's lives into the ground.[465] After working at the White House, Zuckerberg pays him and David Plouffe, Obama's former campaign chief, and so many more.[466] So, if Netflix got canceled because of the show about young girls called Cuties. After being president and maybe even decent parents, the Obama's are Netflix executives.[467] While that show was made and put on Netflix, the Obama's worked there. Facebook just changed its name because of teen girls being mentally abused.[468] See the pattern, what are these people doing talking to young adults, especially girls, how much harm did the Biden Center dish out. He is trying to ruin your sons with opioids and your daughters with degrading self-images. Some still say Zuckerberg is worse than Trump.[469] The Biden Center is now The BidenVerse! From day one, the Biden Center had a plan even though he waited until April of 2019 to announce he was running for president. A little over six months till the election, and Joe threw his hat into the ring. The Biden Center took donations in 2018 for campaigning.

Mark McKinnon: Spoke on The Circus in the White House. He had a PowerPoint presentation calling the Trump White House a Circus and Our President the Head Clown in front of Joe Biden Supporters. Mark is a Hollywood Movie and TV Executive.[470] Host of Show Times "The Circus" about the Trump years in office. He is a Pro-Biden supporter.[471] Mark is also a CNN supporter and Contributor, who said Joe Biden could be more significant than FDR for Americans.

Anthony Fox: Spoke on the Future of Transportation and Autonomous vehicles. Under Obama and Biden, he was the Secretary of Transportation and responsible for the DOT. He now is the CEO of LYFT, the car ride service company. Anthony is pushing for an Infrastructure Bill; he must be Pay to Play for big spending. The ex-DOT Secretary under Obama and Biden now is the CEO of LYFT, the car ride company that would give you a free ride to vote, get a covid shot, and food delivery. Biden made a deal with them.[472] During the pandemic, Lyft grew how much?[473] Remember six feet and social distancing. LYFT was able to pick up and drop off millions of customers through the pandemic. A small car is not six or even three feet distancing. The front seat to the back seat, door handles, windows, seat belts, and handing over tips. All that cross-contact in a little Prius! Was every employee vaccinated? Was every employee who picked up the elderly vaccinated? The workers in retirement communities had to be vaccinated, the police, the truck drivers, all vaccinated. Or they Lost Their Jobs! Was anyone monitoring how many Covid cases came from unvaccinated LYFT employees?

Biden Policy Dinner with Anthony Foxx
Wednesday, February 26, 2020, 5:30 PM to 7:30 PM
Biden Institute- 44 Kent Way, Newark, DE 19716

Beth Myers: Spoke on The Campaign Trail with Mitt Romney and Politics today. She was the Campaign Manager for Mitt Romney.[474] She was the Presidential campaign manager for Jeb Bush. Works with the Shawmut Group, a Massachusetts candidate and politician public affairs consulting firm.[475] Their Approach, "Our team has extensive experience running top tier political campaigns."

Biden Policy Dinner with Beth Myers
Tuesday, September 10, 2019, 5:30 PM to 7:30 PM
Biden Institute - 44 Kent Way, Newark, DE

John Runyan: Spoke on Politics in New Jersey and his time in Congress. Ex-NFL player for the Blue Collar Fanbase Philadelphia Eagles. A Former Congressman from New Jersey said he left Congress because of the games during the Obama & Biden years.[476] He never understood politicians and politics, he said, until he got paid to speak! So, if he is not Pay to Play and doesn't want his son's children to drown in hate, maybe he can "blow it all up!" Big John Runyan and my red, white, and blue Ox can save America. I am calling out a monster of a man to step up, one more down! We can blow this up and restore America's heart and soul to Lady Liberty! Two football offensive linemen can protect our country's back like a rookie QB!

Biden Policy Lunch with Jon Runyan
Friday, November 8, 2019, 1:00 PM to 3:00 PM
100 Discovery Blvd, Newark, DE 19713

Dr. Howard Zucker: Spoke on the Opioid Crisis, Strengthening Environmental Health Research and ending the AIDS Epidemic. When he gave his Biden Center speech, he was the New York State Commissioner of Health.[477] While the Covid Pandemic hit New York and the elderly population, he was getting paid to speak against Trump and criticize how he handled the medical crisis.[478] He wondered if Trump counted all of his dead bodies? Former Governor Cuomo appointed Howard. As people were unaware, he and Governor Cuomo put Covid positive cases in with the greatest generation of American's.[479] As helpless Americans died, they lied and hid the death rate in New York. Howard worked with the NY First Lady Chirlane McCray. Her husband, Mayor de Blasio, named her head of the New York Racial Equity Coronavirus Task Force.[480] How many lives did that program save? Biden, DeBlasio, and Cuomo supported the Covid Pandemic, and every day we heard about the spread and flattening the curve. The only curve they should flatten was in Cuomo's pants. Please have VH1do a where are they now special, please! Should I stop, or can you handle more! What a disgrace to our country and the people who did nothing but love a flag! All I did was love my country! We paid the ultimate price because of being prideful.

Biden Policy Dinner with Howard Zucker
Thursday, February 20, 2020, 5:30 PM to 7:30 PM
Biden Institute- 44 Kent Way, Newark, DE 19716

Samantha Powers: Spoke on being a member of President Obama's Cabinet. She is the US Agency for International Development Administrator and was appointed by Biden in May of 2021, Pay to Play anyone.[481] She was the US representative to the United Nations under the Obama administration. Samantha was not tough on Russia during their first attempt at Ukraine during the Obama terms. They only invaded and took Crimea! Barrack Obama and Samantha Powers were pushovers when it came to Putin. What makes you think anything will change working under Biden. She talks tough on North Korea and Syria but falls silent on China. She was there when Afghanistan fell, during the Taliban takeover, and today during America's southern border crisis. She is a Janet Yellen supporter of Global Equity from American Tax Payers.[482] Samantha also is the author of multiple books. She was the person who told Putin's men to wait until after Barrack wins re-election, then you can have Crimea. Remember the Hot Mic? Obama leaned over and repeated it.

A conversation with former US Ambassador to the United Nations Samantha Power
Wednesday, November 13, 2019, 4:00 PM to 5:30 PM
Mitchell Hall, University of Delaware

Pete Buttigieg: Spoke on bridging the political divide and restoring faith in Democratic facilities.[483] Was appointed the Secretary of Transportation after Biden won the election. Now we have a transportation crisis![484] Pete is Pay to Play and proud of it. He is already looking at the 2024 Presidential elections. The Infrastructure Bill Czar better start fixing some potholes. He has done nothing since being in office, either has Kamala. Do they not know what to do? Pete was behind the Trump Impeachments[485]. He is also an anti-Trumper. He was also against the Anti Vaccine mandate when Trump was president.[486] Pete was originally against Religious and Personal exemptions to the vaccine.[487] He is the new Career Politician, not because he represents America the best he can. Because he can manipulate you and tell you significant political what you want to hear one-liner, he has not done one thing for America. Talking Points, lowering his voice, and looking into the camera. Just like they scripted! A real opportunity wasted because he just does not know what to do; he is not qualified to run the United States highways. The United States has over a million miles of paved roads they maintain. How does that responsibility compare to South Bend, Indiana's 1,276 paved miles? That he was the mayor to, not transportation or DOT. It is like giving a baby the keys to an 18-wheeler! Does Pete need to retake the driving exam? I do not think he would pass!

Biden Institute Special Event featuring Pete Buttigieg, Thursday, October 8, 2020, 1:00 PM to 2:30 PM, online - Zoom
Biden Institute Special Event featuring, Pete Buttigieg
Mayor of South Bend (2012 - 2020), Democratic Candidate for President (2020)

Cathy McLaughlin: Spoke and campaigned for Joe Biden. Her former career was the Tour Manager for New Kids on the Block. How did she get her job to work on the campaign in 2016?[488] Explains why Jen and Donnie Wahlberg trashed Trump all day on Podcasts during his term. There are no Wahlburgers named the Benedict Donald with hollandaise, named after Trump! Cathy works with the Biden Center and the Universities to show programs, influential media feeds, and political forums on topics students in college might like. The director of the Biden Center during the campaign. Cathy set up all the lectures, speeches, payouts to guest speakers. She is the second person who knows the amounts paid to each speaker and the donation amounts from China.[489]

Biden Institute Women's History Month Luncheon
Friday, March 6, 2020, 12:30 PM to 1:40 PM
Trabant Center MPRs - 17 West Main Street, Newark, DE 19716
Spoke On: Politics: Cathy McLaughlin, Executive Director, Biden Institute

Lisa Jackson: Spoke on the Environment, Climate change, and Donald Trump after the election of 2020.[490] She is part of the team to sell the Build Back Better Package. She was the administrator of the EPA under Barrack Obama. Did she look into "Forever Chemicals" at the Biden Center in Delaware? She now reports to Apple CEO TIM COOK on policy and social issues in America. She is currently working on The Racial Equity of Climate change for Apple.[491] Pay to Play instead of building up and building back better. They use excuses and fake sympathy to get advancements, knowing only hard work and dedication create change.

The United States is being told every day about Climate change and what we are doing wrong. What has she done in the office to curve Climate change? How many years before she cared about America's children and their future? Instead of Racial Equity, how about some Racial Honesty! Making victims and teaching excuses only creates teething and childish behaviors. The only hurdle a student in 2022 faces is peer pressure in school, teachers, the internet, social media groups, video games, and immature governments and parents. It is 2022; equity is being given out at the border! How much is an iPad? Give your profits some equity relief.

Biden Institute Special Event featuring Lisa Jackson
Wednesday, April 14, 2021, 6:00 PM to 8:00 PM
online – Zoom
Biden Institute Special Event: featuring Lisa Jackson, Vice President of
Environment, Policy, and Social Initiatives at Apple;
Former Administrator, Environmental Protection Agency

Mike Donilon: Spoke on the Biden campaign during the pandemic about Bidens Racial justice push for America. (**492**) The Biden Administration and the DOJ in 2022 opened injection sites in low-income neighborhoods to do drugs freely without consequences. Racial and Justice in one crack pipe, smoke it up! Mike is the Chief strategist for the Biden Campaign and the other person besides the

NKOTB fan club president who knows, "show me the money from China." He works for the once Axelrod company, now AKPD Message & Media, a political and consulting firm catering to the Democrat party.[493] Mike and Cathy are the two people who sold America on Joe Biden. The outdoor car rallies, the basement gig, great work, guys! He has a company that makes Political TV commercials, social media Ads, annoying pamphlets in your mail, and everything else to advertise a person; they get paid to sell a product. The product is a 78-year-old that cannot read from a teleprompter! If you need to make a person look good for a political job, only the constituents will hurt. A TV ad and a cheap media shot at an opponent cannot win American politics.[494] Mike has made a career out of false advertising. He is responsible for message discipline and development for the Biden administration. He never does interviews, takes questions, or does television interviews with real journalists; Mike hides in the shadows.[495] He knows his product is defective. His product needs to be RECALLED ASAP! He was at almost every luncheon, dinner, and gala at the Biden Center. If you are mad that Joe Biden is president, and your country is failing, He is THE GUY!!![496]

Biden Institute Virtual Conversation with Mike Donilon
Wednesday, September 29, 2021, 5:00 PM to 6:00 PM
online - Zoom
2020: A Campaign Retrospective / / / / Closed to Press/ / / /

David Beasley: Spoke on the hunger crisis in the world; he said it was due to the pandemic, war-torn countries, and famine. He is the Executive Director of the United Nations World Food Program.[497] David is the Former Governor of South Carolina and lives his days Tweeting to rich people to share their wealth to end world hunger.[498] Another South Carolina politician who spoke at the Biden Center, hello SC!! Hunter Biden spoke at the World Food Program. Hunter Biden served as chairperson of the World Food Program USA board in Washington, DC! Hunter Biden works with the United Nations

World Food Program through fundraising, advocacy, education, and tax dollars from the United States!

Biden Institute Special Event featuring David Beasley, Wednesday, April 7, 2021, 12:00 PM to 2:00 PM, Executive Director, World Food Program 2020 Nobel Peace Prize Recipient, online - Zoom

Christopher Krebs: We know him; he was at the Technology Conference in 2017 to spy on Trump and push the "BIG LIE!"[499]. Christopher Krebs spoke on Cybersecurity and Infrastructure Security. He was the Whistle Blower; if you listen, you can still hear him talking shit on Trump. The Biden Center puts in his introduction that Trump fired him because he contradicted him over the voter fraud claim. Donald Trump started the Cancel Culture? Christopher was in on the "BIG LIE" before it happened; we found that out.[500] A Biden Center paid speaker after Joe Won! Ironically, Adam Schiff was mad when his buddy got fired from the White House, no more spying![501] He works for solar wind companies that received billions from the Infrastructure Bill.[502] Another Pay to Play Civil Servant.

Biden Institute Special Event featuring Christopher Krebs Wednesday, March 31, 2021, 6:00 PM to 8:00 PM online - Zoom

Eleni Assanis: Spoke on Joe Biden as a friend, a co-worker, and a great person. Her husband is the president of the University of Delaware, and he makes $967,000 a year; he took a slight pay cut due to Covid-19.[503] Eleni is a Pay to Play spouse. The University of Delaware has many significant donations, and Joe Biden gets paid from the University! How much did the University get from Foreign Donations?[504]

Biden Institute Women's History Month Luncheon

Friday, March 6, 2020, 12:30 PM to 1:40 PM
Trabant Center MPRs - 17 West Main Street, Newark, DE 19716
Hosts: Eleni Assanis, First Lady of UD, and Valerie Biden Owens, Vice-Chair of Biden Institute

Amanda Nguyen: Spoke on Justice for Victims of Sexual violence and anti-Asian Crime. She is the CEO of RISE, a non-profit group that fights for the laws of sexual violence survivors.[505] Why didn't Joe Biden nominate her when the NY governor was being investigated? She spoke on Asian stereotypes and how they are just ordinary people, not those who put out the pandemic that killed millions.[506] China was ordinary until they killed and starved their people.[507] Everyone must push the propaganda to downplay the Covid Virus and the deaths of innocent people. Are women persecuted in China? Does China still kill the firstborn child of the family if a girl is born?[508] If she was assaulted when she went to Harvard, has Harvard done anything about it![509]

Biden Policy Dinner with Amanda Nguyen
Tuesday, May 14, 2019, 5:30 PM to 7:30 PM
Biden Institute - 44 Kent Way, Newark, DE

Dr. Ibram X Kendi: Spoke on How to Be Antiracist. He wrote a book about systematic Racism in America. Ibram is a NY Times bestselling author. Washington Post calls him the (CRT) Critical Race Theory starter. He is a BLM supporter, and his new book is the Anti-Racist Baby. He spoke out for Jessie Smollett when he played the world on a fake Racial attack.[510] Ibram texted out during the January 6th protest that" White Privilege is on Display."[511] Ibram is not racist for saying that? Or is he an Antiracist for saying "White Privilege is on Display"? Equity Pay to Play, and PRO-CRT![512]

Biden Institute Special Event featuring Dr. Ibram X. Kendi Author, How to Be an Antiracist, Monday, October 26, 2020, 6:00 PM to 7:00 PM online - Zoom , hosted by Dr. Michael L. Vaughan, Interim Vice Provost for Diversity and Inclusion

Pablo McConnie-Saad: Spoke on Gentrification and Social Mobility in Philadelphia. He spoke on how we will have an influx of residents, and there will be residential displacement.[513] Pablo spoke on and continues to push the displacement of communities throughout Philadelphia as a graduate of the Biden Center.[514] The face of the illegal immigrant in your backyard and the Illegals crossing the border fence on television are the same ones selling kids to sex rings and cartels. They push Fentanyl on children. People like him cannot fix their own country that is so bad that he left, but he has no problem pointing out America's problems. A GPA of 2.0 is what you need to enter the Biden Center! Is a GPA of 2.0 good enough to run the Biden Center and millions of dollars in donations from China?

Maggie Haberman: Spoke on Post Trump Politics and years in the media. She is the NY Times and CNN reporter who just broke the story on Trump's Blood Oxygen. She showed how the levels were high when he had Covid, one of the first and most common signs that you have a virus, no duh![515] She slammed Joe Biden when the Democrat party first nominated him.[516] She is now a Biden Administration reporter. Maggie broke many stories about Trump during his term, the impeachment(fake), the sex scandal with Stormy(fake), the Russian interference (fake), all fake. Did she break the bank too? What is the reporting, besides lies and misinformation on our youth?[517] She worked with Chris Cuomo and never got anything on him but was all over Trump.

The list of paid speakers, anti-American bashers, and Trump criticizers goes on, enough for three more books. Look up your favorite Americans and the Biden Center while going to the bathroom. When you are done reading about them and get up to flush, it symbolizes two things! The two things that are going down the drain fast are the lies about America and the anti-American pushers that create racism. The hate makers are the Democrat Party. All of the problems facing America in the last two years stem from these people. Every crime, every School Board brawl, every police shooting, and every riot, peaceful or not! Came from the flame lit up at these luncheons, dinners, and zoom calls, instead of taking action and making a real difference. They talk like commentators on TV but do not realize they are the problem starters. The crime in America is them being in power. We have let people in power destroy us because they hate us, plain and simple. You do not put, wish, or act on harm towards someone else unless you have anger in your heart. They plant the hate in the youth of America, speech after speech, always being told Republicans and those people cheated you every step of the way. The hatred grows into anger, and you react to your rage made by the hate and anger.

Do you think Hitler was born hating Jewish people? No, we created that hate in his heart; we made Hitler! Does a child molester come out of the womb touching himself, No? We generate that child molester with smut available everywhere. We show people that it is tolerated by not enforcing laws and stricter sentencing. Are people born with hate for another because of a particular color of skin? No, we created that. If they only put that much effort into rising America, instead they put all that effort, hate, and anger into tearing it and us down. These speakers get paid to lie to whoever would listen. Like Drug Dealers who prey on the weak and innocent, they push drugs so they can stay rich, and you can be weakened and fooled. The lies and stories these people tell are the drugs that make them rich and powerful, and the drugs hurt, hold back and eventually destroy a person and, in this case, a country. We have been fed political lies, manipulation, and disinformation like a person drugged at a bar. They are trying to make us overdose on the lies. They have tried to overdose a nation of believers in America. They knew some of us might die, but just as long as they took out the World War Winners! The drugs of politics have made us all strung out! We are all turning into Hunter's, NO!!!

John Slade White, Todd Stern, Chet Culver, Lonnie G. Bunch III, Michael Moore, Sarah McBride, Sally Yates, Danielle Gray, Chris Jennings, Kristi Solitis Anderson, Danielle Gray, Terri Freeman, Sarah McBride, Ernest Moniz, Gary Locke, Rose Garrity, John McConnell, Michael Haynie, Caroline Tess and so many more.

The Biden Center Institute pays people to push a narrative that Joe Biden is good for you and the Democrat party is the only party of America. How is that working out for us all! The world is upside down, and every day, another problem that was fixed 20 times in the last 30 years, is now a worldwide crisis! From this list alone, you can see how the Biden administration just brainwashed people into believing that he is the best politician for America! He says there is no crime spike in America; trust him, he paid a BLM supporter to speak.[518]

Joe Biden has a mouthpiece for every problem in America! If the people do not trust him, you can trust Jen Psaki! The White House Press Secretary Jen Psaki was a CNN contributor and political analyst from 2017-2020.[519] She tweeted during the 2020 election a picture of her, her husband, and her 4-year-old. The Caption, "our 4-year-old wanted us to vote for someone who likes children, animals and who is strong".[520] This is the manipulation that people like Jen Psaki sell to their children. Hey Jen, did you know that Beau Biden let a child rapist free, a person who raped his 3-year-old daughter, let free.[521] Beau Biden dropped the charges because the rapist's family was a friend and a supporter of Joe Biden, his father.[522] Tell your daughter how your boss's family protects and likes children? Hey, Jen, your boss, and Anthony Fauci criticize Trump, the unvaccinated, the new "Deplorables," and no one else.[523]

Dr. Fauci does cruel medical experiments on innocent beagle dogs. When asked why beagles, Dr. Fauci said they are gentle and kind and allow us to do the experiments without any aggression.[524] A gentle breed and my childhood favorite dog, a beagle, are great family pets. Jen, please tell your daughter how you and daddy voted for an animal lover. Please, Jen, tell her how strong he is. He approved of his one son having sex and cheating on his wife with his dead son's wife! Is Hunter a great Uncle or what? When asked, Joe Biden said," I and Jill are glad they both found peace and closure."[525]. How about that, Jen? Please tell your daughter all the great stuff about your boss JOkE, Biden.

She left CNN to go work for the Biden/Harris Transition team. That is how she can smirk, laugh, and confuse Americans by saying there is no food shortage, gas is the same price, and crime has not risen, only racism has.[526] Joe Biden has every angle of the media to cover for him and lies to you; whatever you are seeing is not valid.[527] Whatever you are hearing is not valid. Whatever you believe is not valid. If you do not believe me, I get a paid speaker to help me sell the "Big Lie." There is no food shortage during the holidays; trust me. There was no real president in the White House during 2016-2020; trust me, I got a speaker for that too.

He cannot tell or show you what he has done for us, but he sure can talk bad on the opponent. Conferences, special election technology meetings, and guest speakers trash President Trump and Republicans behind their backs. A true Politician, JOkE Biden has never looked back and said, "job well done." His first marriage and family, gone. DuPont chemicals killed his eldest son, gone. His other son wooed his dead brother's wife, and she became addicted to drugs, family gone. His term in Delaware, "Forever Chemicals."

The Credit Card company boomed in the '80s, people were in debt for generations, and he closed major companies; he was chasing them out of Delaware.[528]. His job numbers suck because he never created jobs; he only kills them.[529] His days as a Senator when he voted for keeping Delaware schools segregated, even Kamal Harris remembered during the Democratic primary.[530] CNN forgot to cover it! Kamala could not get nominated for President, so she joined the White Devil Biden and became Pay to Play! The botched Afghan exit and weapons hand over to the Taliban. The rebirth of ISIS during the Obama/Biden terms and now the resurgence and restocked Taliban Army again. Can we ever fix something and move on?

We were Energy Independent, then the climate change activist and the anti-Trump protestors stopped real progress! By eliminating the pipeline not stopping oil drilling, the real cause of Climate change, we pay more for gas now. We just pay because they do not understand energy independence.[531] Because Trump did something good, the pipeline and energy independence. Biden had to change progress, economics, barrel reserves, and a war on oil in Ukraine.

A war in 2014 under Obama, and now a war under Biden. See the pattern of pain and stress put on people to create fear and hate.[532] Now, after the war in Ukraine, how will a young generation of Eastern Europeans think of America's loyalty? Destroying Ukraine's future is the plan! The JOkE Biden "I did that" stickers on gas stations, now people will die in Ukraine.[533]

The way he lied about Hunter's Business and his money deals he knows nothing about![534] Joe gets a cut of every painting sold. His days on earth might be looked at as a great American public servant to some. The only people who benefited from his service were Joe Biden and his family. We are not better because of Joe Biden as a politician! All supporters of the "Big Lie" need to come to justice; any politician and council person who allowed crime and riots through their cities must pay. Pay with criminal charges, pay with a public televised trial, and pay with their wallets. The world is not better now than before the 2020 election. Honestly, the only ones who made out, and I quote from a Biden Center paid guest speakers, are the super Elite rich. He repays his friends by hiring them for positions of power, not earned.[535] David Beasley, the Executive Director of the United Nations World Food

Program, is the group that hired Hunter Biden. He put out a tweet in December of 2021, asking the "to the billionaires who made $1.3 trillion during the pandemic, is $6.6 billion too much to ask for to save the lives of millions". Our countries taxes are not a Global Bank for the Democrat Socialist, Communist, Black/Brown/Asian Caucus to hand out. The American people have many options to beat back the lies and beat the anti-American government called the Democrat party of the United States.

We, as Americans, true patriots of freedom and the winner of countless battles, have options; please use these links and groups to retake, conquer and control our country and the world once again. The past lies only make us stronger for what lies ahead, freedom! Enough with the games by the media, the left, and anti-Americans. There are plenty of spaces for you in this world, and America must not be it because you keep on trying to change it! Vote America First, and the world will prosper! Join the Right-side of America once more. The Civil War they started, which they are trying to rekindle again, is not working. Americans have had enough! Join the seventy-five million actual voters and take back America once more! The Patriots of 1776 have emerged again. The farmers and pitchforks are now parents and ballots! See you in 2022, and by the way, I am glad to see you are up and Woke! God Bless America, and God Bless You!

Please keep an eye out for the next book. "Fixing America for our Children." It lays out the 13 biggest hurdles our nation faces after 12 years of Barrack Obama and Joe Biden. We have had enough of walking the hamster wheel, measuring once and cutting three times, and doing things wrong-- twice.

We are Americans; this is not us! The world needs to respect America and its laws. The next book shows you the problem and how it got so bad, what is being done-- or not being done, and the costs involved in fixing the issues. Then it lays out a plan for success, costs analysis, and action methods. Create and follow True Leaders. You follow influencers every day. How about following a great leader? The plan is to keep it simple. If it is not suitable for America, especially the children, we do not do it. The world is challenging, and I understand that each individual contributes in their own way; that is fine; some of us, like 75 million or so, want our country back. So, when things get rolling, you do not have to physically hold a sign or contribute—but stay out of the way of those of us who want to take action! May we all walk the Streets of Freedom, ring the Bell of Liberty, and wave the Great American Flag once more!

ENDNOTES

1-Ben Ziesloft, October 26, 2020, Joe Biden to Harvard 2014...**Tennessee Star**

2-Kate Sullivan, April 30, 2021, Here are the executive actions Joe Biden has signed in his first 100 days..., Christopher Hickey, Richard Chang, Sean O'Key, **CNN Politics**

3-Erin Bradener, May 22, 2020, The Breakfast Club, Charlamagne Tha God podcast..., Sarah Mucher and Arlette Saenz, **CNN Politics**

4-Ariel Niemeyer, December 19, 2014, Courts, the Legislatures and Delaware's Resegregation, a Report on School Segregation in Delaware from 1989-2010..., **John Kuscera, Gary Orfield, Genevieve Siegel-Hawley, Foreword by Gary Orfield, The Civil Rights Project of UCLA**

5-Camille Caldera, October 27, 2020, Committee on the Judiciary, United States Senate floor September 27, 1977, Joe Biden used the filibuster on Delaware Public Schools receiving Federal Money "Busing of School Children"...**USA Today**

6-Bruce Golding, March 30, 2021, Book details how Hunter Biden's wife found out about the affair with Beau's widow, Hunter Biden's book "Beautiful Things"...**NY Post**

7-Ryan Parry, October 1, 2020, It's no coincidence!' Joe Biden's brother Frank finally agrees to pay some of the $1M he owes the family of young father killed in a horrific car crash 20 years ago as the election draws near - after dodging creditors for decades..., Josh Boswell, Alan Butterfield, **The Daily Mail.com**

8-Eric Litke, May 29, 2020, Fact check: Was GOP founded 'to counter the Democrats' plans to expand slavery'?...**USA Today**

9-Becky Little, July 14, 2020, How Woodrow Wilson tried to reverse Black American Progress...**History.com**

10-Alison Dirr, October 24, 2016, Quote from then vice-presidential Nominee Tim Kaine, August 5, 2016, "The Democrat Party is the oldest political party in the world"...**PolitiFact**

11-Gerhard Petters, July 16, 1984, The Democrat Party Platform, after the biggest presidential election loss in history to Reagan in 1984..., John Wooley, **UC Santa Barbara**

12-Hannah Gilberstadt, January 17, 2020, Liberals make up the largest share of Democratic voters, but their growth has slowed in recent years…, Andrew Danniler, **Pew Research Center**

13-Matt Rosenberg, April 11, 2020, A List of Current Communist Countries in the World…**ThoughtCo.com**

14-Leah Rodriguez, October 21, 2021, The10 Best and Worst Countries to Be a Woman in 2021…**Global Citizen.com**

15-Micheal Kranish, May 3, 2019, Inside Bernie Sanders's 1988 10-day 'honeymoon' in the Soviet Union… Julie Tate, **Politico**

16-Martin Luther King Encyclopedia, 2018, Biography of Rustin Bayard March 17, 1912, to August 24, 1987…**Martin Luther King Jr. Research and Education Institute at Stanford University**

17-Jose Pagliery, June 15, 2017, Suspect in the congressional shooting was Bernie Sanders supporter, strongly anti-Trump…Thomas Frank, Carma Hassan, Pete Grieve Andrew Kaczynski, Nathaniel Meyersohn, Mary Kay Mallonee, Brad Parks, Evan Perez, Shimon Prokupecz, David Shortell, **CNN Politics**

18-Elliot C. McClaughlin, June 17, 2020, Honoring the unforgivable: The horrific acts behind the names on America's infamous monuments and tributes…**CNN Politics**

19-Phillip Bump, June 22, 2015, What those Bill Clinton and Al Gore Confederate Flag Campaign Buttons say about 2015 Politics…**The Washington Post.com**

20-Hannah Frishburg, August 28, 2021, JFK's student mistress reveals a 'madly in love' affair after decades of silence…**NY Post**

21-Colby Hochmuth, 11/20/12 12:06, Bronze doors had a long road to the Capitol…**The HILL**

22-Josh Sanburn, July 17, 2019, "The Kennedy Machine Buried What Really Happened": Revisiting Chappaquiddick, 50 Years Later…**Vanity Fair**

23-Patricia Talorico, June 6, 2015, Beau's friends gather to recall a side of him few knew…**The News Journal**

24-2022 Cost of Living in Delaware…**Best Places to Live.com**

25-The Associated Press, Biden explains Indian-American remarks…**NBC News**

26-Jamie Gangel, May 12, 2021, Why Liz Cheney chose to wear this George Washington battle flag pin…**CNN Politics**

27-Tom Vanden Brook, August 30, 2021, What happened to US military equipment left behind in Afghanistan?...**USA Today**

28-Mark Moyar, August 2, 2015, How Obama Shrank the Military, He's used the budget sequester to accomplish what looks to have been his political goal from the start.…**The WSJ Wall Street Journal**

29-Olivia B Waxman, August 30, 2019, The Invasion of Poland Wasn't Hitler's First Aggression. Here's Why That Move Marked the Beginning of WWII…**TIME.com**

30-Dana Bate, January 15, 2019, The death of the Delaware River…Catalina Jaramillo, **WHYY PBS News**

31-Jennifer Goldblatt, February 1, 2004, The Chips Are Down…**NY Times**

32-Barbara Klaw, July 1980, Blood Relations: The Rise and Fall of the Du Ponts of Delaware…**American Heritage**

33-Nathaniel Rich, January 10, 2016, The Lawyer Who Became DuPont's Worse Nightmare…**NY Times**

34-Stacy Kika, December 21, 2010, EPA Announces $3.3 Million Settlement with DuPont for Failure to Report Toxic Chemical Studies…**Environmental Protection Agency EPA RECORDS**

35-Olivia Beach, July 2, 2021, Try Tubing Down the Delaware River…**New Jersey Monthly**

36-James W. Moeller, September 1, 2013, Potomac Power Resources, Pollution…**Washington and Lee Law Journal**

37-Amy Cherry, February 25, 2020, Heightened levels of toxic PFAS chemicals found in 2 additional wells near Dover Air Force Base…**WDEL.com**

38-Frank Kummer, March 3, 2021, Microplastics found in 100% of sampled Pennsylvania waterways, Microplastics were found in 100% of samplings of 53 locations including the Delaware and Schuylkill rivers…**The Philadelphia Inquirer**

39-Meredith Newman, July 10, 2017, Delaware's cancer death rate still higher than the United States…**Delaware online**

40-EPA Records, October 15, 2021, Superfund Sites in Reuse in Delaware…**Environmental Protection Agency of The United States of America**

41-Tim Worstall, November 1, 2013, The Reason That Shovel Ready Stimulus Didn't Work Is That There Wasn't Any Stimulus…**FORBES**

42-Christina Wilkie, August 16, 2021, Biden says Afghanistan war was a lost cause, vows to continue aid and diplomacy… Amanda Macias, **CNBC**

43-Hannah Hartig, September 2, 2021, Decades Later, The Enduring Legacy of 9/11…Carrol Doherty, **Pews Research Center**

44-Guy Gugliotta, April 3, 2012, New Estimate Raises Civil War Death Toll…**NY Times**

45-Kyle Smith, February 21, 2015, Sure, Obama loves America — just not the America we live in…**NY Post**

46-Michael Todd Landis, 2021-2022, ESSENTIAL CIVIL WAR CURRICULUM, Union and Confederate Politics…**Virginia Center for Civil War Studies at Virginia Tech**

47-Camille Caldera, September 16, 2020, Fact check: Biden, like Trump, received multiple draft deferments from Vietnam…**USA Today**

48-Micheal Peck, July 18, 2021, How Israel Overcame and Won the Yom Kippur War…**The National Interest**

49-Brendan Cole, December 3, 2021, Joe Biden Appears to Mix Up the Six-Day War With Yom Kippur War…**Newsweek**

50-Ishaan Tharoor, May 8, 2015, Don't forget how the Soviet Union saved the world from Hitler…**The Washington Post.com**

51-John T. Correll, April 1, 1994, The Decision That Launched the Enola Gay…**Air Force Magazine**

52-Maegan Vazquez, April 29, 2021, The Bidens visit the Carters in Georgia… Kevin Liptak, Jeff Zeleny, Betsy Klein, **CNN Politics**

53-Christine Hauser, September 27, 2021, John Hinckley Jr., Who Tried to Kill Reagan, Will Be Free in June…**NY Times**

54-Matt Swayne, November 19, 2015, Children don't necessarily follow in their parents' political footsteps…**PSU.com**

55-Kennedy Hickman, July 3, 2019, Vietnam War: End of the Conflict…**ThoughtCo.com**

56-JTA and Ron Kampeas, May 9, 2018, Richard Nixon: The anti-Semite Who Loved Israelis and Saved Israel Nixon stands out among presidents for taking the boldest risk for Israel: a much-needed arms airlift during the 1973 Yom Kippur War…**Haaretz.com**

57-Blake Gopnik, July 12, 2016, The Wacky History of Andy Warhol's Anti-Nixon Campaign THE DAILY PIC: There's a rich pedigree behind Kass's pro-Hillary portrait of Trump…**Artnet.News**

58-Bo Erickson, June 4, 2019, When a young Joe Biden used his opponent's age against him…**CBS News**

59-Histor.com Editors, AUG 21, 2018, Yom Kippur War…**History.com**

60-Rep. Kevin Cramer (R-N.D.), November 4, 2015, The US oil export vote: Learning from history and supporting our allies…**The HILL**

61-Grace Panetta, July 15, 2019, Joe Biden worried in 1977 that certain desegregation policies would cause his children to grow up "in a racial jungle"…**Insider.com**

62-United State Senate Records, Senate Salaries since 1789…Between 1986-1991, the US Senate average salary jumped from $75,100.00 in 86' to $125,100.00 in 91'…**US Senate.gov**

63-E. J. Dionne Jr., September 18, 1987, Biden Admits Plagiarism in School But Says It Was Not 'Malevolent'…**NY Times**

64-Tegan George, October 18, 2021, Consequences of Plagiarism for Students & Academics…**Scribbr.com**

65-Steve Chapman, August 31, 2008, Joe Biden's deep (but mythical) blue-collar roots…**Chicago Tribune**

66-Robert Longley, July 2, 2021, Allowances Available to Members of US Congress…**ThoughtCo.com**

67-Tippy.com, 2022, Distance between Washington, DC and Wilmington, DE…**Tippy.com**

68-Luz Lazo, October 18, 2019, Amtrak's chronic delays are costing millions of dollars, report says…**The Washington Post.com**

69-Jerusalem Post Staff, November 1, 2020, Ex-husband of Joe Biden's wife claim two had an affair that split marriage…**The Jerusalem Post**

70-Jim Gilmore, August 5, 2020, Jill Biden Interview where she talks about the 1972 campaign run in Delaware…**Frontline News**

71-Bob Orr, March 24, 2009, Driver In Biden Crash Wanted Name Cleared…**CBS News**

72-David Mikkelson, September 28, 2020, Did Joe Biden Lie About a Drunken Driver's Killing His Wife?...**Snopes.com**

73-Kenneth Garger, April 4, 2021, Hunter Biden convinced the father to publicly support his relationship with his brother's widow...**NY Post**

74-Lauren Fruen, October 28, 2020, 'Hunter is the smartest guy I know: Biden praises his son to Oprah as she refuses to ask him one single question about laptop scandal and his involvement in China business during campaign trail love-in...**Daily Mail.com**

75-DJ McAneny, Oct 12, 2021, Delaware's cancer mortality rates continue to decrease, but national ranking still too high for officials...**WDEL.com**

76-Susan Bernstein, October 6, 2021, What Is Ankylosing Spondylitis?...**WebMD**

77-DHSS, 2017, Study done showing: Prevalence of Selected Chronic Diseases Among Delaware Adults...**Delaware.gov**

78-Fred Clark, November 6, 2008, Return Day...**Patheos**

79-Kevin Conlon, April 2, 2014, Du Pont heir convicted of raping daughter spared prison... Stephanie Gallman, **CNN Politics**

80-Deniz Çam, July 14, 2019, How A Du Pont Heir Avoided Jail Time For A Heinous Crime...**Forbes**

81-Naina Bhardwaj, Dec 20, 2020, Joe Biden's niece, Caroline, pleads guilty and avoids jail for a DUI after she crashes her car into a tree...**Insider.com**

82-Stephen Collinson, June 3, 2021, 'Get a shot and have a beer': Biden's new glass-half-full strategy woos vaccine skeptics...**CNN Politics**

83-Joe Sommerlad, April 5, 2021, Hunter Biden says he 'smoked more parmesan cheese than anyone you know in depths of crack addiction...**Independent**

84-Gov.Info.com, September 26, 2008, Enhanced Partnership with Pakistan Act of 2008, Last Sponsored Bill by Senator Joe Biden...**GOVInfo.com, United States Government Website**

85-Suzanne McGee, April 27, 2021, The Bin Laden Raid: Inside the Situation Room Photo...**History.com**

86-Everett Carll Ladd, December 15, 1989, A Confident America Emerges From the '80s...**The Christian Science Monitor.com**

87-Richard P. Eckman, 2020, Growth, Prosperity, and the Delaware Way! How the Financial Center Development Act Turned a 98-Pound Weakling into a Banking Powerhouse…, Greg Koseluk, **Delaware Banker Magazine**

88-Lane Degregory, October 2, 1994, Buffalo City, NC…**The Virginia Pilot**

89-The Hagley Exhibit, 2022, The DuPont Factories along the Brandywine, Powder Workers, 1820-1860…**The Hagley Museum in New Castle County, Delaware**

90-New York Times Archives, December 7, 1926, PLANT; Ton of Gunpowder Explodes at Carney's Point, N.J. -- Eight Others Injured. Damage said to be $25,000 Cause of Concussion Unknown, All Workmen at the Scene Having Been Victims…**The NY Times**

91-Matt Schulz, January 19th, 2022, The Average Credit Card Interest Rate In America Today…**The Lending Tree**

92-Jane Brooks, Feb. 19, 1989, Farms in Its Future? Delaware Must Decide…**NY Times**

93-Jacob M. Schlesinger, November 23, 2020, DuPont's Up-and-Down History Shaped Biden's Views on, Biden staffed his first campaign with DuPont employees…**Wall Street Journal**

94-Elias Alsbergas, April 22, 2021, Delaware Connections Run Deep As DuPont Family's Darla Pomeroy Heads To Treasury…**The Revolving Door Project**

95-Maureen Groppe, June 16, 2021, Biden insists his presidency is not a third Obama term; his staff picks suggest otherwise…**USA Today**

96-Tim Murphy, November 2019, House of Cards: How Joe Biden helped build a financial system that's great for Delaware banks and terrible for the rest of us…**MotherJones**

97-Sarah Brady Siff, October 15, 2020, Joe Biden and Drug Control: A More Complete Picture (Part 1—the 1970s)…**Points History.com**

98-Natasha Geiling, December 4, 2013, The Confusing and At-Times Counterproductive 1980s Response to the AIDS Epidemic…**The Smithsonian Magazine**

99-William Pett, December 2018, Travel restrictions for people with HIV…**Aidsmap.com**

100-Rev. A. Stephen Pieters, January 1, 1994, HIV/AIDS: Is It God's Judgment? A Christian View of Faith, Hope, and Love…**TheBody.com**

101-Health Resources & Services Administration: Mission Statement, 2022, To improve health outcomes and achieve health equity through access to quality services, a skilled health workforce, and innovative, high-value programs…**hrsa.gov**

102-Oma Seddiq, Oct 7, 2020, Kamala Harris says she will be 'first in line for a coronavirus vaccine if health experts approve it, but 'if Donald Trump tells us we should take it, then I'm not taking it'…**Insider.com**

103-Richard Severo, June 25, 2003, Lester Maddox, Whites-Only Restaurateur, and Georgia Governor, Dies at 87…**NY Times**

104-Associated Press, February 19, 1971, Photos of Jimmy Carter, Carter at his desk in Atlanta, Ga, Governor's office 1971…**Montana Standard**

105-Steven F. Hayward, 2004, The Real Jimmy Carter How Our Worst Ex-President Undermines American Foreign Policy, Coddles Dictators and Created the Party of Clinton and Kerry…**Audio Books by Amazon**

106-Eric Lutz, December 9, 2021, Biden: Saving the world from Autocracy is "THE CHALLENGE OF OUR TIME"…**Vanity Fair.com**

107-Reem Heakal, April 13, 2020, What Is the Glass-Steagall Act?…**Investopedia**

108-Mike Hogan, April 22, 2010, Rep. John Dingell: "Goldman Sachs, Threatened the well-being of the Financial System"…**Vanity Fair**

109-John F. Kennedy, January 20, 1961, Inaugural Address: "Ask Not What Your Country Can Do For You"…**US History.org**

110-Eugene Kiely, July 23, 2012, 'You Didn't Build That,' Uncut and Unedited…**FactCheck.org**

111-Paul Bond, June 27, 2014, Dinesh D'Souza Arranges Fox News' Megyn Kelly Interview With Bill Ayers…**The Hollywood Reporter.com**

112-Richard Cowen, February 14, 2014, Obama weighs in on contentious union vote at Volkswagen plant… Bernie Woodall, **Reuters.com**

113-Orlando Sentinel Editor, April 25, 2019, Democrats' closed-door meeting shows the open government in Florida has no champion…**The Orlando Sentinel**

114-Daniel Chaitin, June 15, 2021, Reporter who broke the story on Clinton-Lynch tarmac meeting found dead…**The Gazette.com**

115-History.com Staff, May 20, 2020, Secret Agents in Hoop Skirts: Women Spies of the Civil War…**History.com**

116-Anne Wicks, Winter 2019, Issue 13, How Schools Can Best Support Children Living in Poverty...**Catalyst Magazine, the George Bush Institute**

117-Sarah D. Sparks, September 10, 2019, U.S. Students and Teachers Top Global Peers for Time Spent in School in OECD Study...**EdWeek.org**

118-Drew DeSilver, February 15, 2017, U.S. students' academic achievement still lags that of their peers in many other countries...**Pew Research Center**

119-Colleen Grablick, October 26, 2021, How Loudoun County schools ended up at the center of Virginia's election...**NPRnews**

120-The White House of Barrack Obama, July 17, 2014, President Obama Announces More Key Administration Posts: Christy McCormick – Commissioner, Election Assistance Commission...**Office of the Press Secretary**

121-NCSC, William and Mary Law, 2022, Advisory Committee Bios...**ElectionLawProgram.com**

122-Jessica Huseman, October 12, 2021, Why did this EAC commissioner talk to the senator behind Arizona's audit?...**VoteBeat.org**

123-Christopher Bling, May 22, 2019, U.S. election cybersecurity agency staff 'strained to the breaking point'...**Reuters.com**

124-Pam Fessler, December 22, 2020, Former Election Security Official Says It Will Take 'Years' To Undo Disinformation...**NPR.org**

125-Eric Tucker, November 4, 2021, Analyst who aided Trump-Russia dossier charged with lying...**APNews.com**

126-Daily Advance Staff, June 14, 2019, Clinton's and Dems have more ties to Russians than Trump...**The Daily Advance**

127-Meghan Kenealley, September 9, 2016, Hillary Clinton Calls Donald Trump's Interview on Russian TV 'Unseemly' An interview he did with Larry King was aired on a state-run Russian station...**ABCNews.com**

128-Erin Laviola, February 1, 2021, Evan Ryan, Tony Blinken's Wife: 5 Fast Facts You Need to Know...**Heavy.com**

129-Jonathan Lemire, November 7, 2020, Biden defeats Trump for White House, says 'time to heal'...Zeke Miller, Will Weissert, **APNews.com**

130-Josh Zeitz, October 27, 2016, Worried About a Rigged Election? Here's One Way to Handle It...**Politico.com**

131-Yuki Noguchi, January 28, 2020, I Can't Work With You! How Political Fights Leave Workplaces Divided…**NPR.org**

132-National Conference of State Legislators, June 14-16, 2017, The Future of Elections: Agenda and Resources…**NCLS.org**

133-John Patrick Leary, August 2008, The Third Way Is a Death Trap…**Jacobinmag.com**

134-Matt Vasilogambros, October 11, 2018, Would You Give Your Ballot to a Stranger?…**PEWTrusts.org**

135-Christina A. Cassidy, May 19, 2021, AP Interview: Disinformation concerns mail voting expert…**Columbian.com**

136-Center for Voting and Democracy, 2022, Details about Ranked Choice Voting…**FairVote.org**

137-Roz Brown, November 14, 2017, On Paper, Albuquerque Ballots Likely Less "Hackable"…**Publicnewsservice.org**

138-Stuart Dredge, September 9, 2015, Tech veteran John McAfee to join 2016 US presidential race as independent…**The Guardian.com**

139-Wendy Underhill, December 11, 2017, Program Director for Elections and Redistricting: "Motor Voter" in the States and Noncitizens on Voting Rolls…**National Conference of State Legislatures**

140-Alex Thompson, November 9, 2021, The Wharton wonks giving the White House fits…Kate Davidson, Tina Sfondeles, **Politico.com**

141-Ali Montag, The Wharton wonks giving the White House fits…**CNBC.com**

142-Adam Goldman, September 21, 2018, Rod Rosenstein Suggested Secretly Recording Trump and Discussed 25th Amendment…Michael S. Schmidt, **NY Times**

143-Omar G. Encarnacion, May 18, 2018, Mauricio Macri Was Supposed to Be Different: Argentina's president promised the world he had the business savvy to jump-start the country's economy. He's ended up begging for a bailout…**ForeignPolicy.com**

144-Andrew Blake, February 11, 2021, Mike Lindell: My Pillow dropped by 18 vendors; Dollar General latest to succumb to 'cancel culture'…**The Washington Times**

145-Jack Allen, Mar 29, 2021, Open letter to Charles Butt of H-E-B Food Stores…**MysouTex.com**

146-Fares Sabawi, September 3, 2020, H-E-B owner Charles Butt writes court in support of sending mail ballot applications to registered voters…**KSAT.com News**

147-Matthew Caulfield, 2021, 'It's a clusterf*ck': The college kid who cracked the election industry…, Eugene Daniels, Ben Wofford, **Podcasts.apple.com**

148-Timothy Caulfield, December 15, 2021, Dr. Oz Shouldn't Be a Senator—or a Doctor: His brand of misinformation has already tarnished medicine. In the halls of Congress, he'd do much worse…**SceintificAmerican.com**

149-Corey Stern, September 13, 2015, What we know about Donald Trump's ongoing relationship with Penn…**thedp.com**

150-Jodi Enda, May 19, 2017, Why Democrats don't like Joe Lieberman…**CNN Politics**

151-Christine Stuart, December 21, 2008, Democrats Vent Against Lieberman…**NY Times**

152-Colin Hay, 2007, Third Way politics…**britannica.com**

153-Washington Post, January 10, 2022, How Democrats can survive the midterm jinx…**thirdway.org**

154-Ben Wofford, June 25, 2021, One Man's Quest to Break Open the Secretive World of American Voting Machines: Why doesn't anyone know what a voting machine costs?…**Politico.com**

155-Glen Thrush, August 1, 2013, Clinton's '08 slaps still sting Obama…**Politico.com**

156-Third Way Polling, September 25, 2019, Poll of Rural Voters' Sentiment on Climate Change…**thirdway.org**

157-Tim McDonnell, January 24, 2022, Oil prices are up but the taps aren't flowing like they should be…**Quartz/qz.com**

158-Tom Vanden Brook, August 30, 2021, What happened to US military equipment left behind in Afghanistan?…**USA TODAY**

159-The Understood Team, 2022, The difference between the Every Student Succeeds Act and No Child Left Behind …Lindsay Jones, **understood.org**

160-Trip Brennan, December 9, 2020, Third Way's Jonathan Cowan on Biden, the Suburbs and Left-wing Critics: The longtime President of D.C.'s top centrist think tank wants moderates to deliver progressive victories…**bluetent.us**

161-David Freedlander, July 7, 2013, Andrew Cuomo Could Beat Trump … If He Can Win Over the Left First…**Politico.com**

162-David Grant, April 14, 2013, How Chuck Schumer plays the congressional chessboard…**The Christian Science Monitor.com**

163-Lauren Gambino, February 19, 2017, Liberal voters warn Democratic officials: resist Trump or be replaced…Adam Gabbatt, **The Guardian.com**

164-Michael Barbaro, January 29th, 2020, Podcast call with Chuck Schumer about the Donald Trump Impeachment: Chuck Schumer on Impeachment, Witnesses and the Truth…**The Daily/NY Times**

165-Molly Ball, October 23, 2017, On Safari in Trump's America…**theatlantic.com**

166-Anne Linskey, June 30, 2020, On Monuments, Biden draws a between those of slave owners and those who fought to preserve slavery…**The Washington Post.com**

167-Daniel White, February 24, 2016, Nearly 20% of Trump Fans Think Freeing the Slaves Was a Bad Idea…**Time.com**

168-U.S. Election Assistance Commission, 2022, EAC's Voting System Testing and Certification program: System Certification Process…**eac.gov**

169-U.S. Election Assistance Commission, 2022, EAC's Voting System Testing and Certification program: System Certification Process…**eac.gov**

170-Bennett Leckrone, March 27, 2018, Ex-Husted aide tapped for top elections security slot…**The Columbus Dispatch**

171-History Detectives, 2022, Causes Of The Civil War: Learn more about why the Civil War was fought…**pbs.org**

172-Associated Press, January 24, 2022, Oxford High School reopens nearly 2 months after shooting…**apnews.com**

173-Robert Cotter, August 6, 2020, Donald Trump: NRA Puppet…Nathan Kasai, **thirdway.org**

174-Christi Zamarripa, 2019, Get Ready to Redistrict: A Seminar for Practitioners and Others…**ncsl.org**

175-Christi Zamarripa, 2021, Census and Redistricting Data FAQs…**ncsl.org**

176-Christi Zamarripa, NCSL Redistricting Seminar: Providence, June 20-23, 2019, Presenters: Wendy Underhill, Christi Zamarripa...**ncsl.org**

177-About Pew Research Center, 2022, Mission Statement...**pewresearch.org**

178-D'Vera Cohn PowerPoint, NCSL Redistricting Seminar: Columbus, Ohio, Oct. 24-27, 2019...**ncsl.org**

179-Mark Fritz, March 15, 2017, Immigrants Will Continue To Play A Major Role In The U.S. Workforce, According To Pew Research Data...**Yahoo! finance.com**

180-D'Vera Cohn, January 27, 2020, Dog Whistle Politics: The Trump Administration's Influence on Hate Crimes...**schorlarship.shu.edu**

181-Mónica Verea, 2018, Anti-Immigrant and Anti-Mexican Attitudes And Policies during the First 18 Months Of the Trump Administration...**scielo.org**

182-Victims of Sexual Violence: Statistics, 2022, Younger People Are at the Highest Risk of Sexual Violence...**rainn.org**

183-D'Vera Cohn, February 20, 2020, Must Adults Aware of 2020 Census and Ready to Respond but don't know Key Details...**pewresearch.org**

184-CBS 2 Chicago Staff, November 22, 2021, 5 Dead, 48 Injured After SUV Plows Into Waukesha Christmas Parade; Darrell Brooks Faces Five Counts Of Murder...**Chicago.cbslocal.com**

185-CBS News, January 19, 2022, Man accused of killing UCLA student at L.A. furniture store arrested, police announce...**cbsnews.com**

186-Caroline Silva, January 25, 2022, 'This one hurts': Mayor, chief frustrated after 6-month-old shot dead in NW Atlanta... Alexis Stevens, **The Atlanta-Journal.com**

187-Matthew Caulfield, 2017, The Business of Voting... Andrew Coppersmith, **trustthevote.org**

188-Joe Biden Center, October 2020, A Roadmap to Rebuilding the U.S. Refugee Admissions Program...**global.upenn.edu**

189-Alex Kotch, January 31, 2020, Centrist Third Way, Funded by Corporate Interests, Attacks Sanders in Iowa...**PRWatch.org**

190-Charlie Warzel, September 29, 2016, Twitter Says This ISIS Beheading Photo Doesn't Qualify As Abuse...**buzzfeednews.com**

191-Dan Balz, November 3, 2021, A sobering reality hits Democrats after Election loses...**The Washington Post.com**

192-D. Hunter Schwarz, January 4, 2022, Could the Republican Party be headed toward a civil war in 2022?...**DeseretNews.com**

193-Ted Barrett, January 6, 2005, Democrats challenge Ohio electoral votes: Move delays official certification of Presidential election...**CNN Politics**

194-Joe Walsh, November 1, 2019, Joe Walsh: In 2016, I was a proud 'deplorable.' In 2019, I'll gladly be 'human scum.'...**USA Today**

195-Anthony Rivas, January 19, 2021, Fired DHS cybersecurity head Chris Krebs says Trump should be convicted for inciting insurrection...**ABCNews.com**

196-Mark Mazzetti, April 15, 2021, Biden Administration Says Russian Intelligence Obtained Trump Campaign Data... Michael S. Schmidt, **NY Times**

197-Dan Mangan, September 26, 2016, Trump brags about not paying taxes: 'That makes me smart'...**cnbc.com**

198-Nick Gass, June 16, 2015, Trump has spent years courting Hillary and other Dems...**Politico.com**

199-Donald Janson, March 20, 1987, Trump Plans Housing for Atlantic City Land...**NY Times**

200-Adam Ambrogi, 2022, Democracy Fund — Founded by The Omidyar Group, 2022, Profile and History...**democracyfund.org**

201-Lisa Rosenberg, July 12, 2012, What You Should Know About the DISCLOSE Act Part 1: What is the DISCLOSE Act?...**sunlightfoundation.com**

202-Adam Ambrogi, Conference: 2019 Ballot Data Convening Attendee: Center For Technology and Civic Life...**Tiana-Epps Johnson-49eh.squarespace.com, hello@techandciviclife.org**

203-United States Senate, Committee on Rules and Administration, page, 591, September 29, 2010, Adam Ambrogi on Examing The Fillibuster: Ideas to Reduce Delay and Encourage Debate in the Senate...**books.google.com**

204-Marc Levy, January 20, 2022, Democrats' issue No. 1 in Senate race: Kill the filibuster...**APNews.com**

205-Press Releases and Statements, November 29, 2006, Analysis of 2006 Election Finds Problems Nationwide...**pewtrusts.org**

206-Denise W. Merrill, January 5, 2022, Secretary Merrill Statement on the One Year Anniversary of the January 6th Violent Insurrection in Washington, D.C.: Her Official website...**portal.ct.gov**

207-Fredreka Schouten, June 29, 2021, Progressive group launches $7 million effort to elect Democratic secretaries of state and attorneys general...**CNN Politics**

208-Chandelis Duster, June 28, 2021, Obama stresses protecting voting rights to avoid 'further delegitimizing' democracy...**CNN Politics**

209-Max Smith, January 16, 2018, Va. election commissioner not retained following dramatic 2017 races...**wtop.com**

210-Travis Fain, October 13, 2016, GOP leader: Fire Virginia's elections chief...**DailyPress.com**

211-Declaration of Edgardo Cortes, May 29,2020, Declaration of Edgardo Cortés in Thomas Curtin v. Virginia State Board of Elections...**AdvancementProject.org**

212-Chase Gunter, February 14, 2017, DHS vague on rules for election aid, say states...**fcw.com**

213-Joseph Johnson, March 3, 2021, Cyber Crimes: Number of breaches and records exposed 2005-2020: Data Breaches vs. Data Exposures...**staista.com**

214-Hamza Tamenaoul, March 11, 2020, Coding in Binary Code! A thing?...**DEV Community.com**

215-Lauren Aratani, February 27, 2021, Electricity needed to mine bitcoin is more than used by 'entire countries'...**The Guardian.com**

216-Ian Haney Lopez, August 13, 2019, Op-Ed: Why do Trump's supporters deny the racism that seems so evident to Democrats?...**LATimes.com**

217-J. Dale Shoemaker, September 24, 2019, Ahead of voting machine decision, six experts and advocates weigh in on Allegheny County's impending purchase...**PublicSource.org**

218-Ron Bandes, June 21, 2017, Expert Sign-on Letter to Congress: Secure American Elections...**info@electiondefense.org**

219-Andy Sheehan, January 14, 2020, Under Threat Of Lawsuit, Allegheny Co. Purging 69,000 Inactive Voters From Rolls...**pittsburg.cbslocal.com**

220-Emily Previti, November 11, 2020, Election law experts: Latest Trump lawsuit a longshot, but could further complicate vote count, certification…**witf.org**

221-W. Ryan Schuster, February 11, 2014, Faculty Profile: A Conversation With Professor Rebecca Green…**law.wm.edu**

222-Dustin Molvaney, November 13, 2014, Solar energy isn't Always As Green As You Think!…**spectrum.IEEE.org**

223-Charles Stewart III, October 26, 2021, 3 Questions: Administering elections in a hyper-partisan era MIT professor of political science: Charles Stewart III discusses the status of US election administration…**News.MIT.edu**

224-State of Nevada, Office of the Secretary of State, 2022, About The Office…**nvsos.gov**

225-Riley Snyder, April 10, 2021, Nevada Republicans vote to censure SOS Cegavske over voter fraud allegations…**theNevadaIndependent.com**

226-Dan Njegomir, September 18, 2017, Behind the Scenes: Meet 'county-facer' in chief Dwight Shellman…**coloradopolitics.com**

227-Associated Press, March 24, 2005, Hundreds in Colorado investigated for voter fraud…**summitdaily.com**

228-Ernest Luning, November 16, 2021, FBI raids home of Mesa County Clerk Tina Peters in election data breach investigation…**coloradopolitics.com**

229-Laura Wagner, November 26, 2016, Clinton Campaign Says It Will Participate In Recount Efforts…**NPR.org**

230-Russell Goldman, August 12, 2009, Anatomy of an Outburst: Why Did Hillary Clinton Get Angry in Africa?…**ABCNews.com**

231-Dan Merica, March 6, 2020, Bill Clinton says he feels 'terrible' that affair has 'unfairly' defined Monica Lewinsky's life…**CNN Politics**

232-Carole Fader, July 1, 2016, Fact Check: Hillary Clinton did defend a man in 1975 rape case…**jacksonville.com**

233-Josh Rogin, June 20, 2014, Exclusive: 'Hillary Clinton Took Me Through Hell,' Rape Victim Says…**theDailyBeast.com**

234-Lauren del Valle, December 1, 2021, Jeffrey Epstein's former pilot testifies Bill Clinton, Donald Trump, Prince Andrew flew aboard Epstein's private plane… Eric Levenson, **CNN Politics**

235-James C. McKinley Jr., December 1, 2021, What is known about Jeffrey Epstein's suicide...**NY Times**

236-Personal Democracy Forum 2018, 2018, The theme of PDF 2018 is "How We Make Good,"...**www.pdf-18.com**

237-Jennifer Cohn, December 17, 2019, How New Voting Machines Could Hack Our Democracy...**TheNewYorkReview**

238-Amy Cohen, August 4, 2015, Indiana Now a Partner in the Voting Information Project... Jen Tolentino, **pewtrusts.org**

239-Rebecca Beitsch, October 4, 2017, Election Officials Attacked From All Sides on Purging Voter Rolls...**pewtrusts.org**

240-Dartunorro Clark, July 16, 2017, Bipartisan Group That Shares Voter Data Shames Trump Panel...**NBCNews.com**

241-Brad Dress, December 15, 2021, AP finds fewer than 475 cases of potential voter fraud in six 2020 battleground states...**The Hill.com**

242-Steve Gorman, May 31, 2017, Kathy Griffin loses CNN deal after photos with fake severed Trump head...**Reuters.com**

243-Keith Esau's Biography, 2022, Amends Gubernatorial Qualifications...**justfacts.votesmart.org**

244-Talia Richman, January 12, 2018, Maryland Lawmakers, Mayor Pugh, Gov. Hogan Condemn Trump's Comments on Immigrants...**cherylkagan.org**

245-Pamela Wood, March 12, 2021, Unlike many other states, Maryland's legislature is moving to make it easier to vote early or by mail...**BaltimoreSun.com**

246-Brian Griffiths, February 14, 2021, Do Democrats want to try to force Baltimore Sun sale by threatening Eminent Domain?...**The Duck Pin.com**

247-Kevin Lewis, August 21, 2019, READ: A List of Disturbing Crimes by Illegal Immigrants in Montgomery County...**wmal.com**

248-Lawrence Lessig, December 12, 2019, Ranked-choice voting (RCV) could guarantee that a candidate is elected by a majority: Ranked-choice voting could guarantee that a candidate is elected by a majority...**BostonGlobe.com**

249-Joe Tasca, February 22, 2021, Rhode Island saw an unprecedented number of business closures in 2020, but it was also a record year for new business filings in the state...**the Public's Radio.com**

250-Tom Byrne, November 3, 2020, Commissioner dies in car crash...**delawarepublic.org**

251-Elaine Manlove, October 1, 2020, Letter: Former Delaware Election Commissioner warns against Trump, urges people to vote...**delawareonline.com**

252-Scott Goss, September 17, 2018, Delaware's first new voting machines in decades are on their way...**delawareonline.com**

253-Detective Breen Police Report, November 3, 2020, Former election commissioner dies in crash...**CapeGazette.com**

254-Betsy Price, April 20, 2021, Election bills zip through House Administration Committee...**Town Square Delaware.com**

255-Aaron McDade, December 8, 2021, GOP Elections Leader in Utah Says Members Trying to 'Fundamentally Destroy the Voting System'...**NewsWeek.com**

256-Ward v. Jackson, November 2020, Findings and rulings of such case...**unamericanbar.com**

257-Jeremy Herb, February 3, 2021, Jamie Raskin: Trump's impeachment defense amounts to 'absurd constitutional arguments'... Manu Raju, **CNN Politics**

258-Stanford University, 2019-2022, Case List of COVID-Related Election Litigation Tracker...**healthyelections-case-tracker.stanford.edu**

259-The Associated Press, December 31, 2020, 'Brutal Day': US Rep. Raskin of Maryland Announces Death of Son...**nbcwashington.com**

260-Meg Tully, August 13, 2018, Maryland Grapples with National Crisis of Mental Illness in Jails...**marylandreporter.com**

261-Dennis Thompson, January 24, 2022, U.S. Teens Were Already in Mental Health Crisis Before Pandemic Hit...**US News.com**

262-Kate Bennett, April 2, 2021, Hunter Biden details his struggle with addiction -- and his dad's love -- in a new memoir...**CNN Politics**

263-Office of the Attorney General of Georgia, January 21, 2022, Carr Joins Multi-State Coalition Urging State Department to Fight Fentanyl Spike...**law.georgia.gov**

264-Rep. Beth Van Duyne, January 1, 2021, Democrats wasted two years on impeachment instead of much-needed infrastructure...**theHill.com**

265-Jesse Paul, February 24, 2021, Colorado elections expert nominated by Joe Biden to serve on U.S. Postal Service governing board…**ColoradoSun.com**

266-Our Staff, October 11, 2021, Video: NBA Coach Doc Rivers interviews Amber McReynolds…**thefulcrum.us**

267-Abigail Abrams, October 20, 2020, Meet the Woman Behind the Country's Effort to Embrace Mail Voting in 2020…**TIME.com**

268-Derek Thompson, September 30, 2020, How Voting By Mail, Could Cost Biden the Election…**theAtlantic.com**

269-Brianna Keilar, 2020 Election, Biden rolls out $1.3 billion for Amtrak…**CNN Politics**

270-Rob Hayes, September 10, 2021, Recall Election CA: Why do your ballot envelopes have holes?…**abc7.com**

271-Libby Denkmann, January 23, 2020, Beverly Hills Sues Over 'Severe Ballot Design Flaw' In LA County Voting Machines…**laist.com**

272-Dora Kingsley Vertenten, October 15, 2020, As few as 1 in 10 homeless people vote in elections – here's why…**theconverstion.com**

273-Alfred Ng, August 10, 2018, US officials hope hackers at Defcon find more voting machine problems…**cnet.com**

274-Elizabeth Weise, December 7, 2017, Illinois' Cook County says it can fix election hacking if it just had the money…**USA Today.com**

275-Jack Gillum, September 14, 2018, The Overlooked Weak Link in Election Security… Jessica Huseman, **propublica.org**

276-Doug Chapin's BIO, 2022, Doug Chapin is working to develop and expand CSPG's Project for Excellence in Election Administration…**eac.gov**

277-Shannon Schumacher, October 30, 2020, From voter registration to mail-in ballots, how do countries around the world run their elections?… Aidan Connaughton, **pewtrusts.org**

278-Presidential Actions at the White House, September 27, 2021, A Proclamation on National Voter Registration Day, 2021…**whitehouse.gov**

279-Todd Blodgett, July 19, 2021, Opinion: Biden White House sets aside ethics with the handling of Hunter Biden artwork sales…**desmoinesregister.com**

280-Salvador Rodriguez, June 4, 2021, Facebook says Donald Trump to remain banned for two years, effective from Jan. 7…**cnbc.com**

281-Official Website of Senator Daniel Ivey-Soto, 2022, About Daniel Ivey-Soto…**iveysoto.com**

282-Josh James, August 29, 2011, Fewer Candidates Taking "Political Courage Test"…**wuky.org**

283-Senator Ivey-Soto Vote, 2019, Authorizes State Investment in Renewable Energies - New Mexico Key Vote…**justfacts.votesmart.org**

284-Senator Ivey-Soto Vote, 2019, Establishes an Electric Vehicle Tax Credit - New Mexico Key Vote…**justfacts.votesmart.org**

285-NBC News and news source, June 3, 2008, Clinton refuses to concede the nomination…**nbcnews.com**

286-Elise Jordan, May 7, 2020, How Donald Trump's Mother Did—and Didn't—Shape His Life…**VanityFair.com**

287-Matthew Reichbach, March 27, 2019, Gov. signs same-day voter registration bill…**nmpoliticalreport.com**

288-Mike Fortner's Biography, 2022, Voting record of Rep. Mike Fortner…**justfacts.votesmart.org**

289-Mike Fortner Vote, August 26, 2018, Requires Increase in Teacher Salaries - Illinois Key Vote…**justfacts.votesmart.org**

290-Mike Fortner Vote, June 26, 2014, Amends Bullying Prevention Measures in the School Code - Illinois Key Vote…**justfacts.votesmart.org**

291-The Associated Press, August 13, 2020, Rep. Andrew McLean, D-Gorham, resigning from Maine Legislature…**BangorDailyNews.com**

292-Ballotpedia, 2020, Kyle Bailey: Maine…**ballotpedia.org**

293-Michael Deal, January 5, 2020, Kyle Bailey: Advocate for Ranked-Choice Voting… George Linzer, **theamericanleader.org**

294-Dick Woodbury and Kyle Bailey, 2014, Committee for Ranked Choice Voting…**influencewatch.org**

295-Fair Vote: For a More Perfect Union, 2022, Timeline of ranked-choice voting in Maine…**fairvote.org**

296-Ballotpedia, 2022, Ranked-choice voting (RCV)…**ballotpedia.org**

297-Zaid Jilani, March 4, 2018, The Oscars use a more fair Voting System than Most of America does: Ranked Choice Voting…**theintercept.com**

298-Mike Shannon, June 24, 2020, Why ranked-choice voting is bad: Consider a current scenario…**TheFulcrum**

299-Politico, November 2020, Joe Biden has been declared the winner, toppling Donald Trump after four years of upheaval in the White House…**Politico.com**

300-Laura Wilson, September 2, 2010, Quick Tip: Don't Leave Blanks in the Grid-Ins…**wilsondailyprep.com**

301-Equal Vote, 2022, Comparing RCV and STAR Voting…**equal.vote**

302-Gabrielle Mannino, September 22, 2020, Court rules in favor of Sec. of State clearing way for RCV in presidential election…**newscentermaine.com**

303-Sophie Lewis, December 7, 2020, Joe Biden breaks Obama's record for most votes ever cast for a U.S. presidential candidate…**CBSNews**

304-Hannah Miao, November 4, 2020, 2020 election sees record-high turnout with at least 159.8 million votes projected…**cnbc.com**

305-Scott McDonald, December 22, 2020, How the Heisman Trophy Winner is Selected, And When The Finalists Are Named…**NewsWeek.com**

306-Susan Cover, October 15, 2021, First-term Gorham House member resigns…**spectrumlocalnews.com**

307-Michael Sheppard, October 15, 2021, Ranked-choice voting advocate in 1st legislative term resigns Maine House seat…**BangorDailyNews.com**

308-Marianne Goodland, February 24, 2021, Former Denver elections chief Amber McReynolds tapped for USPS board of governors…**9news.com**

309-Matt Rivers, December 18, 2021, 'We were cheated, framed, and scammed' Jailed for the killing of Haiti's president, five suspected assassins say they're innocent…, Natalie Gallon, Etant Dupain, **CNN Politics**

310-Penn Biden Center, 2016, Former Deputy Secretary of State Antony Blinken delivers remarks at a World Refugee Day Naturalization Ceremony at the U.S. Holocaust Memorial Museum on June 20, 2016…**global.upenn.edu**

311-LSC Education &Training, January 12, 2022, to January 20, 2022, Innovations in Technology Conference…**globalexpo-net.com**

312-Ismar Volic, September 9, 2020, The Latest Argument For Ranked-Choice Voting? Last Week's Primary…**yeson2rcv.com**

313-Dries Buytaert, 2022, Definition of a Drupal…**drupal.org**

314-Julie Bort, March 25, 2012, Dries Buytaert's Software Powers A Million Important Websites — And He Built It From His Couch…**businessinsider.com**

315-Pine Tree Legal Assistance, 2022, About Pine Street and their services…**ptla.org**

316-Signatures of Lawyers, December 10, 2020, Over 3,500 attorneys call on bar associations to investigate Trump legal team…**practicesource.com**

317-Elliot Spagat, June 4, 2021, Biden taps groups to help pick asylum-seekers to come to US…, Julie Watson, **apnews.com**

318-Pine Street Legal Assistance budget 2020, 2020, Pine Street Legal Assistance Revenue chart, 14/16…**powerpointptla.org**

319-Ballotpedia, 2022, Senator Dee Brown's Record on Voting…**ballotpedia.org**

320-Xanterra Parks & Resorts, 2022, Xanterra Explore…**travelWyoming.com**

321-Tom Tapp, July 6, 2021, Jeff Bezos' Wealth Hits All-Time Record High With Expected Amazon Pentagon Contract, Leaving Elon Musk In The Dust…**Deadline.com**

322-Forbes, 2021, Top 100 richest men in the world: #66 Philip Anschutz…**Forbes**

323-Laurie Bennett, February 4, 2012, Billionaires Channel Millions to Think Tanks…**Forbes**

324-James B. Meigs, February 27, 2021, The real reason why Bill Gates is now the US' biggest farmland owner…**NYPost.com**

325-Catherine Thorbecke, April 30, 2021, How 'Amtrak Joe' Biden's infrastructure push could put rail back on track in the US…**ABCNews.com**

326-Ben Ryder Howe, March 21, 2017, Why Philip Anschutz, Known as the "Anti-Trump," Is Spending a Fortune on Old Hotels…**townandcountrymag.com**

327-Kelly Catalfamo, October 30, 2019, The myth and reincarnation of John Wilkes Booth…**scalawagmagazine.org**

328-Arjun Athreya, October 27, 2020, Who Are the Majority and Minority Stakeholders of the Los Angeles Lakers?…**essentiallysports.com**

329-Bloomberg Billionaires Index, 2022, Phil Anschutz #134…**bloomberg.com**

330-Glenn F. Bunting, July 23, 2006, A Denver Billionaire's Invisible Hand...**LATimes.com**

331-Stephen Goff, February 7, 2001, Anschutz Set To Add United to His MLS Empire...**The Washington Post.com**

332-Niel Westergaard, June 1, 2017, Anschutz Adds to Media Holdings, Buys another Colorado Newspaper...**bizjournals.com**

333-David Brooks, December 15, 2018, Who Killed The Weekly Standard?...**NY Times**

334-Cathy Proctor, October 5, 2011, Anschutz power line project to be part of Obama streamlining effort...**bizjournals.com**

335-Marc Hogan, January 12, 2017, Coachella Owner's Ties to Anti-LGBTQ Causes More Recent Than Previously Reported...**PitchFork.com**

336-Blair Miller, January 6, 2017, Colorado business, entertainment mogul Philip Anschutz denies being 'anti-LGBTQ'...**thedenverchannel.com**

337-Dave Brooks, February 1, 2018, AEG Owner Pulls Financial Support for Some Anti-LGBTQ Groups, But Still Donated $770,000 in 2016...**BillBoard.com**

338-Colorado Pols, July 14, 2021, Nervy Billionaire Phil Anschutz Sues To Claw Back Tax Cash...**coloradopols.com**

339-Marc Hogan, January 31, 2018, Coachella Co-Owner's Latest Charitable Filing Shows Deep Anti-LGBTQ Ties...**PitchFork.com**

340-Sophie Cocke, August 15, 2020, Obama and the beach house loopholes...**staradvertiser.com**

341-Matthew DiLallo, July 20, 2015, How Philip Anschutz Made Billions Seeing What Others Missed...**TheMontleyFool.com**

342-Client Earth Communications, November 11, 2020, Fossil fuels and climate change: the facts...**clientearth.org**

343-Sammy Roth, August 5, 2021, How a federal agency is blocking America's largest wind farm...**LA Times.com**

344-Ben Lefebvre, October 27, 2020, The oil industry actually hasn't done that well under Trump...**Politico.com**

345-Anna Phillips, January 27, 2022, Biden outpaces Trump in issuing drilling permits on public lands...**The Washington Post.com**

346-Ros Davidson, November 9, 2021, Biden to sign US's $1.2 trillion infrastructure bill in boost for Grids and Ports...**windpowermonthly.com**

347-Eli B Martin, September 10, 2010, Wind Farms: Not So Green...**The Harvard Crimson.com**

348-Chris Martin, February 5, 2020, The latest landfill problem comes from the renewable energy industry...Bloomberg, **fortune.com**

349-NS Energy Staff Writer, March 30, 2021, Profiling the top five countries with the highest wind energy capacity...**nsenergybusiness.com**

350-Holly Godbey, November 11, 2017, The American Civil War – the Union told all the European countries if they recognized the Confederacy's legitimacy, it was equal to declaring war against the Union...**warhistoryonline.com**

351-Mark John, December 7, 2021, Pandemic boosts super-rich share of global wealth...**Reuters.com**

352-Tampa Bay Times Staff archive, October 27, 1992 A third of eligible voters didn't register...**Tampa Bay Times**

353-John McCormick, April 27, 2006, Voting Machine maker on Defense...**ChicagoTribune.com**

354-Kim Zetter, July 14, 2008, NY: 50 Percent of Sequoia Voting Machines Flawed...**Wired.com**

355-Brian J. Hancock Miscellaneous Administration And Program, 2022, US EAC Payroll...**openpayrolls.com**

356-Miscellaneous Administration And Program Job Description, 2020, Miscellaneous Administration and Program - Federal Salaries of 2020...**federalpay.org**

357-C-SPAN, October 26, 2004, 2004 Election Procedures...**c-span.org**

358-Mindy Moretti, April 11, 2019, Exit Interview: Brian Hancock...**electiononline.org**

359-Brian Hancock's Linkedin Account, 2022, Director: Infrastructure Policy and Product Development at Unisyn Voting Solutions...**linkedin.com**

360-Press Release, February 27, 2020, NEWS: Benjamin Hovland begins term as EAC Chairman...**eac.gov**

361-YouTube, October 6, 2020, CISA 3rd Annual National Cybersecurity Summit...**waterisac.org**

362-Unisyn Product Overview, 2022, 2005 Certified by the United States Election Assistance Commission...**unisynvoting.com**

363-Jeremy Herb, November 3, 2020, Battleground states report few problems at polls…Fredreka Schouten, **CNN Politics**

364-C-SPAN, March 3, 2016, Thomas Hicks talked about the Election Assistance Commission's (EAC) role in the 2016 presidential primary…**c-span.org**

365-Open Database of the Corporate World, 2022, UNISYN VOTING SOLUTIONS, INC…**opencorporates.com**

366-Bethany Allen-Ebrahimian, December 8, 2020, Exclusive: Suspected Chinese spy targeted California politicians…, Zach Dorfman, **axios.com**

367-Fred Lucas, November 23, 2021, Hunter Biden's Cobalt Deal With China Increases Cost of His Father's Push for Electric Cars…**dailysignal.com**

368-Jenni Bergal, 2017, After Russian hackers targeted state voting systems last year, some officials are renewing their focus on switching to paper ballots, which they say are more secure and leave an audit trail…**huffpost.com**

369-Sidney Milkis, 2022, Theodore Roosevelt: Domestic Affairs…**millercenter.org**

370-Andrew Horn, July 16, 2019, A look at North Dakota's new $11 million election system…**kfyrtv.com**

371-Tammy Patrick, 2013, Appointed by Barrack Obama…**electionsos.com**

372-Jane C. Timm, September 24, 2021, The GOP's election review in Arizona is over. Its influence is just beginning, experts say…**yahoo.com**

373-Margaret Menge, October 15, 2020, Hillary Clinton's Lawyer Launches National Assault on Voter Laws…**insidesources.com**

374-Sam Tabachnik, August 7, 2016, The crusade of a Democratic super-lawyer with multimillion-dollar backing…**The Washington Post.com**

375-Tal Axelrod, October 19, 2020, 10 bellwether counties that could signal where the election is headed…**TheHill.com**

376-David Levine, October 26, 2020, Everything You Wanted to Know About Voting in the U.S. with David Levine and the Democracy Fund's Tammy Patrick…**securingdemocracy.gmfus.org**

377-Ian Chipman, June 3, 2016, David Dill: Why Online Voting Is a Danger to Democracy…**engineering.stanford.edu**

378-George Anders, March 6, 1998, Packard Children Focus Giving On World-Population Control…**Wall Street Journal.com**

379-Jeremy W. Peters, March 31, 2016, HP Inc. Joins Companies Declining to Contribute to G.O.P. Convention…**NY Times.com**

380-Theodore Schleifer, June 11, 2016, Meg Whitman likens Trump to Hitler, Mussolini… Daniella Diaz, **CNN Politics**

381-U. S. Election Assistance Commission, October 12, 2017, Initial Decision on Certification: Dear Chris Ortiz…**eac.gov**

382-Julia Agos, January 13, 2022, Most Pa. Republicans still believe there was widespread election fraud in 2020: poll…Jeremy Long, **pennlive.com**

383-Mairead McArdle, October 9, 2020, Hillary Clinton Maintains 2016 Election 'Was Not On the Level': 'We Still Don't Know What Really Happened'…**Yahoo.com**

384-National Oceanic and Atmospheric Administration, 2016, U.S. saw 10 billion-dollar disasters in 2015…**noaa.gov**

385-Jake Tapper, April 28, 2021, Biden says China is betting the US can't keep up with autocracy… Betsy Klein, **CNN Politics**

386-Victor Fiorillo, January 30, 2018, Uh-Oh: The Curse of Billy Penn May Be Back to Haunt Us…**PhillyMag.com**

387-Ken Finkle, June 30, 2013, Breaking Away from the "Gentleman's Agreement"… **phillyhistory.org**

388-Jeffrey Brodeur, March 17, 1996, Fortune Up In Smoke Former Philadelphia Eagles Owner Loses Mass Fortune Gambling, Drinking…**The Spokesman-Review.com**

389-Austin Thompson, January 1, 2020, When Did Shaking Hands Become a Standard Way of Greeting Someone?...**mentalfloss.com**

390-The Political Writings of William Penn, 1670, stories from William Penn…**oll.libertyfund.org**

391-Ron Avery, December 20, 2010, Slavery stained some unlikely founders, too - Philadelphia …**Philadelphia Inquirer**

392-Michaela Winberg, October 27, 2019, William Penn's plan: How Philly became a model for American cities…**billypenn.com**

393-Thomas Kidd, 2022, William Penn and the Founding of Pennsylvania…**BillofRightsinstitute.org**

394-Doug West, May 12, 2021, William Penn, Quakers, and the Founding of Pennsylvania…**owlcation.com**

395-Jim Powell, 2022, William Penn, America's First Great Champion for Liberty and Peace…**quaker.org**

396-Ben Upton, February 9, 2021, University probed on funds for Biden Center denies China sway…**researchprofessionalnews.com**

397-Jack Kelly, January 22, 2022, Wharton Professor Asks Her Business Students What The Average American Earns—Their Answers Ranged Up To $800k…**Forbes.com**

398-Eric Rosenbaum, March 1, 2019, 1 in 5 corporations say China has stolen their IP within the last year: CNBC CFO survey…**cnbc.com**

399-Maggie Severns, July 9, 2019, Bidens earned $15 million in 2 years after Obama administration… Natasha Korecki, **Politico.com**

400-Imran Siddiqui, January 29, 2021, Penn denies renewed allegations of foreign donations to Biden Center after GOP letter…**thedp.com**

401-Post Editorial Board, April 7, 2021, Biden's $2 trillion pay-to-play plan for unions…**NY Post.com**

402-Laura Roberts, June 15, 2018, Bill Clinton cornered Loretta Lynch at Sky Harbor and it wasn't just to say hello…**azcentral.com**

403-Chris Arnold, April 14, 2010, Tea Party Finds Inspiration In Boston History…**npr.org**

404-Mark Osborne, June 1, 2019, Alexandria Ocasio-Cortez goes back to work as a bartender – for a day…**abcnews.go.com**

405-Washington Examiner, December 20, 2021, On crime, Nancy Pelosi is as clueless as ever…**washingtonexaminer.com**

406-Arlette Saenz, October 4, 2018, Joe Biden to offer contrast to Trump in London foreign policy speech…**CNN Politics**

407-BBC, January 25, 2021, 'Wealth increase of 10 men during a pandemic could buy vaccines for all'…**bbc.com**

408-Navdanya International, April 20, 2021, Bill Gates: Let Them Eat Fake Meat!..**childrenshealthdefense.org**

409-Amy McCarthy, January 10, 2022, KFC's Beyond Meat Nuggets Taste Like Chicken, Eat Like Rubber…**Eater.com**

410-Antony Zurcher, November 9, 2016, US Election 2016 Results: Five reasons Donald Trump won…**bbc.com**

411-William H. Frey, ay 5, 2021, Turnout in 2020 election spiked among both Democratic and Republican voting groups, new census data shows…**Brookings.edu**

412-Joe Kelly, March 7, 2016, How British businesses helped the Confederacy fight the American Civil War…**The Conversation.com**

413-Michael Houston, May 17, 2020, More athletes claim they contracted COVID-19 at Military World Games in Wuhan…**insidethegames.biz**

414-Event 201: Bill Gates Foundation, October 18, 2019, A severe pandemic, which becomes "Event 201,"…**centerforhealthsecurity.org**

415-Damian Paletta, July 6, 2017, At this year's G20 summit, it's Trump against the world…**weforum.org**

416-Gary Abbott, October 18, 2019, Talented US Military Team to Compete in 7th CISM Military World Games in Wuhan, China…**teamusa.org**

417-Molly Nagle, October 13, 2018, 'Middle-class' Joe Biden hits the trail for Dems, but will it win back working-class voters?…**abcnews.go.com**

418-Randall Chase, March 13, 2017, Biden Institute Launched at University of Delaware…**diverseeducation.com**

419-Karl Rove, April 23, 2009, The President's Apology Tour…**Wall Street Journal.com**

420-Daniel Nasaw, April 4, 2012, Who, What, Why: How many soldiers died in the US Civil War?…**bbc.com**

421-Irin Carmon, August 10, 2016, Donald Trump's Worst Offense? Mocking Disabled Reporter, Poll Finds…**nbcnews.com**

422-Gretchen Morgenson, March 1, 2020, How DuPont may avoid paying to clean up a toxic 'forever chemical'…**nbcnews.com**

423-The Daily Mail Staff, April 4, 2014, Beau Biden DEFENDS the judge who only gave a du Pont heir probation after admitting to sexually assaulting his three-year-old daughter…**dailymail.co.uk**

424-Tara Palmeri, March 25, 2021, Sources: Secret Service inserted itself into case of Hunter Biden's gun… Ben Schreckinger, **Politico.com**

425-Micael J. Green, June 24, 2021, Biden's Afghanistan Pullout Could Make the China Problem Harder…**foreignpolicy.com**

426-Michelle Kaffenberger, June 15, 2020, How much learning may be lost in the long-run from COVID-19 and how can mitigation strategies help?…**brookings.edu**

427-Callie Ahlgrim, October 29, 2019, Kanye West claims Democrats have 'brainwashed' black Americans and 'make them abort their children'...**insider.com**

428-University of Delaware: Biden Center, 2021, Transfer into a Biden School Major...**bidenschool.udel.edu**

429-Niamh O, February 16, 2021, The Wharton MBA Program: All You Need To Know About Admissions & Careers...**topmba.com**

430-United States Colleges Ranked by Lowest GPA, 2022, Concordia University Ann Arbor, Ann Arbor, MI: GPA 2.2...**collegesimply.com**

431-Lisa Carter, March 29, 2021, What Was Joe Biden's GPA?...**celebanswers.com**

432-J. Mark Powell, December 7, 2017, The second time Japan attacked Pearl Harbor...**washingtonexaminer.com**

433-Sam Simon, August 10, 2020, How Germany Tried To Get Mexico to Attack the United States in 1917...**historyofyesterday.com**

434-Scott Bomboy, February 26, 2021, How one telegram helped to lead America toward war...**constitutioncenter.org**

435-Michael Peck, March 4, 2017, Mexico Almost Invaded the U.S. in 1917...**nationalinterest.org**

436-David Murrell, July 10, 2019, Penn Paid Joe Biden $775,000 to Expand Its "Global Outreach" ... and Give Some Speeches...**PhillyMag.com**

437-James S. Robbins, November 9, 2021, No collusion: How Americans were fed a false tale about Donald Trump's 2016 campaign...**USA Today.com**

438-Gary Oberg Litchfield, December 23, 2020, READER LETTER: Trump leaves with a long list of accomplishments... Brent Schacherer, **crowrivermedia.com**

439-Cristiano Lima, September 9, 2016, Hillary Clinton walks back 'basket of deplorables' remark: The Trump campaign had demanded an apology — but they didn't quite get one...**Politico.com**

440-Somini Sengupta, November 8, 2021, Obama, in Climate Speech Focused on Youth, Has Words for Republicans, Too... Mark Landler, **NY Times.com**

441-Joseph Curl, May 23, 2017, How much does CNN hate Trump? 93% of coverage is negative...**The Washington Times.com**

442-Andrea Shorter, December 17, 2020, More Than a Number: Losing Our Greatest Generation During COVID-19…**sfbaytimes.com**

443-Paul Kamenar, January 18, 2021, Tony Blinken must Explain Anonymous China Donations to Penn Biden Center: Which he managed…**yahoo.com**

444-White House Briefing Room, April 20, 2021, President Biden Announces More Key Administration Nominations…**whitehouse.gov**

445-Eli Watkins, May 8, 2017, Yates on Trump's travel ban: 'Arguments have to be based on truth'…**CNN Politics**

446-Nate Raymond, December 10, 2021, Group wins new chance to obtain Yates' DOJ emails over Trump travel ban…**Reuters.com**

447-Jeff Stein, November 2, 2017, Donna Brazile's bombshell about the DNC and Hillary Clinton, explained…**VOX.com**

448-Martin Pengelly, November 5, 2017, Donna Brazile tells critics of Hillary Clinton revelations to 'go to hell'…**theguardian.com**

449-Chris Coffey, September 10, 2020, Citizens for Transparency and Inclusion Slams Governor Carney for Runaway Inequality and Economic Decline Across Delaware…**businesswire.com**

450-Brian Schwartz, November 22, 2021, Trump-allied dark money group joins forces with a think tank run by ex-president's former aides…**cnbc.com**

451-University of Delaware, 2018, Julie Mapes Wilgen Award in Human Sexuality & Gender Studies…**hdfs.udel.edu**

452-Brittany Bernstein, January 30, 2022, UPenn May Sue if Transgender Swimmer Is Barred from Women's Championship…**nationalreview.com**

453-Mark Eichmann, May 20, 2021, 'It is inadequate': Delaware launches new effort to diversify judges and lawyers…**whyy.org**

454-Teaganne Finn, January 30, 2022, Senators split on Biden's pledge to pick a Black woman for Supreme Court seat…**nbcnews.com**

455-Dr. Grisel Y. Acosta, November 10, 2020, White Fragility in the Latinx Community: A Lesson (OPINION)…**latinorebels.com**

456-Harmeet Kaur, August 12, 2020, Why people are split on using 'Latinx'…**CNN Politics**

457-Helleniscope Staff, December 11, 2020, Hunter Biden, Karloutsos and Manatos: More Emails From the "Laptop From Hell"…**helleniscope.com**

458-Shannon Osaka, June 8, 2021, Ban Ki-moon wants to solve the climate crisis with kindness…**Grist.com**

459-Embassy of China, September 3, 2016, Xi Jinping, President Barack Obama of US and UN Secretary-General Ban Ki-moon Jointly Attend Deposit of Instruments of Joining the Paris Agreement…**mfa.gov**

460-Bob Inglis, September 26, 2020, Why Christian conservatives like me shouldn't let abortion, socialism turn us off Joe Biden…**greenvilleonline.com**

461-Isabella Grullón Paz, October 18, 2021, All the Republicans Who Won't Support Trump…**NY Times.com**

462-Louis Chan, October 18, 2016, Former Obama Speechwriter Still Making A Difference…**asamnews.com**

463-Christy Cooney, December 1, 2020, Barack Obama once warned not to underestimate Joe Biden's 'ability to f**k things up'…**news.com.au**

464-Daniel Henninger, September 22, 2021, Joe Biden (D., Socialist)…**Wall Street Journal.com**

465-Julia Ries, October 9, 2021, After Facebook and Instagram Bombshells, Should Parents Keep Kids Off Social Media?…**healthline.com**

466-Seth Fiegerman, August 11, 2016, Obama's staff is taking over Silicon Valley…**money.cnn.com**

467-Gina Martinez, December 2, 2021, Cuomo accuser Lindsey Boylan slams female Facebook exec for trying 'to destroy her' by telling then governor's team to 'victim shame her on the record' by releasing her personnel file: Facebook refuses to respond to calls for her to be fired…**dailymail.co.uk**

468-Katie Canales, October 28, 2021, Facebook's New Name Isn't Enough to Save It, Experts Say…**businessinsider.com**

469-Atul Singh, October 2, 2018, Mark Zuckerberg Is More Dangerous than Donald Trump…**fairobserver.com**

470-Dominic Patten, August 3, 2019, Showtime's 'The Circus' Hosts Mock Donald Trump's "Racist Political Campaign"…**Decider.com**

471-Jinitzail Hernández, April 29, 2021, Mark McKinnon: Biden could go bigger than 'anybody since FDR'…**RollCall.com**

472-Aarian Marshall, May 11, 2021, Biden Makes a Deal With Uber and Lyft in the Name of Vaccines…**Wired.com**

473-Jonathan Simmons, November 8, 2021, Uber, Lyft making record profits as consumers pay high prices…**abcnews.go.com**

474-Matthew Jaffe, June 13, 2016, Beth Myers: Romney 'feels he's putting country over party'…**CNN Politics**

475-Beth Myers, 2022, The Shawmut Group Approach…**shawmutgroup.com**

476-Rep. John Runyan, January 24, 2014, Fourth and So Long: I spent 14 years in the NFL. Here's why I'm quitting Congress after four…**Politico.com**

477-Brendan J. Lyons, September 23, 2021, Dr. Howard Zucker resigns as New York's health commissioner…**TimesUnion.com**

478-Will Feuer, August 26, 2020, Cuomo rips into CDC as Trump's political tool says New York won't follow new virus guidance… Berkeley Lovelace Jr., **cnbc.com**

479-J. David Goodman, March 5, 2021, Cuomo Aides Rewrote Nursing Home Report to Hide Higher Death Toll… Danny Hakim, **NY Times.com**

480-Inside New York City Hall, April 27, 2020, De Blasio Defends Naming NYC's First Lady to Racial Equity Coronavirus Task Force…**ny1.com**

481-Laurel Wamsley, January 13, 2021, Biden Nominates Samantha Power To Run U.S. Agency For International Development…**npr.org**

482-Office of Press Relations, October 26, 2021, Administration Samantha Powers on the First-Ever National Strategy on Gender Equity and Equality…**usaid.gov**

483-Diane Stopyra, October 14, 2020, Pete Buttigieg talks about Trust: Former presidential candidate speaks to UD students in Biden Institute event…**udel.edu**

484-Tyler Pager, December 15, 2020, Pete Buttigieg was chosen as Biden's Transportation secretary… Sam Mintz, **Politico.com**

485-Jay Root, September 27, 2019, Pete Buttigieg says he would not pardon President Donald Trump…**TexasTribune.com**

486-Tommy Christopher, May 1, 2019, Mayor Pete Fumbles Badly on Vaccinations, Says Exemptions Should Be Allowed Only Where Vaccines Are Working…**mediaite.com**

487-Dan Merica, May 1, 2019, Buttigieg now says he opposes religious and personal exemptions to vaccines…**CNN Politics**

488-Nathaniel J. Hiatt, August 26, 2016, IOP Executive Director Resigns to Work on Election…**thecrimson.com**

489-Ben Zeisloft, January 31, 2021, GOP lawmakers demand UPenn Biden Center release foreign donation records…**campusreform.org**

490-Ellen Knickmeyer, August 12, 2020, 6 former EPA bosses call for agency reset after election…**apnews.com**

491-Andrew Simon, August 13, 2020, Apple's Lisa Jackson on leadership, justice, and generations of change…**Grist.org**

492-Sam Stein, October 29, 2021, Exclusive: Donilon's plea to Dems… Tina Sfondeles, Alex Thompson, **Politico.com**

493-Kristen Hinman, October 26, 2020, These Are the Most Influential Operatives on the Biden Campaign…**Washingtonian.com**

494-Jonathan Lemire, May 18, 2020, 2016 repeat? Trump revives Clinton playbook to battle Biden… Bill Barrow, **abcnews4.com**

495-Jess Bidgood, March 5, 2021, Quiet and low profile, Mike Donilon is Biden's White House "wise man"… Dan McGowan, **BostonGlobe.com**

496-Niall O'Dowd, June 2, 2021, The trusted Irish American brain behind Joe Biden: Irish American Mike Donilon is the longtime, behind-the-scenes advisor to Joe Biden…**irishcentral.com**

497-Craig Brandhorst, April 23, 2021, In the field with David Beasley: World Food Program executive director, former governor, double-alumnus brings home Nobel Peace Prize…**sc.edu**

498-Pamela Falk, November 5, 2021, U.N. hunger agency chief follows up tweet exchange with Elon Musk with plea to billionaires…**cbsnews.com**

499-Tom Porter, July 16, 2021, Experts Doubt Leaked Docs Claiming Russia Plot to Help Trump in 2016...**businessinsider.com**

500-Alana Wise, November 17, 2020, Trump Fires Election Security Director Who Corrected Voter Fraud Disinformation…**npr.org**

501-Kiran Stacey, January 7, 2021, SolarWinds hires former Trump cyber security chief Chris Krebs: Group's software was exploited by suspected Russian hackers to spy on governments and businesses… Hannah Murphy, **Financial Times.com**

502-Ethan Howland, November 8, 2021, Biden signs $1.2 trillion infrastructure bill with funding for EVs, transmission, hydrogen…**utilitydive.com**

503-Delaware Business Now, April 12, 2021, Trustees extend the contract for President Assanis…**delawarebusinessnow.com**

504-Ebony Bowden, August 3, 2020, Congress demands US universities hand over all records of foreign donations…**NY Post.com**

505-Kristen Rogers, March 31, 2021, Amanda Nguyen is an IGNITE Leader on Fire…**ignitenational.org**

506-Jennifer Liu, March 1, 2021, How millennial Nobel Prize nominee Amanda Nguyen's viral video sparked coverage of anti-Asian racism…**cnbc.com**

507-Neal Nicholson, January 20, 2009, The 5 Most Terrifying Civilizations In The History of the World…**cracked.com**

508-Kallie Szczepanski, December 9, 2019, Female Infanticide in Asia…**ThoughtCo.com**

509-UChicago Pan-Asia Solidarity Coalition, November 29, 2018, U of C Pan-Asia Solidarity Coalition Denounces Lecturer Suing Harvard…**chicagomaroon.com**

510-Post Editorial Board, December 9, 2021, BLM's defense of Jussie Smollett exposes the truth of the school CRT wars…**NY Post.com**

511-BU Today Staff, January 7, 2021, "White privilege is on display." Ibram X. Kendi, Director of BU's Center for Antiracist Research, Sounds Off On US Capitol Attack…**BostonUniversity.edu**

512-Gabe Kaminsky, December 9, 2021, Exclusive: Ibram X. Kendi Raked In $45K From University of Wisconsin, Made School Delete Lecture…**thefederalist.com**

513-Tracey Bryant, February 11, 2021, Strengthening Democracy for a Better World…**udel.edu**

514-Pablo McConnie-Saad, December 1, 2017, Gentrification and Residential Mobility in Philadelphia…**prezi.com**

515-Maggie Haberman, February 28, 2021, Trump Was Sicker Than Acknowledged with Covid-19… Noah Weiland, Mark Mazzetti, Annie Karni, **NY Times.com**

516-Joseph A. Wulfsohn, June 23, 2020, NY Times' Maggie Haberman slammed by Biden supporters for calling him a 'very flawed' candidate…**foxnews.com**

517-Jolie Lash, December 20, 2021, Trump, Bill O'Reilly Booed After Admitting They Both Got COVID Vaccine Booster…**TheWrap.com**

518-Larry Luxner, January 28, 2021, Smithsonian's Lonnie Bunch: 'We're still in the midst of a fundamental debate over what America is'...**atlanticcouncil.org**

519-Jen Psaki, February 27, 2017, Jen Psaki: Without a free press, democracy dies...**CNN Politics**

520-Jen Psaki, March 3, 2020, Our four-year-old wanted us to vote for someone who likes kids and animals and is strong...**Twitter**

521-Amy Lamare, July 7, 2019, How An Heir To The DuPont Fortune Got Off Scot-Free On The Rape Of His Three-Year-Old Daughter...**celebritynetworth.com**

522-Taylor Goebel, October 20, 2020, Fact Check: Joe Biden no longer owns DuPont mansion featured in Eric Trump tweet...**delmarvanow.com**

523-Tanveer Ahmed, January 10, 2022, Sadly, the unjabbed have become the new deplorables...**afr.com**

524-D'Angelo Gore, November 2, 2021, Answering Questions About #BeagleGate...**factcheck.org**

525-Geoff Herbert, January 4, 2019, Joe Biden's married son Hunter dating brother Beau's widow (reports)...**syracuse.com**

526-Athena Thorne, February 1, 2022, Heartless Psaki Laughs at Report on Violent Crime Victims...**pjmedia.com**

527-Pew Research Center, April 28, 2021, At 100 DayMark: Coverage of Biden Has Been Slightly More Negative Than Positive, Varied Greatly by Outlet Type...**pewresearch.org**

528-Maureen Milford, July 12, 2009, GM closing Boxwood Road, last auto plant in Delaware...**abcnews.go.com**

529-Joseph Weber, January 5, 2013, Delaware taxpayers increasingly on the hook as Fisker auto plant idles...**foxnews.com**

530-Kevin Breuninger, June 27, 2019, Kamala Harris attacks Joe Biden's record on busing and working with segregationists in vicious exchange at Democratic debate...**cnbc.com**

531-Emily Folk, September 10, 2018, How important is energy independence in the US?...**theecologist.org**

532-Nafeez Ahmed, March 6, 2014, Ukraine crisis is about Great Power oil, gas pipeline rivalry...**theguardian.com**

533-Paulo Acoba, October 12, 2021, What's with those Joe Biden "I did that" stickers at gas pumps?...**tiremeetsroad.com**

534-Sacha Sloan, November 18, 2021, Hunter's Laptop, Deepfakes, and the Arbitration of Truth…**brownpoliticalreview.org**

535-Erin Brockovich, November 19, 2020, Dear Joe Biden: are you kidding me?... Suzanne Boothby, **theguardian.com**

Love you Christine...the best big sister ever!

11-25-69 – 3-17-2022

CPSIA information can be obtained
at www.ICGtesting.com
Printed in the USA
LVHW081124070422
715599LV00001B/46